Art and Tradition in
Sir Gawain and the Green Knight

Art and Tradition in
Sir Gawain and
the Green Knight

Larry D. Benson

Rutgers University Press
New Brunswick, N. J.

For Peggy

Preface

Sir Gawain and the Green Knight is one of the few Middle
English poems that have not slipped into the obscurity to
which the passing of centuries and changes in taste and
language have condemned most medieval literature. For
readers throughout the world it is, as Émile Pons wrote,
"Non seulement le plus beau poème arturien anglais, mais
une des oeuvres les plus vivantes de la littérature arturienne
de tous pays et de tous temps." [1] Indeed, if such compari-
sons are possible, *Sir Gawain* is more widely appreciated
today than it was in the Middle Ages. Only one medieval
manuscript survives, but in the twentieth century the
poem has appeared in six different editions and has been
translated at least sixteen times into modern English,
French, and even Breton. [2] It has been adapted for the English and German stages, retold as a fairy tale, echoed in the
works of contemporary poets, universally praised, and
studied by scores of scholars in nations ranging from Asia
and Australia to Africa, Europe, and America. [3]

Yet *Sir Gawain* is emphatically a poem of its own time
and place, more deeply rooted in the age in which it was
written than any other medieval work that still appeals to

modern readers. Unlike the *Divine Comedy* or *Piers Plowman*, *Sir Gawain* has no obviously universal subject matter; critics have often noted the "trivial" nature of its plot and sought elaborate explanations for its supernatural elements.[4] The artistry of *Sir Gawain* is even more uncompromisingly medieval than its subject matter. It is possible to read Chaucer's *Troilus* as the "first modern novel" and to admire *The Canterbury Tales* for its "realism," but no one could mistake *Sir Gawain* for a "modern," "realistic" narrative. Romance is dead, but *Sir Gawain and the Green Knight,* the most sophisticated English romance, still survives; alliterative poetry has disappeared, and yet *Sir Gawain,* one of the most traditional works in this forgotten tradition, is now better known than ever.

This is no paradox, for *Sir Gawain* is a work of genius; it would be more puzzling if so excellent a poem had failed to find a modern audience. However, this does create a critical problem: because of the accidents of history, *Sir Gawain* now exists in an artificial isolation. Even the student of Middle English often knows no other alliterative poem except *Piers Plowman* and no other romances except thos contained in the standard anthologies. Compared to them, *Sir Gawain* seems novel both in its style and in its subject matter. This apparent novelty does lend the poem a special appeal for some readers, but it also makes it a more difficult and less satisfying work than it really is. In its own time *Sir Gawain* was unique only for its excellence. It existed within a context of literary traditions that had slowly been created by generations of writers, and the Gawain-poet drew on those traditions for his plots, settings, and characterizations as well as for his meter, syntax, and vocabulary. His is a traditional art, and the romance and alliterative traditions supplied him with a kind of language that he shared with the audience for which he wrote but that has now been forgotten for over half a millennium. The delicate interplay of romance conventions and the even more sophisticated breaches of romance decorum are lost upon readers for whom romance is dead, just as the poet's simple meanings are often lost upon those to whom alliterative verse is an unfamiliar medium. Consequently, to modern readers the Gawain-poet frequently seems obscure when he is most clear, and simple when he is complex. To read the poem without an understanding of its art and of the relations of that art to the traditions that the poet used is to miss much of the meaning and many of the pleasures that *Sir Gawain* offers.

My purpose in this book is to help the reader overcome that difficulty by providing him with a detailed examination of the poem's art in the context of its literary traditions. This is the sort of study from which readers of Chaucer have profited for so long but which until quite recently was impossible for students of *Sir Gawain*; too little was known about the poem's sources, about the alliterative tradition, and about the Alliterative Revival itself. However, in the last two decades or so the great increase in scholarship on *Sir Gawain* and on medieval literature in general has provided much of the necessary material. The availability of new texts allows us for the first time to study the exact relation of the poem to its sources, and that knowledge of what the poem owes to its sources enables us to examine its more general relation to medieval romance. Likewise, the development of new techniques of stylistic analysis and the new knowledge of the alliterative tradition that scholars have gained in recent years make possible the first full examination of the Gawain-poet's style, and an understanding of the poem's relation to its stylistic tradition enables us to consider in full detail the poet's narrative and descriptive techniques. Perhaps most important, this new knowledge of the poem's literary relations allows us to study the main theme and the meaning of *Sir Gawain* in the light of its literary context. These problems of sources, style, and meaning are the subjects that I shall study in the following chapters. My method is mainly comparative; I define the qualities of *Sir Gawain* by comparing it to other romances, to other alliterative poems, and, wherever possible, to the more familiar works of Chaucer.

Throughout this book my assumption is that the more one knows about the poem as a work of art existing in a definite literary milieu the better his reading of it will be.

Of course, I cannot provide a reader with all he needs to know, even though I have restricted myself almost exclusively to literary problems, for we all need a good deal more knowledge than is available even now. We must remain content with no more precise localization and dating of the text than the Northwest Midlands in the late fourteenth century.[5] Consequently our only knowledge of the poet's hearers must be inferred from the poem itself and from what we know of other medieval audiences. We must also operate within the limitations imposed by the fact that so few fourteenth-century texts have survived. The number of romances and alliterative works that must have been known to the poet and his audience but that have since been lost is discouraging to estimate,[6] and certainly the fragmentary nature of what we have is enough to give pause to anyone, like myself, who attempts to study the traditions of medieval vernacular poetry. One would give much for the texts that would solve these problems, but one must work with what he has. Indeed, the student of *Sir Gawain* must even work with no sure knowledge whatsoever of the man who wrote this poem.

Many readers may consider this last problem the most important of all. The question of the Gawain-poet's identity has engaged the attention of a large number of students, and the problem of whether that author also wrote *Pearl, Patience,* and *Cleanness* has been even more frequently studied. The result has been only the proof that unless some startling new documents are discovered the problem will never be solved to everyone's satisfaction.[7] I am not disturbed by this fact, for it seems to me that the question of authorship is not as important as many students believe. It is only a matter of nomenclature. If one of the many proposed identifications of the Gawain-poet could be proved correct, we would gain little more than a name, for little more than the name is known about any of the candidates scholars have suggested. Likewise, only the most minute examination of the poems in Cotton Nero A.x. reveals any differences in style and diction.[8] They are as similar as one could expect of any four poems differing so much in genre and subject matter. If it could be proved that they were written by two, three, or four different authors, we would still have to assume that those authors knew, admired, and echoed one another's work, and we would merely have replaced "the Gawain-poet" with something like "the school of the Gawain-poet." I have preferred to retain the simpler designation.

In this study I concentrate upon *Sir Gawain* and I mention the other poems in the Cotton Nero manuscript only occasionally, but I trust that a knowledge of the poet's artistry as it is revealed in this romance will enable the student to read *Pearl, Patience,* and *Cleanness* with more understanding and delight than they provide even now. I hope too that this knowledge may also serve to make more accessible to the reader some of the other first-rate alliterative poems that still await the audience they deserve.

LARRY D. BENSON

Cambridge, Massachusetts
February 1965

Acknowledgments

My work owes a great deal to many scholars whom I have never met, and my indebtedness to them is, I hope, sufficiently indicated in the notes. But I am also deeply indebted to friends and teachers, to Professors Charles Muscatine, Alain Renoir, and Arthur Hutson at the University of California, who helped me at the beginning stages of this study, and to Professors Morton Bloomfield and B. J. Whiting at Harvard University, who helped me see it to completion. I owe a special debt to Charles Muscatine, who interrupted his own Italian journey to read my manuscript and give helpful advice long after his obligations as a teacher had been so well discharged, and to Morton Bloomfield, who shared with me his wide knowledge of medieval literature and who offered many suggestions that are incorporated in this work. My work would have been less valuable than it is without the generous assistance and encouragement of these friends.

A grant from the Kendall Foundation allowed me the summer leisure that I needed to complete my work, and a grant from the Clark Fund at Harvard University helped me to meet the expenses of typing and microfilming. Frederick R. Goff, Chief of the Rare Book Division of the Library of Congress, kindly granted me permission to print the portion of the prose *Perceval* that appears in the Appendix.

L.D.B.

Contents

The Narrative and Descriptive Techniques 167

The narrative orders in Sir Gawain / Concrete description in the alliterative tradition / The alternating points of view / Narrative technique as characterization / The narrator's voice

The Meaning 207

Renown in the beheading episode / The theme of identity and Gawain's failure / The guide's temptation of Gawain / The new test at the Green Chapel / The return to Camelot

Appendix 249

The prose redaction of the *Caradoc* beheading tale

Art and Tradition in
Sir Gawain and the Green Knight

The Sources

Sir Gawain and the Green Knight is first of all a romance, existing within a tradition that lends a work an authority and range of reference unmatched by any modern genre. This is the first fact we learn as we read the poem, for the Gawain-poet does not begin his narrative until he has devoted two full stanzas, an unusually long "prologue" for an English romance, to an elaborate specification of the connection between his narrative and the romance tradition. His tale, he assures us, is part of the history of Britain that extends from Camelot to Troy; it is one of the many marvels of Arthur and his court, indeed the most marvellous of all, and it has the sober authority of historical fact, as told "In stori stif and stronge" (v. 34). At the end of the narrative the poet asserts once more the traditional nature of his work, which he has told,

> As hit is breued in þe best boke of romaunce.
> Þus in Arthurus day þis aunter bitidde,
> Þe Brutus bokeȝ þerof beres wyttenesse.
>
> (vv. 2521–23)

These assertions are not literally true. There is no exact source for *Sir Gawain,* no single "best boke of romaunce." The poet did draw on one specific source for the beheading tale, but the temptation episode is largely his own invention, and the combination of the beheading and the temptation has no exact analogue.

Yet, in another sense, the assertions are true, for *Sir Gawain* could not exist without the "Brutus bokeȝ." The combination of the parts is the poet's own, but the parts themselves are traditional; the poem's subject is one of the three great "matters" of romance ("De France et de Bretaigne et de Rome la grant" [1]), its episodes are ancient, and its characters are familiar figures who appear in dozens of other romances. The poem, in short, has the proper tone of a romance, which always seems twice-told, even when it is being told for the first time, and the poet's assertion of an exact source is a necessary part of the establishment of that tone, because, as the word "romance" implies, this is a genre that conventionally depends upon the records of tradition rather than the new and original, the "novel." [2] Part of the pleasure in any romance is its novelty, and we miss much if we ignore it, but we miss even more if we ignore the tradition and attempt to read the poem in isolation from its literary background. The poet's insistence on that background shows that he did not want his audience to ignore it, that he wanted his readers to be aware of the aesthetic function of the sources and tradition of his romance.

The function of "sources" in romance

The idea that aesthetic pleasure can arise from knowing the antecedents of a work is so foreign to modern criticism, and the "source study" is consequently in such ill repute that before examining the relation of *Sir Gawain* to its romance sources it may be well to review briefly the aesthetic of medieval romance. Partly this is the aesthetic of all traditional literatures, which are distinguished most sharply from the modern by their preference for the repetition of old tales rather than "originality." Lydia Languish, and her novel-reading sisters, demanded the latest novels, from *The Fatal Connexion* to *Peregrine Pickle;* had she happened upon some medieval romances, she would surely have found, as have some modern critics, that the great majority, and even parts of *Sir Gawain,* are "hackneyed," "merely conventional," and dull. Medieval audiences found romance to their liking not because they had a greater capacity for boredom than Lydia but because they approached the genre with a much different set of expectations. When Criseyde turns to literature for amusement, she chooses the ancient romance of Thebes (II, 100), which is well known not only to Chaucer's audience but even to other characters in *Troilus.*[3] When Pandarus, himself an admirer of romance (III, 980), interrupts this reading, he tells his niece,

> "Al this knowe I myselve
> And al th'assege of Thebes and the care;
> And herof ben ther maked bookes twelve."
>
> (II, 106–08)

One gets the impression that if Pandarus had not been in such a rush to get on with Troilus' suit he would gladly have sat down to hear the old story once more, for the very familiarity of the tale of Thebes is part of its charm for literary traditionalists like Pandarus and most medieval readers.

The touch of pedantry in Pandarus' speech ("herof ben ther maked bookes twelve") and the fact that the story of Thebes is being read to Criseyde by one of her companions indicate the essential difference between romance and other traditional genres. *Beowulf* must have had much the same sort of traditional appeal for its hearers as *Sir Gawain* or the story of Thebes for their audiences, but the tradition invoked in romance, unlike that of the earlier epic or the later ballad, is primarily clerkly, learned, and though the ultimate origins of a particular romance are probably in folk tales, the romance itself exists in and depends on books. In an older culture a king like Hroðgar would entertain his court by singing his lay to the accompaniment of his harp. In the fourteenth century a hero like Robert the Bruce would entertain his troops by reading to them from the "Romanys off worthi Ferambrace" (*Bruce*, III, 437); the connoisseur of vernacular literature has become learned. Indeed, the last and greatest reader of romance is a real pedant; Don Quixote liked nothing better than to spend hours with the barber and the curate (a university graduate) debating the relative merits of romance heroes.

The learning of romance, its dependence on books, is most obvious in the traditional pose of the romance narrator. The older, epic poet draws his material from oral tradition. This, too, is a matter of convention, for the epic audience may be clerical and the poet himself may be a clerk, but he claims that he bases his work on old tales, not previous books. The *Nibelungenlied* begins with "Uns ist in alten mæren wunders vil geseit," and *Beowulf* opens with a brief reference to "We . . . þeodcyninga þrym gefrunon," and both lines are rough Germanic equivalents to Virgil's "Musa, mihi causas memora." The romancer, on the other hand, bases the authentication of his narrative [4] on the medieval respect for written authority, and he poses as merely a clerk, repeating what he has read; his narrative is conventionally an authentic history, and history is the province of clerks. A Wolfram von Eschenbach may claim to be completely illiterate, but he is an exception in a line of poets who present themselves as dependent upon books, whether that belonging to Geoffrey's Archdeacon Walter, that given to Chrétien by Count Phillip of Flanders, or the Gawain-poet's "best boke of romaunce," and even Wolfram had his Kyot, "who saw this story of Parzifal written in the heathen tongue." [5] The Wife of Bath herself adopts the pose of a clerk when she tells us of the "olde dayes of the Kyng Arthour": "This was the olde opinion, as I rede" (v. 862).

This emphasis on the written source differentiates romance from the novel as clearly as from the epic. In its historical situation the modern novel is completely literate; there must have been many illiterate admirers of romance, but there can be no illiterates in the audience of a novel. Yet the conventions of the novel have little to do with literacy; its narrative is authenticated not by previous books but by its apparent freedom from them, its "originality." Its plot may be ancient, and its characters stock types, but the novelist must insist that his work is here made public for the first time, a genuine report from life, a novelty in form and content. If we want to enjoy the latest detective thriller, we accept the convention, even though we know the same boy met the same girl and the same detective solved the same crime dozens of times before. Expecting "realism," we sharpen our sense of the improbable and suspend our knowledge of previous literature. The reader of romance was more bookish. He expected not "life" but "wonders" served up as a faithful report from a familiar antiquity about which the poet's superior learning, his possession of the source book, gave him the authority to speak. As works such as *Sir Thopas* and *The Tournament of Tottenham* show, the medieval reader had as keen a sense of the improbable as we do, but when he turned to romance, he suspended that sense and sharpened his knowledge of previous literature.

That knowledge must have been considerable, for in *Sir Thopas* Chaucer could assume that his audience knew the characters and conventions of romance so well that they could be used for ironic effect. In the north of England, where romance was more assiduously cultivated than in London, an audience at least as knowledgeable as Chaucer's was probably one of the conditions of romance composition and accounts for the sometimes richly allusive technique of poems like *Sir Gawain*. If an audience knew the plot and even the marvels of a tale before it was told, so much the better. Gower and Chaucer unashamedly told some of the same tales to what must have been nearly the same audiences, for they knew that the readers' pleasure in so literary a genre as romance is only partly due to suspense and discovery. A large part of the delight is in hearing the old plots and situations used in new ways. Chrétien serves notice at the beginning of *Lancelot* that his matter is old but his "peine" and "entencion" are new, and when Chaucer's Nun's Priest advises his listeners, "Taketh the fruyt and lat the chaff be stille," he is asking them both to discover the kernel of truth concealed in the chaff of the tale and to admire the virtuosity with which the old materials of the Reynard Cycle have been newly adapted to suit "oure doctrine." [6] The sources of *Sir Gawain* itself are not very obscure; the beheading episode is based on a widely known romance, and the temptation is composed of the most common traditional elements. The poet's audience must have included many whose chief pleasure was in seeing how the traditional materials were used in such untraditional ways.

Such a hearer probably expected a new treatment of the old materials, for despite the romancers' insistence on their fidelity to previous books, the traditional tales were con-

stantly changing and each new romance was indeed an
original work. If the medieval romancer had little of the
modern novelist's fear of plagiarism, he had even less of
the modern scholar's respect for the integrity of his
sources. Perhaps this is partly a matter of definition, because to the medieval writer the faithful transmission of a
tale meant simply repeating the main outline of the action.
Chaucer's clerk, faithfully repeating the tale of Griselda as
he "Lerned at Padowe of a worthy clerk," thinks nothing
of omitting much of Petrarch's materials as a "thyng im-
pertinent." [7] Even much closer translators, like the author
of *William of Palerne,* would add or omit a large number
of small details, changing the tone and meaning of a work
in the process. Sometimes the meaning of a work is
changed in variant manuscripts of the same romance, for
"recopiers" and "retellers" also freely added or omitted details, even though these romancers, like the oral poets of
modern Yugoslav tradition, might claim (and often did)
that they were transmitting the tale exactly as it came to
them.[8] More sophisticated writers, like the Gawain-poet,
made their changes more boldly, preserving most of the
old materials but greatly modifying their function and
meaning.

The skilled romancer is thus "maker" as well as "clerk,"
and he capitalizes upon the modification of material that is
natural to romance by using an existing tale not only as the
clerkly authority essential to the fictional world of this
genre but also as a set of possibilities that, in his role as
maker, he can realize so far as his abilities allow and his
purposes require. It is this process that makes the repetition of old materials possible in a genre that also prized
novelty, "wonders," for it provides for their constant re-
newal; the tale remains generally the same, but each poet
in the tradition passes it on in a modified form, sometimes
with small changes of the sort made by romancers who

really tried to pass it on as it came to them, sometimes with bold changes of the kind that the Gawain-poet made. The result is "the striking contrast between the continuity in the transmission of the *matière* and the corresponding degree of instability in the position of the *sen*" in medieval romance.[9]

Consequently, the study of sources can be more than a simple matter of finding parallels and ultimate "originals," for when we know a poet's exact source, as we now do for the Gawain-poet's beheading tale, we have something like a modern author's notebooks and rough drafts; we can specify exactly what changes the poet made and thus define more clearly his artistic methods and purposes. The other versions of a tale, the poem's more distant analogues, are in some ways even more valuable, for the history of a romance tale is not governed by necessity. Thus the analogues are not only stages in the development of a tale, they are other realizations of the possibilities it offered a romancer, and they can help us to recognize what a poet is doing by showing us what he chose not to do, what possibilities he chose to ignore. Even when there is no direct source, as in the Gawain-poet's temptation episode, the analogues provide us with some of the knowledge a poet could assume his audience would have, and they thus allow us to recognize what traditional situations the poet is using and how he modifies them by emphasizing or rejecting their conventional parts. We cannot hope to become as learned about the genre as Pandarus or the audience for whom Chaucer wrote *Sir Thopas*, but with the study of the Gawain-poet's sources we can at least begin to understand something of the literary relations of *Sir Gawain*.

The origins of the beheading tale

The history of the beheading tale that appears in *Sir Gawain* is the history of Arthurian romance in microcosm. Originally it derived from an ancient and widely distributed folk tale that was first given literary form in the Irish *Fled Bricrend (Bricriu's Feast)*. Thence, like so many Celtic tales and motifs, it was taken into twelfth-century French romance. In the thirteenth century it passed from French to German poetry, and in the fourteenth century it was taken from French into English. In all, the tale appears in eleven surviving works—two Irish (both in the *Fled Bricrend*), four French (*Caradoc, La Mule sanz frain, Hunbaut*, and *Perlesvaus*), two German (*Diu Crône* and Colin and Wisse's *Parzifal*, which includes a translation of *Caradoc*), and three English (*Sir Gawain and the Green Knight, The Grene Knight*, and the mutilated version in *The Turk and Gawain*). There must certainly have been other versions that are now lost, but for our purposes the most important are those in the *Fled Bricrend* and *Caradoc*, which lead directly to *Sir Gawain*.[10] The others show the variety of uses to which the beheading tale could be put, but these show how the tale acquired the form in which the Gawain-poet knew it.

Ultimately that tale derived from folk tradition, perhaps, as some scholars have held, from a seasonal myth of the recurrent battle of Summer and Winter, or, more likely, from the widespread "exchange of blows" folk tale, of which Kittredge collected examples from as far afield as the Solomon Islands.[11] If the Gawain-poet or his audience thought about such matters at all, they probably would have connected the beheading in *Sir Gawain* with the "exchange of blows," for that primitive tale was still current in English romance. In *Richard Coeur de Lion* Richard is challenged to an exchange of blows. A bare fist is the weapon; the challenger is to strike the first blow, Richard to return the blow on the day following. He returns it with such force that he breaks the challenger's jaw and kills him (vv. 746–98). *A Geste of Robyn Hode, The Turk and Gawain,* and Chapman's play, *Alphonsus Emperor of Germany,* contain similar episodes, and in *Schir William Wallace* Wallace meets a club-carrying "carl" who is foolish enough to allow the hero to strike him with his own club as he stands unarmed. Wallace kills him outright.[12] Perhaps some such simple test of strength suggested to the Gawain-poet some of his minor changes in the beheading tale—such as the Green Knight's claim that he has won when Gawain flinches (v. 2278). However, so simple a tale can account for no more than a minor detail such as this. For the most part the Gawain-poet was dependent not upon a primitive tale but on a highly developed literary tradition.

That tradition first appears in the *Fled Bricrend,* which contains the two earliest surviving versions of the beheading tale. Of the two the "Uath" or "Terror" episode is the simpler and probably earlier version, and even though the author of the *Fled Bricrend* must have had some literary sources (he mentions "other books" that contain the beheading tale [13]), we may take this as the first stage in the literary development of the tale:

> To settle a dispute over who shall have the "champion's portion" at Bricriu's feast, Loigaire, Conall, and Cuchulainn go to "Terror, son of Great Fear." He proposes a test: "I have an axe, and the man into whose hands it shall be put is to cut off my head today, I to cut off his tomorrow." Only Cuchulainn accepts. Terror puts spells on the axe and lays his head on a stone. Cuchulainn strikes off the head, which Terror picks up along with his axe and carries

into a nearby loch. The next day he returns, and Cuchulainn stretches himself out on the stone. Terror brings the blunt edge of the axe down on Cuchulainn's neck three times without harm and awards him the champion's portion and the "sovereignty of the heroes of Erin." [14]

The primitive exchange of blows supplies the central incident of the episode, but the author has incorporated it into the literary framework of his saga, and he has changed the purpose of the traded blows from what may have been a ritual act or a mere demonstration of strength to a formal test of Cuchulainn's prowess. Only the most simple modifications were required. The contest between the three heroes is the subject of the whole saga, and most of its episodes are tests of the same three heroes, tests in which Cuchulainn invariably succeeds. The author needed merely to add these elements to the exchange of blows in order to adapt it to the pattern of the *Fled Bricrend*. The result of this simple amalgamation is that the folk tale has become a literary work; it now has a conflict (the dispute of the heroes), an agency of resolution (the beheading test), a resolution (Cuchulainn's triumph), and a theme (the proof of the hero's prowess).

Furthermore, it now has the symmetrical form which is to survive even in *Sir Gawain;* in the first half of the action there is a bargain and a beheading, in the second half a fulfillment of the bargain and another, this time symbolic, beheading. This balanced structure is implied even in the folk tale, but the shift of the conflict from the beheading itself to the contention for the champion's portion allowed the author to maintain the balance and extend it to the challenger and the hero. When the conflict is centered in the exchange of blows, as in *Richard Coeur de Lion*, the hero's victory is a defeat for the challenger and the symmetry is destroyed. In the *Fled Bricrend* the exchange of blows serves only as a means of resolving the conflict, and

Cuchulainn's victory is a defeat for Conall and Loigaire but not for Terror. The hero and challenger merely exchange positions, and each is successful. By submitting to the first blow the challenger proves his supernatural powers; by bravely and loyally submitting to the return-blow the hero proves his human ones.

The other version of the beheading tale in the *Fled Bricrend,* that known as "The Champions' Bargain," contains all these elements and several more additions:

> One night when Loigaire, Conall, and Cuchulainn are absent, a huge, ugly *bachlach* (carl) comes into Conchobar's hall. He is dressed in an old hide, with a black mantle about him; he has a large bushy head, like a great tree, and big yellow eyes; in his left hand he carries a huge block, in his right an enormous sharp axe. He announces that he has supernatural power and that he has heard so much about the valor of Conchobar's men that he has come to ask a boon: aside from Fergus and Conchobar, whom he exempts because of their rank, he wants someone to come forward that "I may cut off his head tonight, he mine tomorrow."
>
> Though Duach of the Chaffer Tongue remarks that no one would accept such a bargain, Munremar mac Gerreind springs forward to accept it. On Duach's urging, the challenger agrees to reverse the order of blows. Munremar then strikes off the head, which the challenger snatches up along with the block and axe and carries from the hall. When he returns the next night, Munremar is nowhere to be found. On succeeding nights Loigaire and Conall also accept the bargain and then fail to submit to the return-blow.
>
> On the challenger's fourth visit, Cuchulainn is present. The carl enters and taunts the court—"Your valor and prowess are gone," and he asks for Cuchulainn by name. Cuchulainn leaps forward, accepts the challenge, and strikes a mighty blow. Then he seizes the head and smashes it with the axe, but the carl rises and departs.
>
> Cuchulainn is waiting in the hall the next night, for, he

says, he would rather have death than dishonor. The carl
enters and calls out, "Where is Cuchulainn?" "Here am I,"
the hero replies. The challenger says that Cuchulainn
fears to die, but he also admits that he has kept the bargain. Then Cuchulainn lays his head on the block, which
is so large his neck stretches only halfway across. The
challenger insists that he stretch out his neck. "You keep
me in torment," Cuchulainn cries, "Dispatch me quickly!"
But still the challenger insists, and with a great effort
Cuchulainn extends his neck across the block. Then the
bachlach raises his axe and brings the edge harmlessly
down on the hero's neck, and announces that for "valor,
bravery, and truthfulness" Cuchulainn deserves the champion's portion. "It was Curoi mac Dairi who in that guise
had come to fulfill the promise he had given to Cuchulainn."

The differences between this and the "Terror" versions
of the beheading tale are partly due to their differing
functions in the book. In his continuing dispute with
Conall and Loigaire over the champion's portion, Cuchulainn always wins, but, as in the "Terror" episode, his vic-
tories are all private. Loigaire and Conall are always able
to claim a foul and demand a new test. "The Champions'
Bargain" is the last in this series of tests. The shift in scene
from the lonely loch to Conchobar's court allows Cuchulainn public and irrefutable proof of his merit. And the
fact that the challenge is delivered to the entire court,
along with the addition of Munremar to the list of those
who fail, increases the magnitude of Cuchulainn's feat by
showing him to be the superior not only of Loigaire and
Conall but of the whole body of Ulstermen. With these
changes the tale now provides a suitable conclusion to the
adventures that began at Bricriu's feast.

The magnitude of Cuchulainn's feat is also emphasized
by a variety of minor additions to the tale. Partly they are
dramatizations of what was only stated in the "Terror"

version. This is apparent in the narration of the failures of the other heroes prior to Cuchulainn's victory, an expansion in the narrative that also builds suspense for the climax. The same procedure appears in the extended description of the challenger, which dramatically presents the terror merely implied by the name in the earlier version and which increases the suspense by delaying the revelation of the purpose of this frightening visit. The by-play between Duach and the challenger has the same function, and Duach's rejection of the impossible bargain and the subsequent agreement to change the order of the blows communicate both the difficulty of the test and the challenger's confidence in the outcome. However, the most striking means of building suspense and emphasizing the magnitude of Cuchulainn's feat is the use the author makes of the interval between the first and second blows. He reminds us of the possibility that Cuchulainn could escape as others have done, and he thus establishes the fact that honor as well as bravery is now involved. "It is better for me to have death than dishonor," the hero says as he waits. Thus the author of the *Fled Bricrend* not only retells the beheading tale, he puts it to a new use, gives it a new theme, and freely adapts the plot to its new purpose. This is a procedure that poets repeat throughout the history of the tale.

The beheading tale in Caradoc

The expanded version of the beheading tale in "The Champions' Bargain" evidently supplied the source for the earliest and best-known of the French versions, that which appears in *Le Livre de Caradoc,* a part of the popular First Continuation of Chrétien's *Perceval.* Of course, there is no way of determining how the French poet came upon the Irish tale, for the history of Arthurian literature is cursed by a druidical mist that obscures the passage from Celtic tale to French Arthurian romance. It is hardly likely that the author of *Caradoc* based his work directly on "The Champions' Bargain." There must have been intermediary versions, probably by Breton jongleurs, but what those works were we shall probably never learn.[15] Nevertheless, *Caradoc* and "The Champions' Bargain" do share so many details of action and even, in one passage, of diction,[16] that one will not go far wrong if he assumes that the source used by the author of *Caradoc* was some version very similar to the adventure in Conchobar's hall in the *Fled Bricrend.*

Until quite recently it appeared that the beheading episode in *Caradoc* was drawn from some lost romance that also supplied the source for *Sir Gawain.* Scholars knew *Caradoc* only from Potvin's text, which was based almost entirely on but one manuscript.[17] A comparison of this text to *Sir Gawain* showed that each shared certain features with "The Champions' Bargain" that did not appear in the other, and a common source seemed the only explanation. However, the First Continuation of *Perceval* was so popular that manuscripts quickly multiplied and within a few years there were four distinct redactions—the "short," "mixed," and "long" metrical redactions, and a prose redaction, made in Paris in 1530 from an older metrical version. Roach's edition of the First Continuation has now made all three metrical redactions available (the prose version of *Caradoc* has never been reprinted; I include the chapters relevant to *Sir Gawain* in the Appendix), and it is now clear that the small changes that each redactor introduced resulted in three distinct versions of the beheading episode. The earliest is that in the nearly identical "short" and "mixed" redactions, known to scholars from Potvin's text. The "long" version is considerably different, and almost every passage that differs from the earlier version agrees with *Sir Gawain;* those details of "The Champions' Bargain" that occur in Potvin's text but not in *Sir Gawain* are also absent from the "long" redaction, and most of the apparently "Celtic" features found in *Sir Gawain* but not in the earlier redactions also appear in the "long." [18]

The latest version of the beheading episode is that preserved in the prose redaction. It is generally similar to the "long" version, but it contains a number of significant additions, such as the challenger's green costume. Nearly every one of these additions also occurs in *Sir Gawain*. Evidently the Gawain-poet knew a manuscript of *Caradoc* similar, if not identical, to that used by the Paris printers. That such a manuscript did exist in England is shown by *Golagros and Gawane*. That poem, written around 1450 in an alliterative stanza similar to that of *Sir Gawain,* has exactly the same relation to the First Continuation; it is based on an episode that occurs in that collection, and it agrees with the "long" redaction where that version differs from the "short" and "mixed" and with the prose where it differs from the "long." [19]

The version of the beheading tale that the Gawain-poet knew had therefore undergone a considerable literary development, first in the major shift from Irish saga to French romance and then in the smaller but significant changes wrought by the later redactors. The importance of these minor changes is shown by the following summary, in which the features common to all redactions of *Caradoc* are printed in italics, those found only in the "long" and prose redactions in roman type, and those unique to the prose within brackets:

> *One Pentecost Arthur is holding a high feast at Cardueil to celebrate the knighting of his nephew Caradoc. Guenevere and many famous knights are there. The king refuses Kay's invitation to eat, telling him of his custom of not*

eating until some marvel has appeared. As Arthur and his knights stand talking, a tall, strange knight comes riding through the door on a war horse.

He is singing a song. [He wears a garland of flowers, and he is dressed entirely in green, trimmed with ermine.] *He wears a long sword,* "with which the head would be cut off" and which is adorned with a belt of rich silk—"les renges ou saincture de fine soie." [His accoutrements are trimmed with gold and many fine pearls.]

He greets Arthur and praises him as the best and highest king in the world. *Then he requests a boon.* The king replies that whatever the challenger may ask, he will not fail to find it here. The challenger then says that he [will give his sword] to whoever will strike *a blow now in exchange for receiving one later. Kay remarks* [under his breath] *that only a fool would accept such an offer. The strange knight taunts the court,* saying that now it will be told everywhere that Arthur's court has failed to grant the little gift he has asked.

The king is troubled and the knights are amazed. Then the strange knight draws his sword and "offers it here and there" around the hall. Caradoc can contain himself no longer. *He leaps forward and seizes the sword.* "Have you been chosen as the best knight here?" asks the stranger. "No," Caradoc replies, "mais pour ung des plus folz."

The knight bows for the blow. The king and all his barons are troubled and in another moment Yvain would have run forward to snatch the sword from Caradoc's hands, but before he can do so *Caradoc strikes a mighty blow.* The head does not fly far, but before anyone can prevent it *the body reaches its head and replaces it.* The stranger turns to the king, and he warns him not to be false and to make sure that he receives his due in a year. *Then he turns to Caradoc and warns him to be ready in a year. The court is deeply troubled over the hero's impending doom, but he shows no sign of fear.* [The narrator comments on how all the laughter and joy of the court is turned into sorrow. "Oh how unfortunate is he who through his blow or foolish play ("folle plaisance") brings sadness and pain on all, and in the end this one

pleasure is turned into a hundred pains." Then he condemns the challenger in similar terms.] *Caradoc shows
no concern* [saying only that he will accept his fate—"Il
en actendra la fortune"].

*After a year that Caradoc spends in adventures, to
which the narrator merely alludes, the challenger returns
to the court. He has his sword drawn, and he has lost none
of his "fresche color."* He greets Arthur and asks him to
have Caradoc step forward. He tells Caradoc to prepare
for the blow, as is only right, he says, since now Caradoc
must see how I can strike. The hero comes forward, tells
the challenger he is ready, and tells him to do his worst—
"Faictes du pis que vous pourrez." *The king intercedes on
Caradoc's behalf, but without success. The challenger
raises his weapon, and Caradoc urges him to strike
quickly, accusing him of cowardice* and complaining
that he is made to suffer two deaths—"De deux mors
me faictes mourir." *Then the queen emerges from her
chamber to plead for Caradoc's life. The challenger
refuses,* and tells her abruptly that if she does not dare
watch, she should go to her rooms and pray for Caradoc's soul. The queen covers her head and returns to
her chamber, where she nearly dies of grief for Caradoc.
Caradoc lays his head on a table ["bloc" in the prose],
*and the challenger strikes him lightly with the flat
of the sword and publicly praises him for bravery and
trustworthiness. Then he takes him aside and reveals that
he is the disguised magician Éliavres and that he is Caradoc's natural father. Caradoc, who has always thought he
was the son of King Caradoc, is saddened and angered at
this news. Deeply depressed, he returns to the rejoicing
court.*[20]

Even from this summary it is apparent that the version
of the beheading tale that the Gawain-poet inherited was
a highly sophisticated work. Yet the outlines of "The
Champions' Bargain" are still discernible, for the Celtic
tale lent itself rather easily to a romance adaptation. No
changes need be made in the basic plot, for the tale involves a test, the romance situation *par excellence,* of loy-

alty and bravery, the greatest of chivalric virtues. Of course, the author of *Caradoc* had to omit the failures of Loigaire, Conall, and Munremar, which were essential to the contest for the champion's portion but which serve no purpose once the episode is detached from the *Fled Bricrend*. Likewise, Cuchulainn's neck-stretching feat must be omitted, for it hardly suits a romance knight, and instead the interventions of the king and queen provide the interruptions that build suspense for the return-blow. Aside from these, few changes were needed. Even the characters and setting of "The Champions' Bargain" fell easily into conventional patterns. Conchobar became Arthur and his hall Cardueil. The Ulstermen became knights of the Round Table and Cuchulainn a *preux chevalier*. Even "Duach of the Chaffer Tongue" fit the pattern; he became the sharp-tongued Kay, the Duach of Arthurian romance. The challenger seemed just as clearly to fit this scheme, for his ugliness, hairiness, gigantic size, and axe are the conventional marks of the literary *vilain*, the traditional opponent of the romance knight.

In some ways the disguised Curoi fits the pattern too well, for his resemblance to the *vilain* presents the romance adaptor with his one serious difficulty. The test of chivalric virtue seems to require an uncourtly challenger, and the exchange of blows seems to demand a symmetrical structure such as it has in the *Fled Bricrend*. But in romance, which exists to demonstrate the superiority of chivalry, the *vilain* must always suffer defeat, especially if he is allowed to enter the court and taunt it in the way Curoi does. The romancers never found a permanent solution to this problem, and though the heroes, the form of the challenges, and the nature of the tests remain generally uniform in the romance versions of this tale, the challengers and the conclusions vary widely. In Paiens' *La Mule sanz frain* the challenger is a *vilain* who resembles the Irish *bachlach,* and Paiens can retain a trace of the original symmetry only by moving the scene far from Arthur's court and thus sacrificing much of the action of *Caradoc* and "The Champions' Bargain." In *Hunbaut* even this trace is gone. Indeed, this romance seems to show that with the challenger as a *vilain* a knight need not even accept the proposed bargain. "I shall make no agreement" ("Je n'en ferai nule aramie," v. 1504), Gawain disdainfully tells the *vilain,* thereby justifying the trick that allows him to escape the return-blow. In *Perlesvaus,* on the other hand, the challenger is a completely chivalric gentleman, and the balanced structure of the tale is so completely realized that the hero and his challenger end by kneeling to beg one another's pardon. This is an even more symmetrical conclusion than in the Irish tale, but the point of the tale is completely lost.[21]

The author of *Caradoc* was able to avoid these difficulties by retaining the element of disguise that appears in "The Champions' Bargain." Éliavres is an enemy to the Round Table, as basically opposed to Arthur's chivalric court as are the *vilains* of *La Mule* and *Hunbaut.* However, he disguises himself not as a grotesque churl, as Curoi did, but as a remarkably handsome knight, as courtly in appearance as the challenger in *Perlesvaus.* Consequently, the poet could use an anti-courtly challenger and yet retain the many features of the Irish tale he would have had to omit with a monstrous *vilain* in that role. He thus passed on to the Gawain-poet both the fully developed tale and a significantly ambiguous challenger.

He also passed on a tale rich in new meanings. Mainly they are due to the new use to which he puts the tale. The central plot of *Caradoc* turns on the relations between the hero, his mother, and the magician who is his natural father—the Alexander-Olympias-Nectanabus triangle of the Alexander romances. Éliavres is kindly disposed to his son, but when Caradoc learns of his parentage he inflicts a terrible punishment on his father, and later he must suffer for this intemperate act, since he is finally to attain Christian humility rather than an Alexander's pride. The challenge tale, which involves a disguised magician, Curoi, who is kindly disposed to the hero and who reveals his identity to him at the end provided the author of *Caradoc* with an excellent means of bringing father and son together, of demonstrating the hero's prowess in an introductory adventure, and of setting the main plot in motion by the revelation of Éliavres' identity and relation to Caradoc. Consequently, the beheading is no longer the climax to a life of adventure, as it was when Cuchulainn finally won the champion's portion; it is now an initiation into that life. Caradoc has received the accolade of knighthood only the evening before, and the beheading, which occurs at the feast celebrating his new state, is the first chivalric act of his career, the fictional equivalent of the public demonstration of skill and strength that followed the ceremony in real life and the symbolic equivalent of the accolade itself. Furthermore, Caradoc's experience brings him pain and sorrow, the sad knowledge of his parentage rather than the unalloyed triumph enjoyed by Cuchulainn. For Caradoc the beheading is not only an initiation into chivalric life but a means of discovering himself.

This new function accounts for the allusions to the theme of the "Dümmling" or "fol chevalier" that the poet adds to the tale. In the early redactions the theme is suggested by Arthur's warning that Caradoc should not accept the challenge, for, he says, there are better men in the court. The later redactions omit the warning and substitute Éliavres' demand to know if Caradoc has been selected as the best knight in the court. No, the hero replies, as one of the "plus folz." Caradoc probably means "fol" in the sense of "foolhardy," and his speech is a development of Kay's remark that only a fool would accept such a bargain, but the word echoes ironically at the end of the episode when he learns that he is also "fol" in the sense of "foolish," ignorant even of his own parentage. Like many another young hero in Arthurian literature—Lancelot, Tristan de Nanteuil, Libiaus Desconnus—Caradoc has been raised in ignorance and must discover his own identity.[22] The most famous of such heroes is Perceval, whose first adventure is the duel with the strange Red Knight who rides suddenly and threateningly into Camelot in somewhat the same manner as the green-clad Éliavres. Only after proving his merit does he learn who he is—Perceval le Gallois—and only then is he ready to undertake his great adventures. Certainly it was the example of *Perceval* that suggested this theme to the poet, and his allusions to the themes of foolishness, identity, and self-discovery must have gained much of their original force from the direct relation of *Caradoc* to *Perceval* in the First Continuation.

To show that Caradoc is initiated into life as well as knighthood the poet adds another set of allusions, those to the theme of nature and its seasonal cycle. The Irish *bachlach* had traces of a seasonal deity about him, as appears in his description—"the bushiness of a great tree upon him"—and in his boast of control over the elements—"the whole household shall have light and yet the hall shall not be burned."[23] In *Caradoc* the Celtic deity becomes a romance magician, but the seasonal theme is developed considerably. The time, unspecified in the Irish version, is set at Pentecost, the traditional high spring holiday of the Round Table in French romance, and in place of a single day between the first blow and the second there is a year's interval, clearly implying the rebirth of nature in the spring. The later redactors made the theme even more explicit by giving Éliavres the costume of a celebrant of May; on his head he wears a chaplet of flowers, and he is clothed entirely in green. If, as seems likely, the beheading episode in the later prose romance *Perlesvaus* is derived from *Caradoc,* we have in that work the final realization of the possibilities of the seasonal theme, for the author of *Perlesvaus* explicitly links the beheading with the redemption of a wasteland.[24]

When one considers that the attractive Éliavres is an evil character and that Caradoc's new knighthood leads him to a humiliating discovery and a reckless act, the complexity of the life that Caradoc discovers becomes apparent. Unlike Perceval and the other "fair unknowns," Caradoc is disconcerted and shamed by his discovery of his parentage, and in the penitential scenes later in the romance this shame is developed into a major theme: Caradoc learns more about his own relation to life and evil, and he is brought to condemn himself as the "worst knight in the world." [25] Only after this deep and painful penitence (at a chapel hidden far in the forest) is he released from the serpent his mother attached to his arm (the serpent of evil that all inherit). Only then is he able to return to Arthur's court, which he left immediately after the return-blow, and resume the life of a knight.

The Gawain-poet's treatment of the beheading tale

The Gawain-poet must have been attracted to the beheading tale in *Caradoc* at least partly because of the implications with which the author had invested it. The entire First Continuation was very popular in England; it supplied the sources for a number of other romances, including at least two others concerning Gawain, *The Jeaste of Syr Gawayne* and *Golagros and Gawane,* and *Caradoc* itself is ultimately related to *The Boy and the Mantle*.[26] The poet clearly had a wealth of tales to choose from. However, no other part of the First Continuation was so rich as *Caradoc* in possibilities clustering around the problem of the relation of knighthood to life. The original author and later redactors of *Caradoc* were by no means the blunderers that critics have thought them;[27] they developed the beheading tale from a simple test of loyalty and bravery to an initiation into chivalric life by means of that test, and they offered the Gawain-poet not only a good plot but a significantly ambiguous hero and challenger, an important subject, and a series of actions that involve the themes of foolishness, identity, self-discovery, and nature—all of which passed along with the plot itself into *Sir Gawain*.

In general, the Gawain-poet followed his source very closely. He changed the time of the action from Pentecost to New Year's, the traditional high holiday of the Round Table in English romance,[28] he omitted Sir Kay from the action, and he made many significant additions. Yet the outlines of *Caradoc* are easily discerned in *Sir Gawain*, for the Gawain-poet, like the author of *Caradoc* before him, retained as much as he could from his source, using it as a framework on which to build his own narrative.

Both works begin with the feast, at which Guenevere has an important role, and both mention Arthur's custom of not eating until some marvel has appeared. Then, as the king and nobles are at the dais talking—"parlerent," "talkande" of "trifles ful hende"—the green-clad challenger rides into the hall carrying a weapon that, like himself, is both threatening and attractive; it is belted with fine silk in the French, lapped about with a rich "lace" (a cord that serves as a belt) in *Sir Gawain*. After praising the king, he proposes that someone cut off his head now in exchange for a return-blow a year later (*Sir Gawain* and the later redactions of *Caradoc* are the only romance versions in which the challenge is stated without a prior reversal of the order of blows, as in "The Champions' Bargain"). When no one speaks, the challenger looks about for an opponent—wagging his beard and turning in his saddle in *Sir Gawain,* offering his sword about the hall in *Caradoc.* Finally, Arthur's nephew (Caradoc and Gawain are both so related) accepts the challenge, labelling himself a fool in his opening speech ("plus folz," "of wyt feblest"). He strikes off the head, and the challenger retrieves it before anyone can prevent him (as Gawain prevents the body from reaching the head in *Hunbaut*).[29] The challenger warns the hero to be ready in a year and rides out of the hall.

The court is left sorrowing for the hero, and the narrator intrudes to condemn him for the folly of his undertaking: "En le fin le seul plaisir est en cent tourmens converti"; "Gawan watȝ glad to begynne þose gomneȝ in halle, Bot þaȝ þe ende be heuy, haf ȝe no wonder" (vv. 495–96). But the hero remains calm, saying that he will accept his fate ("la fortune," "destinés derf and dere," v. 564). When the antagonists meet for the second time, the challenger reminds the hero of his bargain, and the hero announces that he is ready—"Vous me voiez; faictes du pis que vous pourrez"; "I schal stond stylle/ And warp þe no wernyng to worch as þe lykeȝ" (vv. 2252–53). The challenger twice delays the blow, and the hero angrily accuses him of cowardice and tells him not to delay so long. The challenger finally strikes a harmless blow and then praises the hero and reveals both his own identity and his relation to the protagonist—his father in *Caradoc,* the agent of Morgan la Fay, "þyn aunt," in *Sir Gawain.* The hero, successful in the test but disturbed by the knowledge he has gained from it, sadly returns to the rejoicing court.

The differences between *Sir Gawain* and *Caradoc* are

more important than the similarities, for the Gawain-poet's changes in the inherited plot, mainly additions, radically alter the tone and meaning of the tale. The additions themselves are of an unusual nature, so unconventional that the more orthodox romancer who wrote the fifteenth-century adaptation of our poem, *The Grene Knight,* omitted almost all of them and restored the beheading tale to nearly the shape it had in the French romance. Yet the Gawain-poet's technique is conservative, and most of his unconventional additions are based on hints provided by *Caradoc.* For example, the poet's most significant addition to the opening scene—Arthur's attempt to accept the challenge—presents the king in a rather unflattering and definitely unconventional role. In no other version of the beheading does Arthur take such a part in the action. Yet in the later redactions of *Caradoc* he is deeply involved in the challenge. When the stranger demands his boon, he prefaces his request with praise for the king, and Arthur consequently feels personally responsible when the challenger taunts the court for its failure ("Le roy fort se dehaite"). Evidently he is in some way responsible, for when the challenger recovers his head he turns first to the king and warns him to keep the bargain: " 'Sire,' faict il, 'maintenant me debvez mon droict rendre.' " A trace of this action remains in *Sir Gawain,* where the challenger also turns to the high table and faces the dais (v. 445) even though his speech, containing echoes of Éliavres' words to Arthur, is addressed to Gawain. The author of the later version of *Caradoc* does nothing further to develop Arthur's role, perhaps depending on Caradoc's relation to Arthur as both vassal and nephew to account for the king's involvement. Yet he did make Arthur's role explicit enough that his action in *Sir Gawain* is more a matter of development than of complete change.

Even some of the details of Arthur's actions are adapta-

tions of what the poet found in *Caradoc.* The king's reply
to the Green Knight's request for a boon helps to establish
the tension between him and the challenger: "If þou
craue batayl bare/ Here fayleʒ þou not to fyʒt" (vv. 277–
78). But it differs more in tone than in content from the
reply in *Caradoc:* "Que vos demander me voudrez/ Ce
saichier que ja n'i faudrez" (vv. 7157–58).[30] When the challenger taunts the court, Arthur's reaction is the same in *Sir
Gawain* as it was in *Caradoc:* "þe lorde greued" (v. 316);
"Le roy fort se dehaite." Even when the king rushes forward to seize the axe—"Lyʒtly lepeʒ he hym to and laʒt at
his honde" (v. 328)—his action is the same as that of
Caradoc, who "could restrain himself no longer" and "Si
vet corant au chevalier/ An sa main prant le branc d'acier"
(vv. 7191–92). Arthur takes up the challenge in a manner
more suitable to the Kay than to the Arthur of most romances, and it is therefore not surprising that his speech
to the challenger should echo the sentiments of Kay in
Caradoc: "Pour fol le chevallier tendroie qui ceste chose
entreprendroit"; "As þou foly hatʒ frayst, fynde þe be-
houes" (v. 324).

Gawain's interruption of the king just as he is about to
strike seems to have been suggested by *Caradoc,* for in the
French poem a similar interruption very nearly occurs.
When the strange knight bows and Caradoc prepares to
deliver the blow, we are told that in another moment
Yvain would have rushed forward to seize the sword: "Et
a petit chose tint que Yvain ne lui court l'espee hors des
mains oster." Nothing further is done with this suggestion
in *Caradoc;* apparently the later redactors introduced it
partly to strengthen the parallel between the first scene
and the last, in which the return-blow is interrupted twice,
and partly as a replacement for the scene in the earlier
redactions in which Arthur and his barons attempt to dissuade Caradoc from the adventure, since that attempt con-

flicted with the later redactors' other important set of additions, the king's responsibility to see that the bargain is accepted and fulfilled. However, in *Caradoc* we have only the hint that Yvain might interrupt the undertaking and transfer the adventure to himself. In *Sir Gawain* the transfer actually takes place, and Arthur, who has Caradoc's role as well as his own up to this point in the action, is replaced by Gawain.

The transfer makes Gawain explicitly the surrogate for the king. The hero is thus no longer a free agent like Caradoc, who, impelled by foolhardiness, snatches the weapon from the challenger's hands. Instead, Gawain asks Arthur for permission to undertake the adventure, arguing that it is "more seemly" that he should do so. Arthur consults with his barons, obtains their consent, and solemnly invests Gawain with the adventure in a ceremonial manner that emphasizes the fact that the hero represents the king and court:

> Þen comanded þe kyng þe knyȝt for to ryse;
> And he ful radly vpros, and ruchched hym fayre,
> Kneled doun bifore þe kyng, and cacheȝ þat weppen;
> And he luflyly hit hym laft, and lyfte vp his honde,
> And gef hym Goddeȝ blessyng, and gladly hym biddes,
> Þat his hert and his honde schulde hardi be boþe.
>
> (vv. 366–71)

In the early versions of *Caradoc* the hero had acted against the advice of the king; in the later redactions his responsibility to fulfill the bargain on behalf of the king is implied; in *Sir Gawain* the hero is formally presented with the adventure that he undertakes as Arthur's representative. By the speeches and actions assigned to Gawain and by the characterization of him in the description of the Pentangle, the poet takes care to make the champion of Arthur's court a model knight, the representative of chivalry in general

as well as of Camelot in particular. This is possible because
he also changes the hero from the untried, unknown
Caradoc, who has received the accolade only the evening
before, to the famous Gawain, renowned for his chivalry
throughout the world of romance.

This leads to an apparent contradiction. The narrator
states that Gawain is the best of knights even before the
hero proves the fact by bowing for the return-blow. Yet
the Gawain-poet retains the trace of the "fol chevalier" in
the hero's character, and in Gawain's first speech he labels
himself "þe wakkest, I wot, and of wyt feblest,/ And lest
lur of my lyf" (vv. 354–55). Likewise, the poet retains the
narrator's comment, preserved in the prose version, on the
foolhardiness of the hero's undertaking:

> This hanselle hatȝ Arthur of auenturus on fyrst
> In ȝonge ȝer, for he ȝerned ȝelpyng to here.
> Thaȝ hym wordeȝ were wane when þay to sete wenten,
> Now ar þay stoken of sturne werk, stafful her hond.
> Gawan watȝ glad to bygynne þose gomneȝ in halle,
> Bot þaȝ þe ende be heuy, haf ȝe no wonder;
> For þaȝ men ben mery in mynde quen þay han mayn
> drynk,
> A ȝere ȝernes ful ȝerne and ȝeldeȝ neuer lyke,
> Þe forme to þe fynisment foldeȝ ful selden.
>
> (vv. 491–99)

The Gawain-poet reemphasizes the king's involvement in
the action by including Arthur in his comment, and he
generalizes Gawain's particular situation by the *sententia*
that extends the application to "men" at large. The burden
of the comment nevertheless remains the same as that in
Caradoc; both the French and the English writers stress
the contrast between the light-hearted beginning ("glad
. . . gomneȝ"; "par sa couppe ou par une folle plaisance")
and the heavy end ("en le fin le plaisir seul est en cent
tormens converti"). This insistence upon the foolishness

of the undertaking and the warning that the end will be heavy are perhaps suitable to an untried knight, a "fol chevalier" like Caradoc, but they seem unsuitable to Gawain, who has proven his worthiness in the past, who embodies all the virtues represented by the Pentangle, and who will, if the conventions of romance are fulfilled, certainly triumph again.

From Gawain's point of view the conclusion is as heavy as the narrator promises. In *Sir Gawain*, as in *Caradoc*, the adventure initiates the hero into a new knowledge of himself. Caradoc learns of his parentage, a fact that fills him with anger and sorrow, and he later undergoes a penance that brings him to recognize his own unworthiness and that thus completes his initiation. At the end of *Sir Gawain* the hero also learns something about himself and he is also brought to the heavy knowledge of his own unworthiness. In his first speech, that in which with extravagant courtly humility he labels himself the least of knights, he acknowledges only Arthur's blood in his veins. This kinship, Gawain says, is his only claim to merit. After the return-blow is delivered, when Gawain is brought to true humility, he is forcibly reminded that Arthur is not his only kin, that the blood of Morgan la Fay also flows in his veins. She is the symbol of the evil that Gawain discovers in his flesh, a discovery that angers and shames him as much as Caradoc's had done. In this sense, Gawain, like Caradoc, also has a trace, though a slight one, of the "fol chevalier." He learns that he is indeed feeble of wit, "fol" both in the sense of "foolhardy" and in the sense of "ignorant," of failing to reckon with his own humanity, with the "flesche crabbed" (v. 2435) symbolized by the evil Morgan.

The Gawain-poet was not completely successful in his use of this character.[31] She became necessary to the poem once the hero was changed from Caradoc to Gawain, for

the well-known biography of the famous son of King Lot
made it impossible for the poet to make Gawain a son of
the evil enchanter Éliavres. However, Gawain did have a
relative almost as close who was an evil enchantress, his
aunt Morgan, and so she was brought into the poem, useful not only as a replacement for Éliavres but also, since
she is both the equal and the opposite of Arthur, as one
of the parallel contrasts in which the poet delighted and
which his theme required. She also allowed the poet to
retain the symmetrical structure of the beheading tale as
he had found it in Caradoc, since she provided an "over-
plot" within which the beheading could be contained as
part of a scheme against Guenevere. The struggle of good
and evil could thus be shifted away from the beheading;
with the revelation of Morgan's defeat (evil must always
be defeated in the romances) the narrative reaches a logical conclusion, since in this larger context the beheading
episode is simply a means of resolving the conflict.

The difficulty is that Morgan appears too late in the action, and Guenevere's role is too slight to justify the importance she suddenly assumes at the end of the adventure. In *Caradoc* Guenevere is far more important. She is
devoted to the hero, and she presents him with rich gifts
when he is knighted. She is therefore distracted with grief
when she thinks he must die, and she rushes into the hall
to interrupt the blow and plead for his life. When the challenger cruelly refuses her, there is a hint of antagonism in
his reply ("If you do not care to watch this, go to your
chamber and pray for his soul"), and the poet tells us that
she is so overcome by grief that she nearly dies. This was
probably the hint that led the Gawain-poet to create Morgan's plot against the queen's life.

Morgan, of course, expects that the sight of the challenger's suffering rather than the prospect of Gawain's will

cause the queen's death, a weakening but necessary change once the scene of the return-blow is shifted away from the court. Perhaps this is part of the reason for the bloody and frightening quality of the first beheading scene in *Sir Gawain,* in which the challenger displays his gory head to the court rather than immediately replacing it, as Éliavres does. This evidently does upset Guenevere, for Arthur takes special pains to comfort her after the challenger's departure, but she is apparently no worse for her experience. To provide for the rest of the action of the romance, the poet extends Morgan's plot against the queen to a plot against the whole Round Table (vv. 2456–59). This part of her scheme is integral to the action of the poem, and it does emphasize for the audience some of the dominant themes of the work. Yet, thematically important as it is, it does not help much so far as the plot is concerned, and the reader cannot avoid the feeling that the last-minute revelation of Morgan's scheme is too weak a foundation for this poem. Even the uninspired author of *The Grene Knight* realized this, and he supplied an entirely new motivation for the evil enchantress.[32]

However, the poet's perfunctory handling of Morgan's motives shows only that he was less concerned with integrating her into the action of the poem than with the principal advantage her presence allowed him. Bringing her into the poem allowed the Gawain-poet to make two characters out of the disguised enchanter Éliavres. Morgan inherits his function as an evil magician, and the Green Knight becomes solely a challenger. He has none of Éliavres' evil, even though he remains an enemy to knighthood, and there is no need to punish him later in the romance, as Éliavres must be punished. At the end of *Sir Gawain* the hero and the challenger embrace and part as friends;

Gawayn on blonk ful bene
To þe kyngeȝ burȝ buskeȝ bolde,
And þe kynȝt in þe enker grene
Whiderwarde-so-euer he wolde.

(vv. 2475–78)

Such a conclusion, as Kittredge wrote, is "delightful but contrary to all custom." [33] Customarily the hero's opponent is completely overcome—killed, disenchanted, or, at the very least, brought back to Camelot as a captive or as a reformed enemy who is now enrolled in the Round Table. This last alternative is the fate of Bredbeddle, the Bercilak of *The Grene Knight.* In our poem the Green Knight is as much a *vilain* as a knight, and he is therefore an even more likely candidate for reform or punishment than Bredbeddle or Éliavres. Yet Morgan removes the responsibility for the action from him, just as he absolves his lady from blame by taking the responsibility for her acts. Morgan thus becomes a convenient scapegoat for the potential evil in the scheme against Gawain and the court. Since she barely appears in the action of the poem, we do not become concerned with her, as we do with Aggteb in *The Grene Knight* or with Éliavres in *Caradoc,* and we are not intent on seeing her punished; but since she is the evil plotter we can blame her for everything and accept without difficulty the good-natured conclusion, however contrary to custom it is.

This unconventional conclusion is the Gawain-poet's most important modification of the beheading tale, and almost all his other additions serve to lend significance to the equality at which Gawain and the Green Knight finally arrive. All the additions concerning the hero help generalize him from a particular, untried knight like Caradoc to a representative of knighthood itself. Arthur's new role and Gawain's subsequent assumption of the challenge make him the explicit agent of the king and the court. His courtly actions and elaborate opening speech, in contrast to the few words of the close-mouthed Caradoc, demonstrate his loyalty and courtesy and prove that he is a suitable representative of this court. The change of name from the relatively obscure "Caradoc" to the famous "Gawain" underscores the change from a specific hero to a defender of Camelot's honor. The complex account of his armor presents the idealized appearance appropriate to such a champion, and, finally, the account of the Pentangle, in which the narrator characterizes Gawain as a perfect knight, completes the process and shows us that Gawain represents not only the court but perfect chivalry.

The additions concerning the challenger establish him as the equal of this perfect knight. He is described with as much care as Gawain, and he now has speeches as long and as impressive, in their uncourtly way, as Gawain's. Furthermore, he now has a castle where the festivities rival those at Camelot and where there is a woman more lovely than Guenevere, and he has a "green chapel" to which Gawain must come at the end of the poem just as the Green Knight came to Camelot at the beginning. But in addition to this, he is the embodiment of qualities antithetical to the perfect courtesy of the hero, for though he retains Éliavres' beauty and is richly dressed and "merry" in appearance, he is also "aghlich," fiercely bearded, and superlatively churlish in speech and action.

Consequently, the parallel between the hero and his challenger is more than a simple development of the balanced structure that the poet found in *Caradoc* and that derives ultimately from the Old Irish version. In *Sir Gawain*, far more clearly than in *Caradoc* and far more significantly than in the Irish versions, the challenger and the hero are complete opposites. The characterization of Gawain and the Green Knight is central to the poem, and it must therefore be examined in detail in the next chapter.

At present we need only note the antithesis that the poet has built. It suggests that he is using the beheading tale with a new theme, one that concerns the ideal of knighthood itself and the relation of that ideal to the churlishness represented by the Green Knight.

The source of the temptation episode

The temptation scenes and the related activities at Bercilak's castle are clearly the Gawain-poet's most important additions to the beheading tale. In *Caradoc,* the year's interval between the two blows is dismissed in a single sentence: "The tale tells us that he did so many chivalric deeds that no chevalier on earth had done so much in so little time, and his fame was so great that everyone believed his accomplishments to have been done by divine rather than physical means." In place of this bare report *Sir Gawain* has the brilliant festivities at Bercilak's castle, the hunting scenes, and the temptation itself, in which Gawain, assisted by Mary, succeeds by divine as well as physical means. However, Gawain's deeds are not as "chevallereux" as Caradoc's must have been, for at Bercilak's castle the hero finds himself in a situation completely different from that in the beheading episode. There he had encountered the world of *Märchen* in the person of the terrifying, invulnerable, and apparently supernatural Green Knight. Gawain's task is difficult, but his duty is clear, for that world is a familiar milieu for the knights of Arthur's court. In the temptation scenes, on the other hand, his opponent is anything but terrible, only too vulnerable, and disconcertingly natural—a fleshly, even comic figure from the world of novella who seems at times to be trying to change this romance into a fabliau. His duty is by no means so clear, and the Gawain of heroic and sententious resolution we see at Camelot becomes a Gawain of ridiculous bewilderment, peeping furtively from under the blankets and coyly submitting to the kisses of this woman so unlike the usual ladies—the enchanted maidens, idealized queens, and fairy mistresses—known to the knights of Arthurian romance.

The exact source of this episode has long been a moot question in Gawain-studies, and a great variety of ultimate originals have been suggested,[34] but only the Anglo-Norman romance *Yder*, first cited by Kittredge, provides any significant parallels:

> Yder sets out to find someone who will grant him arms (like Caradoc, he is on his first adventure). He comes upon King Ivenant in the forest. The king agrees to knight Yder on one condition: Yder must first go to Ivenant's castle, where he must resist the advances of the queen, who will attempt to seduce him. Yder goes ahead of the king and reaches the castle alone. He is well received and shown to a bed, where he soon falls asleep. He is awakened by the queen, who is richly but lightly dressed ("sanz guimple fu e sanz chemise," v. 313) and who offers him her love. He refuses, but she becomes more insistent, and he finally puts an end to the temptation by kicking her in the belly. Everyone in the castle thinks this is very funny: "Mult s'en rïent, mult s'en esjöent" (v. 384). When the king returns, he compliments Yder on his success, and then he knocks the queen to the floor. Then Yder bids farewell to the queen, but he will speak to her only through a door. The king laughs, grants Yder arms, and the hero rides away.[35]

The obvious crudity of this episode contrasts so sharply with its sophistication in *Sir Gawain* that critics have been inclined to look elsewhere, hoping to find a source "nearer the tone and spirit of the *Gawain* passages." [36]

However, tone is too complex a quality to be transported from one romance to another, as a comparison of *Sir Ga-*

wain to *Caradoc* and to *The Grene Knight* demonstrates. The tone and spirit of the temptation episode in *Sir Gawain* are the poet's own creation; the plot appears to be that of *Yder*, for the other analogues resemble *Sir Gawain* only in containing similar traditional elements. The theme of a host, usually a hunter, who manages a test of the hero is common in romance, from the Welsh tale of *Pwyll* to the Guinganbresil episode of the French *Perceval*, the German *Diu Crône*, and the English *Carl of Carlisle*.[37] The attempts of a hot-blooded wife to seduce a young man who is obligated to resist her advances is even more common, appearing in literature from the time of the first "Joseph and Potiphar's Wife" to Fielding's *Joseph Andrews*.[38] It is only in *Yder* and *Sir Gawain* that the two themes clearly coincide; the sexual tests in such works as *The Carl of Carlisle* are not attempted seductions at all, and the attempted seductions in such works as *Perlesvaus* have no trace of the hunter-host. Furthermore, the other tempted knights in romance have only a general obligation to the husbands; Yder and Gawain have specific, contractual agreements, and only they encounter hostesses who act with the knowledge of their husbands, absent hunting, and enter the heroes' bedrooms and attempt to seduce them. It is apparent that *Yder* or some work very closely related to it provided the basic situation used in the temptation episode in *Sir Gawain*.

Yet it is equally clear that the *Yder*-story is not the direct source of this episode, for it supplied no more than the general situation and the beginning of the temptation in *Sir Gawain*. On that simple framework the poet builds a far more complex temptation than appears in any other medieval work. First he reshapes the episode from *Yder* to make it parallel to the beheading. Yder, like Caradoc, is an untried young knight engaged in his first adventure. In *Sir Gawain* the hero is a proven champion, the model of knighthood and the exemplar of courtesy. His antagonist is not the simple hot-blooded queen of *Yder* but a more complex character who, like the frightening but "merry" Green Knight, is a combination of idealized and uncourtly, even churlish characteristics. Nevertheless, like the beheading episode and unlike *Yder* or any other temptation tale, the episode ends with Gawain and his opponent equally successful. Gawain manages to preserve both his continence and his courtesy, and yet the lady does trick him into accepting the lace and betraying his host. At the conclusion of the romance, Gawain and his temptress emerge as friendly equals; Gawain sends his respects to the lady (as in *Yder*, the hero refuses an invitation to see her again), and the Green Knight vouches for her friendship to him (vv. 2404–11). Considering the usual fate of unsuccessful temptresses in medieval romance, this conclusion is even more obviously contrary to custom than the reconciliation of Gawain and Bercilak.

In addition to this general parallel between the beheading and temptation episodes, the poet inserts a number of direct links between the two sets of scenes. The lace, which binds the outcome of the temptation with the beheading, was not difficult to invent. It is the common (and often magical) love token of medieval romance. Usually that token is a ring, and the lady first offers Gawain a ring, but the lace is more appropriate to this romance, since it obviously suggests the lace that adorns the challenger's weapon. Probably the cloth that adorned Éliavres' sword ("les renges ou saincture de fine soie"—"the girdles or belt of fine silk") suggested both the lady's girdle and the belt ("lace") on the axe. The hunting scenes, which are essential both to the conversations and to the relation between them and the return-blow, are drawn from what appears to be an English romance tradition as it appears in works like *Sir Tristrem, Somer Soneday,* and *The Parlement of the Thre Ages.*[39] The exchange of winnings, the most obvious link between the beheading and the temptation, is far less common. It appears only in *Sir Gawain* and the Latin *Miles Gloriosus,* but the resemblances between the two exchanges are close enough to suggest that the poet knew and drew on some version of the Latin work for this important detail.[40]

The substitution of the exchange of winnings for the agreement between Yder and King Ivenant changes considerably the character of the tale. The king tells Yder exactly what he can expect at the castle, and Yder knows precisely what he must do to pass the test. In *Sir Gawain* the warning is omitted, and Gawain thinks that the agreement is more a joke than a serious obligation, a bargain made, as Gawain says, "þer spared watȝ no drynk" (v. 1935). The problem posed by the temptation has therefore become an internal, psychological one. Gawain himself must find reasons for resisting the lady, and he has no support in the expectation of any immediate reward of the sort awaiting Yder and no clear guide in the terms of his bargain with the host. When the lady presses Gawain closely, he thinks not of his apparently joking agreement with her husband but of the more general moral problems raised by his situation:

> For þat pryncece of pris depresed hym so þikke,
> Nurned hym so neȝe þe þred, þat nede hym bihoued
> Oþer lach þer hir luf, oþer lodly refuse.
> He cared for his cortaysye, lest craþayn he were,
> And more for his meschef, ȝif he schulde make synne,
> And be traytor to þat tolke þat þat telde aȝt.
>
> (vv. 1770–75)

The temptation, which in *Yder* had been a simple test of continence, has become in *Sir Gawain* a complex trial involving not only continence and a bargain with the host but courtesy, loyalty, and the dangers of sin.

Perhaps we have here the reason that the Gawain-poet decided to add the temptation to the beheading tale. The poet had changed the hero of *Caradoc* from an individual knight to a representative of Arthur and the Round Table, a model of chivalry, and he had thus generalized the test from a trial of a particular knight to a test of knighthood itself. However, the beheading episode, even with the Gawain-poet's changes, tries only a part of Gawain's perfect knighthood. It is an excellent test of loyalty, but it tests that virtue mainly on the basis of the hero's courage and fortitude. Even the relatively crude Cuchulainn could pass that test. If Gawain's knighthood was to be fully tested, the poet had to find some means of trying those more peaceful virtues that distinguish a gentleman from a mere warrior. The temptation in *Yder* could be modified to provide such a test. With the Gawain-poet's changes it becomes as good a trial of loyalty as the beheading, but here the test is conducted not in the realm of violence and high romantic adventure but in that of courtesy and sometimes low comedy, and here the necessary virtues are those of the hall and bower rather than of the battlefield.

The poet was able to make the tale from *Yder* fulfill this new function because the theme of sexual temptation, a very common one in romance, had acquired a variety of well-known associations on which the poet could draw. For example, Gawain resists the lady partly because he fears a disaster—"meschef, ȝif he schulde make synne." It is this fear that integrates the temptation with the beheading. Nothing is said at Bercilak's castle to imply that succumbing to the lady's advances will in any way affect the return-blow. However, a sexual temptation is a clear invitation to sin, and, as Gawain realizes, one who faces death must avoid sin, especially the sin of incontinence. The purpose of this is not to die in a state of grace but to avoid death altogether. The idea that continence is a guarantee of survival is an ancient folk belief that survives in medieval romance,[41] and even some quite sophisticated people held this belief in the Middle Ages.

The memoirs of Aeneas Sylvius (Pope Pius II) contain an amusing example. Aeneas had been sent to Scotland on a diplomatic mission early in the fifteenth century (c. 1435). Fearful of shipwreck, he chose to journey overland from Scotland to England. When he crossed the Tweed, he took lodging in a small town. After dinner his host and his host's men left to take shelter in a tower some distance away, for they expected an attack by the Scots. The women stayed behind, because, Aeneas explains, "They think the enemy will do them no wrong—not counting outrage a wrong." Aeneas remained with the women.

> But after a good part of the night had passed, two young women showed Aeneas, who was by this time very sleepy, to a chamber strewn with straw, planning to sleep with him, as was the custom of the country, if they were asked. But Aeneas, thinking less about women than about robbers, who he feared might appear any minute, repulsed the protesting girls, afraid that, if he committed a sin, he would have to pay the penalty as soon as the robbers arrived. Some time after midnight there was a great noise of dogs barking and geese hissing, at which all the women scattered, the guide took to his heels, and there was the wildest confusion as if the enemy were at hand . . . [but] very soon the women returned with the interpreter, saying that nothing was wrong and that the newcomers were friends, not enemies. Aeneas thought this was the reward of his continence.[42]

Gawain's desire to avoid sin is probably motivated by the same superstition as Aeneas', since, as his bad confession shows, he is an even poorer theologian than the future

Pope.[43] Gawain does not know that the temptation is connected with the beheading, but he does realize that to succumb to the lady's advances will considerably lessen his chance of surviving the return-blow.

Gawain is almost as concerned for his loyalty as for his life, and he fears becoming a "traytor to þat tolke þat þat telde aʒt" as much as he fears committing a sin. This was no problem to Yder, who is obligated entirely to himself, but, as Gawain knows, one owes a special loyalty to his host. This principle, especially in regard to the women of the household, is widespread in literature, appearing in works that range from the crude "Imperious Host" tales collected by Kittredge to Henry James' *The Europeans,* in which the sophisticated Felix fears that he is guilty of "disloyalty" even in considering a proposal of marriage to his host's daughter.[44] In the many medieval examples of the "Potiphar's Wife" tale, to which *Sir Gawain* is related, the tempted knights repulse the ladies not because of chastity but because of loyalty to the lady's husband.[45]

The temptation as a test of courtesy

Gawain's problem is further complicated by the fact that he must guard not only his life and his loyalty but his "cortaysye, lest craþayn he were." In none of the analogous tales is courtesy of any importance. In *Sir Gawain* it is the most important aspect of the temptation. Gawain is characterized as the perfect courtier, and when he arrives at Bercilak's castle his reputation for courtesy has preceded him. All rejoice that their visitor is "þat fyne fader of nurture" and that those who hear him will "lerne of luftalkyng" (vv. 916–27). Almost immediately Gawain demonstrates that his reputation is justified. When the two ladies appear in the hall, he greets them courteously and "knyȝtly he meleȝ."

> Þay kallen hym of aquoyntaunce, and he hit quyk askeȝ
> To be her seruaunt sothly, if hemself lyked.
>
> (vv. 975–76)

Gawain's request is an act of homage to the forms of polite society, in which the polished courtier is a servant of ladies, even the ugly ones like the ancient companion of Bercilak's wife. Naturally Gawain pays more attention to the beautiful wife than to her repulsive companion, but even so he seeks only an affair of "fin amour," devoid of fleshly ties and reduced to the level of polite conversation, "Wyth clene cortays carp closed fro fylþe" (v. 1013). The lady, however, is determined that she will learn more than this from the master of "luf-talkyng." "Dos," she urges him when they are alone, "techeȝ me of your wytte,/ Whil my lorde is fro hame" (vv. 1533–34).

This emphasis on Gawain's courtesy explains why *Yder*, like every other analogue adduced for the temptation scenes, provides the pattern for only the beginning of the action, the first half of the first day's temptation. In *Yder*, as in *Sir Gawain*, the woman offers the hero her love, he refuses, and the test is ended. As soon as Gawain reminds the lady that she is married, she recognizes the futility of any further attempt on his continence:

> "Þaȝ I were burde bryȝtest," þe burde in mynde hade,
> "Þe lasse luf in his lode."
>
> (vv. 1284–85)

In some editions these lines are drastically emended, for if the lady realizes that Gawain will not yield to temptation there seems little reason for her to continue her efforts through the rest of this day and for two days more.[46]

She continues because at this point the nature of the temptation changes, and she begins to direct her attack not so much toward Gawain's continence as toward his courtesy. If continence were all that mattered, if Gawain were the ideal Christian battling the flesh, any one of a number of crude but moral acts would solve his problem. He could kick his temptress in the belly, as Yder does, refuse to speak to her, as does the tempted Gawain· in *Perlesvaus,* or he could lecture her on the duties of a wife, as do the heroes of so many of the English "Potiphar's Wife" tales. When one is dealing with evil, courtesy does not matter, and the quicker one puts an end to the temptation the better. But Gawain is no Guyon and Bercilak's castle is no Bower of Bliss. A failure in courtesy is as serious to this hero as a failure in loyalty or continence. The lady is so insistent and so attractive that Gawain is at his wits' end and "wroth with himseluen,"

> Bot he nolde not for his nurture nurne hir aȝayneȝ,
> Bot dalt with hir al in daynté, how-se-euer þe dede turned.
> (vv. 1661–62)

A simple "no" would end the temptation, but Gawain will not desert his "nurture" and betray his famous courtesy.

Indeed, Gawain is too concerned for his courtesy. Halfway through the third day's interview the lady suddenly changes her tactics again, and "smeþely con he smyle" when Gawain thinks he has won and can courteously tell the lady that he intends to have no paramour (vv. 1788–91). Then he accepts the lace. It takes the nick of the axe to remind him that courtesy, like continence, is only a part of the temptation. Nevertheless, it is the most important part, and his main problem in these scenes is to resist the lady's advances without deserting his model courtesy.

The pattern of action that Gawain follows is therefore much different from that apparent in *Yder.* He finds himself in what appears to be the traditional "Potiphar's Wife" situation, of the sort that appears in works like *Le Chastelaine de Vergi*. The Gawain-poet may never have read that lovely and widely influential poem, but *La Chastelaine* is useful to the student of *Sir Gawain*, since it clearly presents the tactics that the perfect courtier traditionally uses in this delicate situation.

The unnamed hero of the French romance is a guest in the household of the Duke of Burgundy. The duchess, observing his excellent qualities, soon develops a passion for him. One day she engages him in a private conversation, and she tells him that he is so generally admired that he deserves an "amie" in a very high station. The hero, pretending to misunderstand, replies that he has never considered such an idea ("Je n'ai mie/ encore a ce mise m'entente," vv. 66–67), and, pressed further, he claims that he is unworthy of such an honor—"Ne je ne sui duc ne conte/ qui si hautement amer doie" (vv. 76–77). The duchess becomes more insistent, and she comes as close to a direct statement as the standards of romance allow even so abandoned a woman as she—"Dites moi se vous savez ore/ se je vous ai m'amor donee" (vv. 84–85). Confronted with almost a direct statement, the knight can only reply that he would be pleased to have her love but that she is, after all, married to his lord and host:

> "Mes de cele amor Dieus me gart
> qu'a moi n'a vous tort cele part
> ou la honte mon seignor gise,
> qu'a nul fuer ne a nule guise
> n'enprendroie tel mesprison
> comme de fere traïson
> si vilaine et se disloial
> vers mon droit seignor natural."
>
> (vv. 91–98)

["But may God preserve me from that love which on my part and yours would bring wrong or shame to my lord, that in any manner I should be so base as to commit so churlish and disloyal a betrayal of my right and natural lord."]

Thereupon, the lady, perceiving that her attempt has failed, sets about plotting the knight's downfall in the customary manner of a disappointed "Potiphar's Wife," an act for which she justly loses her life (by decapitation) at the end of the poem. The rest of the plot turns on the problems of loyalty to which the knight alludes in the speech quoted above, since loyalty—the obligation to keep one's plighted word and the conflicts to which this leads—is as important in *La Chastelaine de Vergi* as in *Sir Gawain*.

Gawain uses exactly the same tactics as the hero of *La Chastelaine*. First he attempts to evade the lady by deliberate misunderstanding—"I be not now þat ȝe of speken" (v. 1242)—and then he claims to be unworthy of such an honor: "I am wyȝe unworthy, I wot wel myseluen" (v. 1244). Finally, he must remind the lady of her own position: " 'Ywysse, worþy,' quoþ þe wyȝe, 'ȝe haf waled wel better' " (v. 1276). The reminder is a signal to the lady that her attempt has failed. "Fi," the duchess immediately replies, "Et qui vous en prie?" (vv. 99–100); and Bercilak's lady realizes there is "þe lasse luf in his lode." The pattern of defense that both heroes use was so firmly established in medieval literature that it survived until well into the modern period. It appears in the eighteenth-century *Joseph Andrews*, in which Lady Booby tells Joseph, "You are a handsome young fellow and might do better; you might make your fortune." He first misunderstands, then becomes humble, and finally, when she becomes more insistent, he reminds the lady of her position: "I should think your lady condescends a good deal below yourself." [47]

Although Gawain willingly plays the Joseph both in the

conventional defense he adopts on the first day and in his similar tactics throughout the rest of the temptation, his opponent does not adopt any such fixed and easily classifiable role. The lady refuses to take the forms of courtesy with any of Gawain's seriousness, and with a charming disregard of consistency she alternates between pedantically lecturing Gawain on the rules of courtship and then ignoring them herself.[48]

She begins in a most shocking manner by shamelessly offering herself to the hero with no regard at all for the rules of that courtly love in which she seems more expert than Gawain. Even the heroines of the "Potiphar's Wife" tales recognize that it is the male's prerogative to take the initiative in a courtship, and they pay verbal homage to the proper form by taking refuge in the conditional. Lady Booby's "What would you think Joseph, if I . . ." has ancient grammatical precedents in works like *Generydes* (vv. 482–83), "If I myght fynd/ That ye wold loue me . . ." or in *La Chastelaine de Vergi*, "Si lo que vous soiez amis/ en un haut leu, se vous veez/ que vous i soiez bien amez" (vv. 70–72). Bercilak's lady bothers with none of this; she goes to Gawain's room, locks the door, and announces that Gawain is her prisoner. It is a situation reminiscent of the "Fairy Mistress" tale or of the predicament in which Alexander finds himself (in *Kyng Alisaunder*) when Candacee discovers him in her tent:

> "And þou art yfalle in hond myne
> Þe to solace and no pyne,
> For here vnder þis couertour
> Y wol have þe to myn amour,
> Now þou art in my baundoun, leoue sir."
>
> (Ms. L, 6431–35)

Gawain could probably have handled a "fairy mistress" with no difficulty, for she is a common figure in romance,[49] but in the next few lines the lady has shifted her tactics again, and she seems not so much a "fairy mistress" as the heroine of a fabliau. Her husband is away from home, her attendants elsewhere in the castle, and, she resolves,

> "I schal ware my whyle wel, quyl hit lasteȝ,
>> with tale.
>> Ȝe ar welcum to my cors,
>> Yowre awen won to wale;
>> Me behoueȝ of fyne force,
>> Your seruaunt be and schale."
>>> (vv. 1235–40)

A moment before, Gawain was her prisoner; now, she claims, she is his. But she is no helpless damsel. Her resolution and her brisk concern for the physical details of the assignation—the locked door, the absent husband—are worthy of a Wife of Bath. "Fyne force," not "fin amour," controls the lover in her view, and her only gesture toward assigning the knight to his proper role as a wooer is to cast him in the part of a ravisher ("Me behoueȝ of fyne force"), a kind of knight who would more endear himself to Chaucer's Alisoun than to the refined ladies of romance. On the second day she defines the courtship in the same manner:

> "Ma fay," quoþ þe meré wyf, "ȝe may not be werned,
> Ȝe ar stif innoghe to constrayne wyth strenkþe,
>> ȝif yow lykeȝ,
> ȝif any were so vilanous þat yow devaye wolde."
>>> (vv. 1495–97)

She insists upon flaunting her disregard of the courtly code. That the audience is meant to be aware of this is apparent from the lady's diction. "Seruaunt" in the first speech above recalls Gawain's earlier use of the word and reminds us that the knight, not the lady, is supposed to be the servant, and "vilanous" in the second speech above invokes the proper courtly judgment on her action. Gawain must remain true to his courtesy, yet his only alternatives seem to be either "lach þer hir luf, oþer lodly refuse" (v. 1772), and, with the love defined in the way the lady insists, it is as "lodly" to accept as to refuse.

Churlish as the lady's purposes may be, her tone is never crude, and she is no simple "Potiphar's Wife" or fabliau heroine. Gawain's strategy is based on the "Potiphar's Wife" situation, but hers is based on an equally common romance situation, one that suits the famed and courtly Gawain and that very nearly justifies her enthusiastic and indecorous pursuit of the hero. The lady pretends that she loves Gawain for his reputation—"Priuilye paramour/ & she neuer hym see" (vv. 47–48), as it is put by the author of *The Grene Knight*, who expands this aspect of the temptation and makes it the motive for his whole poem. Bercilak's lady begins her courtship by telling Gawain that she knows of his great fame: "For I wene wel, iwysse, Sir Wowen ȝe are,/ Þat alle þe worlde worchipeȝ, quer-so ȝe ride" (vv. 1226–27). Now that she has the famous Gawain with her—"Now ȝe ar here, iwysse, and we bot oure one" (v. 1230)—she cannot restrain herself, and she flatly offers him her love. Such an argument is not only flattering, it considerably complicates Gawain's problem, for it casts the lady not in the role of an evil temptress or a simple lecher, like the queen in *Yder*, but in that of a traditional romance heroine whom Gawain must therefore respect and whom he cannot "lodly refuse."

Modern readers know such a heroine from Malory's *Morte Darthur*, in which the four queens love Lancelot in the way Bercilak's lady pretends to love Gawain.[50] The Gawain-poet knew this situation from the romance of *Brun de Branlant*, which occurs just before *Le Livre de Caradoc* in the First Continuation of *Perceval*. In that romance Gawain is travelling through a wild forest when he

comes upon a lovely *plaisance* in which there is a beautiful
tent and an even more beautiful girl. She has loved Gawain for many years, although she has never seen him, for
she loves him only for his reputation and knows him (as
Candacee knows Alexander) only by his portrait. When
she discovers that her visitor is the famous Gawain, she
rushes to him, throws her arms about him, and announces:

> "Sire," fait elle, "en abandon
> Vos met mon cors et vos presant
> M'amor a toz jors loiaumant." [51]
>
> (vv. 6322–24)
> ["Sir," she says, "freely I give you my body and present
> you loyally with my love forever."]

Her offer is as blunt and takes nearly the same form as
Bercilak's lady's "ʒe ar welcum to my cors." In *Brun*, the
lady's conduct is pardonable, for she is only a young girl,
innocent of the rules of courtship and charming in her
naïveté. However, Gawain realizes the breach of decorum
of which she is guilty, and he is careful to invoke a proper
tone of formal reserve in his reply:

> "Et je reçoif, ma douce amie,
> Liez et joianz, sans vilenie,
> Ce presant et ce riche don."
>
> (vv. 6325–27)
> ["And, my sweet friend, happily and joyfully, without
> churlishness, I receive this present, this rich gift."]

The narrator also, by repeating "sans vilenie," emphasizes
that the relation is not churlish despite its beginning:

> Des jeus d'amours sanz vilenie
> S'ont puis ansamble tant parlé
> Et bonement entr'eus jöé
> Qu'ele a perdu non de pucelle,
> S'a non amie et damoiselle.
>
> (vv. 6332–36)

[Of the games of love, without churlishness, they have spoken so much together and so well played that she has lost the name "girl" and is now a "lover" and "lady."]

The outcome of the meeting in *Brun* is obviously much different from that in *Sir Gawain,* for in the English poem Gawain is confronted not with an unattached *pucelle* but with the wife of his host. Gawain's problem, however, is the same. In each poem the atmosphere is perfectly courtly up to the moment the woman speaks. Then, with none of the conventional rhetoric of courtship, the woman bluntly offers the hero her "cors." The prince of courtesy must thereupon strive to reestablish the proper tone. When he accepts the lady in *Brun,* he must reassure her, the audience, and perhaps himself with "Et je reçoif . . . sans vilenie." Even more delicately, when he refuses the offer in *Sir Gawain,* he must do so with careful attention to the "fourme of his castes" (v. 1295). He never quite succeeds in imposing his courtly pattern of conduct on the lady in *Sir Gawain.* He does succeed in this episode of *Brun,* but the author of the First Continuation evidently had some doubts about the propriety of the situation, for when the episode is recounted later, it has become a rape rather than a seduction.

The emphasis that Bercilak's lady puts upon rape may possibly be designed to recall this version of the episode in the First Continuation, since it was a very famous incident in Gawain's career. In it he fathered Libiaus Desconnus, and it forms part of *The Jeaste of Syr Gawayne.* More likely her words are intended to emphasize her physical, unidealized view of the situation. In *Brun* the "vilenie" of the girl can be glossed over, but Bercilak's lady is no simple girl. She is skilled in the steps of the "olde daunce," and the fame that led the girl in *Brun* to fall in love with Gawain becomes a powerful rhetorical weapon against him in *Sir Gawain*. The lady uses Gawain's fame not only to account for her supposed passion for him but as a means of urging him to accept her love, and she insists repeatedly that he live up to his reputation, a matter that we must consider in more detail in the chapter on the poem's theme.

Such additions account for much of the complexity and individuality of the temptation in *Sir Gawain*. The poet began with the simple tale that appears in *Yder*, which supplied him with the general situation of a hunter-host whose wife tests the hero with a sexual temptation. He modified this plot by fitting it to the structure of the beheading, giving it both the same conclusion and the same kind of characters as that episode. By drawing on a variety of other traditions to develop the action, on the courtly paradigm for the tempted hero as it appears in *La Chastelaine de Vergi* and on the uncourtly model of *Brun de Branlant* (at least it becomes uncourtly with Bercilak's lady in the part of the love-struck girl), the poet changes the nature of the test itself. Courtesy becomes as important as continence, and Gawain's problem becomes not merely to resist the sexual temptation but to do so without deserting his courtly code. Then, by a final reversal, the original exchange of winnings becomes the most important element of all, and Gawain fails not because he is incontinent or discourteous but because he accepts and conceals the lace.

At the end of the poem, both the temptress and the hero are equals. She, like the Green Knight, is an attractive but essentially uncourtly character, the antithesis of the perfect gentleman whom she woos. But we finally learn that she is not responsible for the apparent evil of her actions; she is following Bercilak's orders, just as he is following those of Morgan la Fay. We do not blame her for what she has done, and we are more amused than shocked by the way she ignores the conventions of courtship. Traditionally such a temptress should be punished for her actions, but the tradition contains none so delightful as Bercilak's lady, and it is fitting, though contrary to custom, that she and Gawain, like Gawain and the Green Knight, should end as friends.

Even so, that conclusion is an index to the poet's handling of his traditional materials throughout his work. Like the romancers before him, he reshapes his inherited tales to produce a new theme. But the purpose to which he puts this new theme and old materials is markedly unlike that in any previous romance. Our principal concern in the following chapters will be to define that purpose more clearly, but even from the poet's changes in the plot alone we can see that his main interest is in the balance he establishes between an ideally chivalric hero and an equally superlative but in some ways churlish opponent. Our next task is therefore to examine these characters more closely; to do that we shall have to consider the poet's relation to romance tradition in more general terms than a study of sources allows.

Literary Convention
and Characterization
in "Sir Gawain"

The Gawain-poet's debt to romance tradition is most clearly and significantly evident not in his dependence on specific sources such as *Caradoc* but in his use of the general stock of literary conventions that were the common property of all romancers. We have already considered some of them in our discussion of the temptation episode, but their influence is not restricted to that part of the narrative; the poet drew on them for much of his settings, his actions, and, most important, his characterizations. Critics of *Sir Gawain* have seldom paid much attention to this fact, though it is just what one would expect of a poem written in so notoriously conventional a genre as romance; W. P. Ker speculated that when two romancers met to talk shop their first words must have been, "Where do you put your Felon Red Knight? Where do you put your doing away with the Ill Custom? Or your tournaments?" [1] No doubt the Gawain-poet would have joined in the conversation enthusiastically, and certainly he could have given those romancers some pointers on the use of the "Potiphar's Wife," the "Imperious Host," and even the "Felon Red Knight." The conversation might soon have turned to more technical and less obvious matters, for romance is such a conventional genre that a poet need not merely repeat the conventional patterns. He can play upon them, invoking them by allusion, modifying them by combination, and sometimes even redefining them by some obvious addition to or subtraction from the stock pattern.

However, this technique depends on an audience that shares the poet's knowledge of literary conventions. With such an audience the Gawain-poet can characterize Guenevere's ideal beauty by specifying but one detail: "Þe comlokest to discrye/ Þer glent with yȝen gray" (vv. 81–82); the "yȝen gray" alone evoke the whole stock *descriptio feminae pulchritudinis* with the gray eyes, golden hair, snow-white skin, and delicate limbs that were the conventional marks of literary beauty, as familiar to the audience as to the poet.[2] Without such an audience the mention of only the gray eyes, so unusual in real life, is simply puzzling, and the reader must either interpret the "yȝen gray" symbolically (one critic took them to mean "innocence accused"[3]) or ignore them. The second alternative is as gross an error as the first; it is as if a reader of the popular fiction of the 1950's invariably took "gray flannel suit" as only an article of clothing or "Madison Avenue" as only a place name.

The conventions that the Gawain-poet used to create his main characters are even less known today than the stock figure of the beautiful woman, and the conventional features of Gawain and the Green Knight therefore seem even more puzzling than the queen's eyes. The Green Knight is especially difficult for critics, and the many attempts to explain features such as his "rede yȝen" have made him more of a shape-shifter in criticism than he is in the poem. To one critic the Green Knight's strange appearance reveals his relation to folk ritual; to another it proves his direct descent from Curoi, and the ritualistic interpretation "must be assigned to limbo." [4] And to almost all it seems to place the Green Knight outside the conventions of romance, as if he were a character without a literary history who rushes as suddenly into medieval literature as he rides into Camelot. Gawain's character is somewhat less mysterious, but the range of critical disagreement has been almost as great.[5]

A knowledge of the conventions that the poet used to create the characters of Gawain and the Green Knight will not solve all the problems these figures pose, for the hero and his challenger are more complex than the conventions on which they are built. Yet even their complexity depends on our recognition of those conventions, which the poet could assume his audience knew and which he invoked to define his characters. Let us begin with the most difficult character in the poem, the Green Knight.

The description of the Green Knight

The Green Knight seems so completely mysterious that the modern reader is apt to overlook the fact that the Gawain-poet takes great care to make the conventions that the challenger embodies as clear as possible to his audience. When the Green Knight first enters Camelot, the action is suddenly suspended, and over ninety lines are devoted to a carefully detailed portrait. In this long passage the conventions are fully presented rather than evoked by allusion, and the characteristics that Bercilak displays both as challenger and as host are thus firmly established at the very beginning of the action. Of course, Bercilak remains a puzzling figure despite his obvious conventionality. The plot requires that the challenger be a mysterious character, and the Gawain-poet realizes that the most fascinating mysteries are those in which everything is obvious but the solution. He shows us the parts of which the Green Knight is composed, but he carefully maintains the challenger's essential ambiguity, and we are never sure whether Bercilak is a benevolent or a malevolent figure until he reveals himself to Gawain, and to us, at the end of the poem.

This ambiguity is part of the Green Knight's essential character, and his long opening portrait establishes this fact at the same time that it makes clear the conventions he embodies. This is because the portrait of the Green Knight presents not one but two conventional figures, distinct from one another in both appearance and implication. The description begins as if it were to be the usual romance portrait, the simple and unified head-to-toe *descriptio* of medieval poetics:

> Þer hales in at þe halle dor an aghlich mayster,
> On þe most on þe molde on mesure hyghe;
> Fro þe swyre to þe swange so sware and so þik,
> And his lyndes and his lymes so longe and so grete,
> Half etayn in erde I hope þat he were.
>
> (vv. 136–40)

To this point Bercilak is nearly a monster, fearful and gigantic, and the portrait is an ordinary straight-forward catalogue of his terrifying characteristics. Then, in the next line, the narrator abruptly abandons this catalogue and begins anew:

> Bot mon most I algate mynn hym to bene,
> And þat þe myriest in his muckel þat myȝt ride;
> For of bak and of brest al were his bodi sturne,
> Both his wombe and his wast were worthily smale,

And alle his fetures folȝande, in forme þat he hade,
        ful clene.

                        (vv. 141–46)

This passage is not only parallel in structure to the previous
one, it covers the same ground, going from the breast to
waist just as the first went from neck to leg. But whereas
the previous passage makes the Green Knight a grotesque
figure, these lines make him the "myriest" of men by going
back to list features that the first description passed silently over.[6]

This alternation between the beautiful and the grotesque appears throughout the rest of the long description. After the "ful clene" the description is again interrupted. The grotesque aspect returns, and we learn that
this merry figure is "oueral enker grene." Then the narrator turns again to the merry side of the challenger, who,
we are now told, is "al grayþed in grene" in a lovely costume trimmed with jewels, ermine, and gold—an outfit
that would do credit to Gawain. At this point the description apparently ends, for the poet now turns his attention
to the Green Knight's equipment. But then the portrait is
resumed. Again it starts at the top (the poet follows the
top to bottom order of the rhetorical *descriptio* in each
section), but this time it begins with the head, which had
not previously been mentioned, and we discover that the
handsomely dressed challenger has a great bushy beard
and hair that covers his upper body like a cape:

Fayre fannand fax vmbefoldes his schulderes;
A much berd as a busk ouer his brest henges,
Þat wyth his hiȝlich here þat of his hed reches
Watȝ euesed al vmbetorne abof his elbowes,
Þat half his armes þer-vnder were halched in þe wyse
Of a kyngeȝ capados þat closes his swyre.

                        (vv. 181–86)

There is no exact repetition in these sections. Each describes features that were previously ignored, and each thus casts what precedes into a more complex, ironic perspective. As a result, our impression of the Green Knight is constantly changing. First we see him as a monster (vv. 136–40), then as a handsome knight (vv. 141–46), then as a completely green man (vv. 147–50), again as an attractive character (vv. 151–67), and finally as a grotesquely bearded churl. Each of these five sections presents a sharp and clear visual image, as one would expect in the work of a poet so justly celebrated for his power of visual representation. What is surprising in the work of such a poet is that the portrait as a whole is significantly blurred, and it is impossible to visualize a coherent figure of the challenger.

The first and last sections of the portrait present a complete description of an ugly old churl, the second and fourth an equally complete portrait of a handsome young man. These two descriptions are merely placed side by side, and they remain independent of one another. This is shown by one obvious inconsistency. In the fourth section of the portrait the poet describes the Green Knight's beautiful hood and mantle:

> A meré mantile abof, mensked withinne
> With pelure pured apert, þe pane ful clene
> With blyþe blaunner ful bryʒt, and his hode boþe,
> Þat watʒ laʒt fro his lokkeʒ and layde on his schulderes.
> (vv. 153–56)

In the next section, which is quoted in the previous paragraph, we are told that the upper part of the challenger's body is covered by his great beard and grotesque head of hair that encloses his body like a "kyngeʒ capados." The mantle would therefore have been covered by this hair. Of course, the poet could have resolved this difficulty merely by specifying that the mantle as well as the hood was thrown back over the shoulders, but he did not do so because his interest is not in smoothly combining the two figures. Alone, each is completely and accurately described. Together, they are contradictory, and what is a handsome hood and mantle in one passage becomes a grotesque, cape-like head of hair in the other.

That is why good critics have disagreed so widely in their interpretations of the Green Knight. Seen from one angle, he is an attractive character who, it seems, could have been patterned on one of the contemporary noblemen with whom he has been identified; from another angle, he is a frightening figure who does indeed resemble some of the supernatural "originals" that have been adduced to explain him. He is composed of contradictions; even his axe is at once a terrifying weapon, "hoge and vnmete" (v. 208), and a lovely work of art, engraved with "gracious works" and adorned with a rich lace (v. 216). In his actions in the plot the same contradictions appear, for he is both Gawain's threatening opponent and his jolly host, and he begins as the hero's unpitying enemy and ends as his indulgent friend, more comic than frightening. Yet the two figures that the poet combines in the Green Knight control and define his contradictions, because they are familiar and meaningful stock characters, rich in associations for a medieval audience.

The literary green man

In the handsome parts of the Green Knight's portrait the Gawain-poet reproduces almost all the characteristics he found in the challenger of *Caradoc*. Like Éliavres, Bercilak is a merry figure, richly dressed in a costume "verd fourre de erminnes" and decked out with the golden, bejewelled equipment that adorned the French challenger. Only the chaplet has disappeared, replaced, as we learn in the next section of the description, by the grotesque hair and beard, but even they still have some of the vegetative associations of the chaplet, for the beard is like a bush and the hair is green as grass. The Gawain-poet retains so many of Éliavres' features only partly because they provide a convenient framework on which to build the attractive aspect of the Green Knight. He does so mainly because they are more than merely physical features; they are conventional characteristics rich in implications of the attractive vitality that Bercilak, partly at least, represents. In Éliavres the poet recognized, as his own audience must also have recognized in the Green Knight, the handsome, richly dressed, and merry figure of the literary green man, the stock figure of the green-clad youth who so often appears in late medieval poetry.

In the earliest versions of *Caradoc* this conventional figure was merely invoked by allusion; the tall and handsome challenger is crowned with a golden chaplet that suggests the garland of flowers conventionally worn by the green man. Brief as this suggestion is, it was enough to lead the later redactor of *Caradoc* to expand the description slightly by adding an even more obvious feature of this stock character, the rich green costume. The Gawain-poet, whose more concentrated plot allowed him more leisure for description and whose purposes required that the challenger's vitality be emphasized, needed only to fill out the entire conventional pattern to which *Caradoc* alludes.

That this was the Gawain-poet's procedure is shown by the striking similarities between the handsome aspect of Bercilak and a fully described green man, Youth, the antagonist of Elde and Medill Elde in *The Parlement of the Thre Ages*.[7] Youth's general characteristics—his green cos-

tume, his chaplet of flowers, his beauty—are the same as
Éliavres' (he even sings a song, as Éliavres does in *Cara-
doc*). The particular details with which the author of *The
Parlement* fills out this pattern are almost the same as
those that the Gawain-poet uses for the Green Knight.
Youth, like Bercilak, is a "ferse freke,"

> A bolde beryn one a blonke bownne for to ryde,
> A hathelle on ane heghe horse with hauke appon hande.
> He was balghe in the breste and brode in the scholdirs,
> His axles and his armes were i-liche longe,
> And in the medill as a mayden menskfully schapen.
>
> (*Parl*, 110–14)

Like the Green Knight (v. 170), Youth stands in his stir-
rups, and he does so in order to emphasize his height
(vv. 115–16), but he is clad for peace rather than battle
and, also like the Green Knight, he has "no hatte bot his
here one" (v. 117). His equipment is as richly adorned with
gems as Éliavres' or the Green Knight's, and he wears the
same costume:

> He was gerede alle in grene, alle with golde by-weuede,
> Embroddirde alle with besanttes and beralles ful riche.
>
> (*Parl*, 122–23)

The green costume is the most significant feature of his
appearance, for in the balance of the poem the narrator
refers to this character not as "Youth" but as "the gome
gered alle in grene" (e.g., v. 194), a phrase that the Gawain-poet also uses to designate and characterize the
Green Knight (e.g., v. 2227). Youth also shares the Green
Knight's interest in fighting (he too tells the audience that
he has armor at home), and he is an enthusiastic hunter, as
expert in hawking as Bercilak is in the chase.

Such resemblances are probably not due to "borrowing." There are major differences between Youth and Ber-

cilak (Youth is a pining lover, for example), and the conventional figure they both embody was common enough that a poet need not have depended on specific works to learn the characteristics. One finds the same green-clad figure throughout fourteenth-century literature. In the romances there are innumerable "Maying" knights and ladies, richly clad in green and garlanded with flowers, and often, as in contemporary life, they carry boughs of greenery into the court (as the Green Knight brings in his holly).[8] Perhaps because of its association with spring, the green costume also came to be symbolic of love, and sometimes (as in Gower's *Mirour de l'Omme*, vv. 17893 ff., and Dunbar's *Twa Mariit Wemen and the Wedo*) of love that borders on lechery. In *The Flower and the Leaf*, for example, the adherents of the flower (the faithless lovers) are dressed in a costume exactly like that worn by Youth and Éliavres, and, like Youth, they are fond of hunting and hawking. In all such figures, however, the basic implication is that of youthful, natural vitality. Thus, when Henryson in *The Testament of Criseyde* characterizes the youthful Jupiter as the admirable and vital opposite of the aged Saturn—"Fro his Father Saturne far different"—he draws upon the literary green man to define his qualities, providing him with a garland, burly face and brows, a hunting spear, and "His garmound and his gyis ful gay of grene" (v. 178).

There are two other late texts that explicitly show the youthful associations of the literary green man and that imply something of his earlier history.[9] The first is the sixteenth-century *Interlude of Youth*, in which the main character announces in his first speech:

> "My name is Youth, I tell thee,
> I flourish as the vine-tree:
> Who may be likened unto me
> In my youth and jollity?

> My hair is royal and bushed thick;
> My body pliant as a hazel stick;
> Mine arms be both big and strong,
> My fingers be both fair and long;
> My chest big as a tun,
> My legs be full light for to run."

(p. 6)

Here again appears the tall and jolly Youth (in a work with the same moral burden as *The Parlement*). The close relation to vegetation, reflected in the green costume and flowery chaplet of Youth in *The Parlement* and his fourteenth-century analogues, appears in the vine tree and hazel of this figure. Instead of a chaplet he has a bushy head of hair, as does Bercilak, and we should note that it is "royal," like Bercilak's "kyngeʒ capados." Probably the hair shows the relation of this Youth to the wild man, a more grotesque figure who is related to the green man and who is perhaps reflected in the concern with hunting shown by Youth in *The Parlement* and by many of the other green men in late medieval literature.

That these resemblances are not fortuitous is shown by the parallel between Youth in *The Interlude* and the character called Blue Breeches in the *Revesby Folk Play*. In his first speech Blue Breeches announces:

> "I am a youth of jollitree;
> Where is there one like unto me?
> My hair is bush'd very thick;
> My body is like an hasel stick,
>
> "My legs they quaver like an eel,
> My arms become my body weel;
> My fingers they are both long and small:
> Am I not a jolly youth, proper and tall?"

(p. 116)

The folk play (which in the form we know it dates only from the eighteenth century) also contains a ritual beheading faintly reminiscent of that in *Sir Gawain,* although Blue Breeches is not involved in it.[10] Leaving that aside, the general resemblances between Youth in *The Interlude* and Blue Breeches in the folk play do seem to indicate the existence of a less sophisticated tradition of portraiture in which "youth" is conventionally represented as a tall, jolly, and handsome character closely associated with vegetation and with the wild man. This character, with his bushy hair and association with nature, stands in about the same relation to Youth in *The Parlement* as the Irish *bachlach,* who has the "bushiness of a great tree upon him," to the sophisticated challenger in *Caradoc.* In each case the relatively crude work contains a bushy-haired figure with explicitly arboreal associations, and the analogous sophisticated work contains a literary green man.

The ultimate original of such characters as Blue Breeches may well have been the "green man" or "May King" of folk ritual, for the folk play does seem to be a descendant of some ancient fertility ceremony. Furthermore, the ritual green man appears in folklore throughout the world, from the Aztec "Corn King" to the analogous figures of ancient and modern Europe.[11] He is usually regarded as a vegetation spirit representing fertility, and the rite in which he takes part usually involves his sacrificial death, often by beheading. He customarily appears decked out in greenery, covered with leaves like a great bush. Often the leaves cover the entire body, but sometimes they cover only the head and shoulders, as is shown by a modern May King whose photograph appears in Christine Hole's *English Customs and Usages.*[12] He is mounted on a horse, and he wears a covering of leaves quite similar in shape to Bercilak's hair and beard. Such facts as these have led many scholars to regard Bercilak as a ritual green man; indeed, Speirs goes so far as to claim that Bercilak "*is* the Green Man" (his italics), taken directly from a ritual that the poet "may have seen with his own eyes." [13]

If the poet did see such a ritual, it is doubtful that he regarded it as much more than a country dance, for by the fourteenth century the pagan implications of this figure had long since disappeared. Naturally, fourteenth-century moralists denounce May dances and such festivities as the works of the devil, but the seventeenth-century pastors of Hawthorne's "Merrymount" did the same, and such denunciations should be taken with the same degree of literalness as a modern evangelist's denunciation of the cinema. Speirs, the most convincing advocate of the ritualistic interpretation of the Green Knight, believed that he had found concrete proof of the green man's paganism in the roof bosses of medieval churches photographed by C. J. P. Cave. Cave's photographs revealed in hidden and inaccessible places, visible only to searchlight and telescopic lens, the recurrent carving of a foliated face—"a face with leaves sprouting from its eye-lids, eyebrows and ears, the face of the Green Man." [14] This foliated face, which Speirs identified with the Green Knight, is hidden in these churches, he explains (following a theory very cautiously advanced by Cave, who in turn had it from Lady Raglan [15]), because it is a pagan charm that the stone-carvers felt free to use high above the prying eyes of ecclesiastical authorities.

However, the most orthodox authorities could have seen just as many of these foliated heads in the prayer books they were reading as they might have found hidden away on the roof, for it is a common decorative motif in medieval art, and it appears in both painting and carving throughout the period, from the twelfth-century Canterbury Psalter to Cardinal Farnese's Book of Hours in the sixteenth century.[16] On some pages, such as the famous Beatus Page of the Windmill Psalter, they could have seen the full figure, foliated and taking its strange complexion from the leaves in which it appears.[17] Originally the figure may have been a pagan charm, but by the poet's time it had become an amusing and theologically harmless grotesque, objectionable only to reformers like Bernard of Clairvaux, who objected to all worldly distractions.[18]

Such evidence of the peasant green man as does survive is useful only for showing how very far the literary green man is removed from the ritual figure. Even Blue Breeches in the crude folk play is only remotely connected to the original. He now represents not the forces of nature or the assurance of good crops but the vitality, here slightly comic, of youthfulness. Characters such as Bercilak or Youth in *The Parlement* are even more remote from the folk original. One may still detect the faint traces of the ultimate origin of these literary figures, but the original has obviously been refined and adapted to a courtly milieu.

The refinement was at least a century old by the time *The Parlement* and *Sir Gawain* were written, for Ulrich von Lichtenstein's autobiographical poem *Frauendienst* shows that even in the thirteenth century and even in Germany, where Mannhardt found the peasant green-man cults so strong, the figure of the green man could be used for a disguise like Bercilak's without ritual overtones. Ulrich's first real adventure was the tourney at Friesach, which began on May 1st in 1224. He met with such great success on the first day that he was hard put to find a way to make the second day as exciting. He wanted to do something at once original and noble—"daz niemen hete ê anderswâ/ getân, und daz wære ritterlîch" (p. 81). His solution is to adopt a disguise, and the next morning he rides into the tourney with clothing and equipment "grüene als ein gras" (p. 83). His attendants are dressed in the same fashion, and even the horses are green ("Mîn knehte grüen, ir pferd alsam," p. 83; Ulrich must mean only that the trappings are green).

The effect was all he desired. Not even his own brother recognized him, and everyone marvelled at his appearance, each knight asking the other:

> "Waiz iemen wer der ritter was
> der hiute grüen alsam ein gras
> zuo uns her ab dem perg reit?
> Sîn maienvarbiu wâppencleit
> diu wâren dêswâr wunnenclîch."
>
> (p. 86)
>
> ["Does anyone know who that knight was, the one who, green as the grass, came riding to us today down from the hill? His May-colored armor was indeed wonderful to see."]

The emphasis on "grass-green" and the explicit relation of the color to the May season have led to the identification of Ulrich's disguise as that of the "May King"—the green man.[19] It is this, but its connotations are courtly rather than popular. Ulrich wanted to do something unusual, but he was determined to maintain his high standards of chivalry—"und daz wære ritterlîch."

By the fourteenth century Ulrich's disguise would not have seemed so unusual, for the green man had become thoroughly assimilated to courtly poetry. *Le Songe vert,* a fourteenth-century work that may have been written in England and that has been attributed to John Gower,[20] shows that even the ritual of rebirth with which the figure was originally associated had been adapted to sophisticated verse. The poem begins on an Easter morning, with the narrator disconsolately mourning the death of his lady. He longs to join her in death, and he is about to drown himself when he suddenly swoons. He has a vision in which he meets Venus and her court. They urge him to cast off his black mourning clothes and become a lover once more. He refuses, and the debate becomes hotter until, without warning, he faints. "Alas," cries Venus, "I have killed him." Her attendants then revive him with water from the stream and a marvellously shining electuary, and they strip off his black attire and clothe him completely in green—"Entire de vert de color" (v. 961). The narrator's sorrow is gone; he accepts the new love that Venus offers him and he thanks her for restoring his life. She and her court then disappear, leaving him alone in a dry, wasted terrain. Then he awakes and discovers that he is still clothed in green, that the dry hedge is now covered with verdant leaves, and that the birds are singing joyfully to greet him. He returns home, where he is met by rejoicing servants and finds that his hall is miraculously decked with flowers and that all his black wardrobe has turned to green. By the skillful assimilation of the motif of love with that of the Wasteland (the return of vegetation) and the May Day rites implicit in the rejoicing of nature and the servants at the narrator's return, the usual lover of lyric verse, who conventionally dies and lives again for love, becomes in this poem the green man, who had originally died and lived again in peasant ritual.

Of course, the author of *Le Songe vert* probably did not draw directly on any ritual, for the green man's relation to Spring with its implications of rebirth were already well established, and it led to his connection with the Wasteland motif in several other poems. In the alliterative *Death and Life*, for example, Death is black and foul, whereas Life is a lovely figure "comlye clad in kirtle and mantle of goodliest greene that euer groome ware." Gray grasses turn green wherever she walks, and singing birds and rejoicing beasts surround her as she brings in spring and restores life to all those whom Death has struck down. Perhaps the Wasteland motif is to be detected in all the literary green men, since all are associated with youth, life, and the kind of vitality these qualities imply. Certainly it must have been these associations, along with the arboreal characteristics of the Irish challenger,[21] that led the author of *Caradoc* to make his challenger a green man, and that in turn must have influenced the author of *Perlesvaus* in his decision to connect the beheading with the redemption of a Wasteland.

However, the Gawain-poet chose not to develop this theme any further, and it is probably simple vitality that the handsome side of the Green Knight most immediately suggested to a medieval audience, for this is the basic implication of all green men in medieval literature, whether that vitality is expressed in love, youth, or the restoration of a Wasteland. Perhaps some members of the audience, recalling the associations of the figure with death and rebirth, would recognize in the Green Knight's attractive aspect the assurance that he would survive the beheading. Certainly all would have recognized the pleasing connotations of this stock figure, the attractive vitality that exists alongside and complicates the grotesque terror invoked by the other aspect of Gawain's strange challenger.

The literary wild man

Éliavres may also have supplied the suggestion for the grotesque side of Bercilak's character. The later redactor of *Caradoc*, realizing that the challenger in the beheading tale is basically an opponent to chivalry, adds some hints of uncourtliness to Éliavres' appearance and actions. He gives him a beautiful sword decorated with green silk, but he also tells us that this is the sword "dont puis eust la teste couppee." Likewise, he makes Éliavres handsome and courtly but he also provides him with a stern speech to Arthur, an abrupt refusal of the king's plea that he be "courteous" and spare Caradoc, and a brusque dismissal of Guenevere which suggest that his disguise conceals an anti-chivalric nature as well as his ordinary appearance. These are only hints, but they are hints that a romance audience could hardly overlook. The host in *Sir Gawain* is composed of the same mixture of courtly and uncourtly elements. Like Éliavres, he is usually courteous in speech but occasionally lapses into uncourtly forms. Likewise, his appearance has traces of a more threatening nature than his fine castle and hospitality would lead one to expect, and the description in which he is first presented is organized on the same principle of alternation between pleasant and grotesque elements as the portrait of the Green Knight:

> Gawayn glyȝt on þe gome þat godly hym gret,
> And þuȝt hit a bolde burne þat þe burȝ aȝte,
> A hoge haþel for þe noneȝ, and of hyghe eldee;
> Brode, bryȝt, watȝ his berde, and al beuer hwed,
> Sturne, stif on þe stryþþe on stalworth schonkeȝ,
> Felle face as þe fyre, and fre of his speche;
> And wel hym semed, for soþe, as þe segge þuȝt,
> To lede a lortschip in lee of leudeȝ ful gode.
>
> (vv. 842–48)

Although Gawain does not notice the implications of his host's appearance, the audience cannot fail to recognize in the host the figure of the huge, bearded, and fiery-eyed Green Knight, in whom Éliavres' traces of churlishness have become explicit and fully developed. The Green Knight is invariably churlish in speech and action, and he is not just fierce-looking, he is a frightening "half-etayn" with a bush-like beard, a strange covering of hair, and a huge axe. This part of the portrait of the Green Knight and the allusions to it in the description of the host lend meaning to the later traces of churlishness in the host's conduct, for these are conventional features, so meaningful to a medieval audience that the author of *The Grene Knight* had to omit them completely when he revised *Sir Gawain*. He intended his Sir Bredbeddle to reform and enter the Round Table at the end of his poem. As he recognized, the Green Knight of *Sir Gawain* is hardly a suitable candidate for reformation, because in the grotesque side of the description of the challenger the Gawain-poet presents the familiar figure of the stock enemy of knighthood—the "wild man" of medieval romance.

This character is used even more frequently in medieval art and literature than the green man. As "wodwose," "carl," "wild man," *homme sauvage*, or, most common, *vilain*, he appears in a great variety of contexts.[22] He is always large, sometimes a giant, remarkably hairy, strange in color (black ordinarily), marked by a grotesque head and beard, and armed with a club or with a huge axe such as the "granz hace danois" carried by the gigantic *vilain* in *Cléomadès* (v. 2940). He is portrayed as a fierce fighter and mighty hunter, and he usually has a strange power over wild beasts. His natural habitat is deep in the forest, but in Arthurian romance he often appears as a bridge-ward or porter with whom the knight must do battle. These characteristics were as widely known as those of the handsome knight or beautiful woman, and the briefest, most allusive description sufficed to imply the whole stock figure. In *Hunbaut* (where the wild man appears as a bridgeward who challenges Gawain to the beheading game), the romancer needs only to mention the fact that the challenger is a *vilain* who carries an axe and "Grans ert et noirs, lais et hideus" (v. 1473). In *Sir Gawain* we have the same figure, armed with an axe and "hideus" ("aghlich"), "lais" ("sware and þik"), and "grans" ("half-etayn"). He is also strange in color, fierce in manner, and crowned with the beard and hair that conventionally mark the *vilain*. Gawain clearly recognizes the stock figure of the wild man in the Green Knight, for later in the poem he describes him as a "Sturne knape/ To stiʒtel and stad with staue" (vv. 2136–37), substituting a stick or club for the axe since, though wild men often carry axes, the club is their favorite weapon.[23]

The wild man is also a recurrent figure in folklore and myth, and he seems to have had the same sort of ritual origin as the green man. In popular belief the two figures are closely linked, and in folk ritual they are interchangeable.[24] The crude Blue Breeches and Youth in *The Interlude of Youth* show how easily the great shock of hair could be substituted for the leaves or chaplets of flowers. In medieval art the wild man often wears both hair and leaves, and wild men were sometimes divided into "leafy" and "hairy" categories.[25] It may have been this relation between the wild man and the green man that suggested to the Gawain-poet the vegetative associations and the green color that he gives to Bercilak's hair and beard. However, in literary works the two figures are quite distinct. A close association with nature is the only quality they share, and even this reveals a contrast. Spring and greenery are the natural phenomena associated with the green man; he develops from the pleasant aspects of nature, and in literature he becomes an attractive, youthful figure. The wild man seems to have developed from the sterner side of nature. Winter is the more suitable season for him, and, in folklore, he delights in storms and rides with the Wild Hunt. He is old rather than youthful, grotesque rather than beautiful, and he is usually a hostile figure, the enemy of the knight and the opponent of the values represented by the romance courts.

This literary development began long before the Gawain-poet's time. Indeed, the wild man seems to have entered romance, as the challenger did, from Celtic literature.[26] Curoi was a "wild hunter" in Celtic tradition, and when he appears in the *Fled Bricrend* disguised as a *bach-lach*—a "carl" or "herdsman" [27]—he has a black cloak, a huge and bushy head, and "an old hide next to his skin." These same features reappear in one of the earliest romance wild men, the huge *vilain* whom Calogrenant encounters in the forest of Broceliande in Chrétien's *Yvain:*

> "Une vilain qui rassonbloit mor
> Grant et hideus a desmesure. . . .

> "Si vi qu'il ot grosse la teste
> Plus que roncins ne autre beste,
> Chevos meschiez et front pelé,
> S'ot plus de deus espanz de le,
> Oroilles mossues et granz
> Auteus come a uns olifanz,
> Les sorciz granz et le vis plat. . . .

> "Barbe noire, grenons tortiz. . . .

> "Vestuz de robe si estrange
> Qu'il n'i avoit ne lin ne lange,
> Ainz ot a son col atachiez
> Deus cuirs de novel escorchiez
> De deus toriaus ou de deu bués."
>
> (vv. 289–90, 295–301, 305, 309–13)

["A churl who looked like a Moor, exceedingly large and hideous. . . . I saw that he had a huge head, bigger than that of a horse or any other beast; that his hair was in tufts and his forehead bare for more than two spans; that his ears were big and mossy, like those of an elephant. His eyebrows were heavy and his face was flat. . . . His beard was black and his whiskers twisted. . . . He was dressed in a strange garb made neither of cotton nor of wool but of two newly flayed hides of bulls or beeves that hung from his neck."]

Chrétien's wild man had a wide and lasting influence on romance, from works such as *La Mule sanz frain* to *Le*

Livre d'Artus and Spenser's *Fairy Queen.*[28] The tradition
was so well established that when the author of the alliterative *Wars of Alexander* found a wild man mentioned in
his source he added as a matter of course some of the details that first appeared in *Yvain:* "With laith leggis & lange
& twa laue eres;/ A heuy hede & a hoge as it a horse ware"
(vv. 4748–49).[29]

However, Chrétien's portrait did not completely fix the
character of the wild man. There seems to have been a
progressive humanization from the half-animal, half-hu-
man creatures of Celtic myth to Chrétien's herdsman, in
which the animal features are present mainly in similes, to
the wild man of the later Middle Ages. A rich growth of
hair replaced the animalistic head, and frequently the
hair was used to replace even the hides worn by such early
wild men as Curoi and Chrétien's herdsman. The *vilain*
in *Aucassin et Nicolette* shows the beginning of this development. Like his ancestor in *Yvain*, he is "lais et hidex"
with a bushy head of coal-black hair, and he is dressed in
hides. But the hides have now assumed a different shape:
"Et estoit afulés d'une cap a deus envers"—he was dressed
in "a double-folded cape" rather like the Green Knight's
hairy "capados" (XXIV, 13–21). In the *Fled Bricrend* the
hide worn by Curoi is merely an article of clothing. In
Yvain Chrétien specifies how the hides are worn, hanging
from the neck. In *Aucassin et Nicolette* the hides have become a cape of the sort that still appears on the wild man
in Lovelich's *Merlin:* "And vppon hym a clowted cote/
that heng adown abowten his throte" (vv. 3153–54).

Often this "cap a deus envers" was replaced by a growth
of hair. In *Rigomer* Lancelot meets a wild man whose hair
and beard are his only clothing, hanging down to his waist,
where they are fastened with a belt (vv. 2288–2319). By
the fourteenth century this strange growth of hair had become so common that the English translator of *Yvain*, the

author of *Yvain and Gawain,* felt compelled to add it to Chrétien's wild herdsman; the only change he makes in this part of Chrétien's text is the substitution of a marvellous growth of hair for the wild herdsman's strange garments: "Unto his belt hang his hare,/ And efter þat byheld I mare" (vv. 253–54). The tradition was strong enough to survive even in Spenser's *Fairy Queen* (IV, vii, 7) and so well known that in *Wynnere and Wastoure* the "wrethyn locckus" are enough to invoke the entire stock figure of the wodwose (v. 71). When Merlin disguises himself as a wild man in Lovelich's *Merlin,* he wears the cape cited above,

> And thereto he hadde a ful gret berd
> Þerwith to han mad many men aferd.
>
> (vv. 3155–56)

When Bercilak bursts into Arthur's court, his cape-like head of hair and his broad beard are perhaps as frightening to Arthur's courtiers as his green complexion is amazing, for they are the marks of the fierce and hostile wild man "Þerwith to han mad many men aferd."

This conventional figure had acquired a number of stock associations and traditional roles in medieval literature by the time of *Sir Gawain.* His ritual character had, of course, been lost. It survived among the peasantry of continental Europe until well into the nineteenth century, but in the sophisticated art and literature of the late Middle Ages the wild man had developed so far from his origins that he could be used for everything from a heraldic symbol to a prop for an elaborate practical joke in Boccaccio's *Decameron* (IV, ii). He was perhaps especially well known to the nobles and clerics who, like the Gawain-poet, were fortunate enough to read the illuminated books of the fourteenth century,[30] for the heavily bearded, long-haired wild man, carrying his club or his axe and hunting or

sporting in the forest, is one of the most common grotesqueries in fourteenth-century art. In the "Sherborne
Missal," an English work of the fourteenth century, there
is even a drawing of a wild man in a situation reminiscent
of *Sir Gawain*.[31] He is shown standing upright in the stir-
rups of a handsome saddle that is mounted on the foliage.
In one hand he holds a long sword; in the other he grips
by the hair and holds up, as if it were speaking, his heavily
bearded, severed head. This decapitated but living wild
man, holding his head by the hair, reappears, this time
shown only from the waist up, in Jean Pucelle's Book of
Hours.[32] It is hardly likely that such wild men represent
any beheading game or ritual. They are probably merely
the marginal parody of sacred themes so frequent in the
grotesquerie of illuminated manuscripts, for the beheaded
but living saint (Denis is the prototype) is quite common
in church art.[33] Nevertheless these illustrations do show
that the beheaded but living wild man of *La Mule sanz
frain, Hunbaut,* and especially *Sir Gawain* has some prece-
dent in medieval art.

Indeed, fourteenth-century art and literature provide
precedents for almost every aspect of Bercilak's role in
Sir Gawain. When Arthur assures Guenevere that the challenge and beheading are only "enterludeȝ" and that "Wel
bycommes such craft vpon Cristmasse" (v. 471), the audience was probably reminded of how often the wild man
appeared in court masques and dramatic entertainments.
As Elizabeth Wright pointed out some years ago, the
Green Knight himself lends substance to Arthur's reassur-
ance, for his elaborate and exaggerated posturing does indeed remind one of a character in a dramatic entertain-
ment.[34] The wild man was so fashionable a figure in such
performances that even the heir to the throne of France
wore a wild man's costume in the tragic "Dance of the
Wild Men" held at the French court near the end of the

fourteenth century (one of the flaxen costumes took fire, some of the dancers were burned to death, and the prince himself was nearly killed).[35] The wild man's association with winter made him especially suitable for Christmas plays, and he appears in Christmas entertainments at Edward III's court as early as 1348.[36]

The late Middle English Christmas play *A Mumming of the Seven Philosophers* preserves another of the wild man's traditional roles, that of teacher to the courtly knight. In this play the "King of the Wilderness" is represented as brother to the "King of Christmas," and he appears at the court's Christmas banquet to warn it against pride, which is attacked in language similar to that used in the condemnation of Arthur's court at the beginning of the Second Fit in *Sir Gawain*.[37] The wild man is of course a king of the wilderness; hence the Green Knight's "kyngeӡ capados" and the poet's later, apparently puzzling, reference to Bercilak as "kyng," a reference that all editors have unnecessarily emended to "lorde." [38] The wild man as a wise man, a natural philosopher chastizing the artificiality and pride of the courtier, was a rather popular theme in the later Middle Ages. It seems to have derived mainly from the Alexander romances, such as *Alexander and Dindimus,* in which the learned Brahmin lives in the sylvan isolation commonly identified with the wild man, and it seems to have had an especially strong appeal to the later period, in which the chivalric ideals of the earlier Middle Ages no longer held unquestioned dominance.[39]

In whatever role the wild man appears, whether as a comic figure, a philosopher, or—by far the most common —as the pugnacious foe to knighthood, he is basically the same, for he always represents a mode of life completely opposed to that represented by the knight. In the frequent battles between a wild man and a knight, a common theme in fourteenth-century art and the subject of at least one lost English romance,[40] "The wild man is interpreted as a symbol of unruly passion while the knight is consciously treated as a protagonist of an opposite manner of life." [41] When Gawain battles the "etayneʒ" on the way to Bercilak's castle, he is probably reminded of the Green Knight, who is "half etayn." When he battles the "wodwos, þat woned in þe knarreʒ" (v. 721), he must also remember the Green Knight, who is half wodwose as well and who clearly champions a set of values completely opposite to those of the polished courtier.

Because in the later romances wildness was a matter of attitude and manners rather than social class, one could combine a nobleman with a wild man in the same character. For example, the carl in *The Carl of Carlisle* is, like Bercilak, lord of a fine castle and husband of a lovely wife. But he is also a wild man. His castle is located deep in the wilderness; he has a strange power over wild beasts (his "pets" are a bull, a lion, a bear, and a wild boar); and he is evidently a hunter, since he has a hunting spear handy for one of the tests to which Gawain, his guest, must submit. Moreover, the carl is a "dreadfull man" with a twisted nose and a great beard:

> Betwyne his browus a large spane
> His moʒth moche, his berd graye,
> Ouer his brest his lockus lay
> As brod as anny fane.[42]
>
> (vv. 252–55)

He is "ij tayllors ʒerdus" across the shoulders, and nine tailor's yards in height, with long legs, huge arms and fingers, and thighs thicker than any post in the hall.

> Whos stoud a stroke of his honde
> He was not wecke I vnderstond.
>
> (vv. 268–69)

The resemblances between this carl and the Green Knight extend even to the poets' comments on their strength ("Hit semed as no mon myʒt/ Vnder his dynttes dryʒe," *SG*, 201–02), and the more general similarities to the host in *Sir Gawain* have led some critics to assume a direct link between the two works.[43] There may be a tenuous relationship, since each poem contains an "Imperious Host," a hunter who subjects his knightly guest to a test of obedience.[44] Yet the Gawain-poet could easily have developed the host in the temptation tale from a simple hunter, as he is in *Yder,* to a wild hunter without drawing on *The Carl of Carlisle.* The resemblances are due not to borrowing but to the fact that both poets were using the same set of conventions.

A character who resembles Bercilak even more closely than the carl is King Claudas, Arthur's opponent in the vulgate *Lancelot.* He shares some features with the carl—the exact specification of his height and his ugly nose—but in other respects he is remarkably similar to Bercilak. He is a tall and handsome knight from the neck down, but, like the Green Knight, he has a wild man's head:

> li contes dist quil auoit bien .ix. pies de lonc a le mesure dies pies de lors. si auoit le viaire noire & gros. Et les sorchiex velus. & les iex gros & noirs, lun loig del autre. Il auoit le neis court & reskignie & le barbe rousse. & les cheueus ne bien noir ne bien rous. Mais entremeles dun & dautre. Si ot le col gros & le bouche grande. & les dens clers & enchises. Mais les espaules les pies & tout lautre cors ot il si bel & si bien fait com len ne poroit miex diuiser en nul homme. Et ses teces estoient & boines & mauuaises. . . . volentiers aloit au moustier. mais ne faisoit mie grantment de bien a poure gent. Moult volentiers leuoit matin et manioit. ne ia ne iaust as esches ne as tables ne a autres ieus se moult petit non. En bois aloit volentiers. (pp. 26–27)

[The story says that he was a good nine feet tall, according to the foot measure of those days. His face was black and large, and his eyebrows were bushy. His eyes were large and black with a large space between them. He had a short and ugly nose, and his beard was red. His hair was neither all black nor all red; rather the two were intermingled. He had a large neck and a large mouth, and his teeth were white and sharp. But his shoulders and his legs and all the rest of his body were as well made as one could imagine. His habits were both good and evil. . . . He was fond of going to church, but he did not give much to the poor. He liked to rise early and to eat. He did not care for chess nor for tables nor for other such games; he was fond of going to the woods.]

Claudas' favorite weapon is the axe, and his full name is "Claudas de la terre desert," just as the challenger is "Bercilak de la Hautdesert." [45] Yet there need be no direct relation between the two. Even the recurrence of "desert" in both names is merely an explicit reference to the wilderness with which their appearance implicitly links them.

The wild man as vilain

Such characters as Claudas and Bercilak could be easily distinguished from the various courtly knights with a suggestion of wildness in their characters, such as Doddinaual li Sauvage in *Sir Gawain*,[46] because in the later romances, in which the hero had become less a warrior and more an exponent of refined and courtly manners, the speech and action of a *vilain* distinguish him as clearly from the courtiers as does his grotesque appearance, and it becomes possible for a character to be a *vilain* without looking like one.[47] In *Sir Gawain*, in which the word "vylanye" always implies morals or manners rather than social class, this distinction allows the poet to establish the essential relation between the host and challenger and to establish their basic identity, at which the host's appearance only hints.

"Dangiers li vilains" of *Le Roman de la rose* was by far the most influential of those unmannerly wild men, and his influence can be detected even in the challenger of our poem.[48] When Dangier first appears in *Le Roman*, he bursts onto the scene with the same sudden violence as marks Bercilak's entry:

> Atant saut Dangiers li vilains
> De la ou il s'estoit muciez.
> Granz fu e noirs et hericiez.
> S'ot les iauz roges come feus,
> Le nés froncié, le vis hisdeus,
> Et s'escrie con forsenez.

(vv. 2920–25)

[With that sterte oute anoon Daunger,/ Out of the place where he was hid./ His malice in his chere was kid;/ Ful gret he was and blak of hewe;/ Sturdy and hidous, whoso hym knewe;/ Like sharp urchouns his her was growe;/ His eyes reed sparclyng as the fyr glowe;/ His nose frounced, ful kirked stod./ He com criand as he were wood. (*The Romaunt of the Rose,* vv. 3130–38)]

Dangier has the appearance that we expect of a wild man, complete with a club (*Roman,* v. 3157) and the fiery red eyes, like the Green Knight's "red yȝen" and the host's "felle face as þe fyre," which conventionally mark the fierce *vilain*.[49] But more important is the churlish energy of his speech and action, which differentiates him as clearly from l'Amant as does his appearance.

His superlative rudeness is most obvious in his speech, a most significant aspect of character in works like *Le Roman de la rose* and *Sir Gawain*, where nobility of speech is so important. He consistently addresses l'Amant as "vassal" and "felon," and he uses "tu" even when he grants that gentleman's humble request. Likewise, the Green Knight refers to Arthur not as "the king" but as "þat haþel" and he invariably addresses him in the familiar form—"in fayþ I þe telle." But both Dangier and the Green Knight would be churlish even if they used the proper forms, for their manners are revealed in their delivery as well as their words. Both accompany their speeches with the frowns and grimaces that so often mark the *vilain* of this period. When Dangier speaks, he shakes his head disdainfully (v. 2948); when enraged, he rolls his eyes (v. 3733). The wild man in *The Sowdane of Babylone* has the same mannerism: "Alagolofur rolled his yen/ And smote with his axe on the stone" (vv. 2175–76). The Green Knight does the same:

> And runischly his rede yȝen he reled aboute,
> Bende his bresed broȝeȝ blycande grene,
> Wayued his berde for to wayte quo-so wolde ryse.
>
> (vv. 304–06)

The bent brows and waving beard are also marks of the angry *vilain*. For example, the churl "Rud Entendement" in *The Pilgrimage of the Life of Man* first appears with his "browhes fersly bente" (v. 10334), and when enraged,

> Grucchynge, he grunte wyth his teth
> His grete malys for to kythe,
> And shook his berd fful offte sythe.
>
> (vv. 10470–72)

Not only does the conventional *vilain* roll his eyes and grind his teeth; like Dangier, he also frowns (v. 3733), and the Green Knight increases the terror of his appearance in the same way:

> þenne tas he hym stryþe to stryke
> And frounseȝ boþe lyppe and browe.
>
> (vv. 2305–06)

The noble gentlemen of romance seldom betray their emotions in this manner; they may blanch, or redden, or weep, but they almost never distort their features with churlish frowns. Even when Arthur becomes as "wroth as wynde" (v. 319), there is no trace of even so much as a bent brow. The *vilain* is less decorous, and the Gawain-poet drew freely on the conventional grimaces of the churlish wild man to characterize the Green Knight.

However, the most important distinction between a *vilain* like Dangier and a gentleman is the frenzied energy of his action. Dangier first appears in *Le Roman* leaping up and "criand as he were wood," and the violence of that entry characterizes him throughout the work. The same is true of the Green Knight, who first comes riding through the door calling out for the king, and of the host, who continually shouts and rushes about. This contrast between the reserved, dignified movement of the gentleman and the hasty violence of the churl is frequently employed in medieval narrative; when a character in the *Purgatorio* breaks into sudden action, his movement has "la fretta/che l'onestade ad ogni atto dismagha" ("the haste that mars the dignity of every act," iii, 10–11), and we recognize the momentary loss of the aristocratic dignity that befits him. Likewise, when Chaucer's noble Theseus rides to battle, his actions are described with relatively neutral verbs—"rit" "cam," "alighte"—that convey little more than the idea of decorous courtly activity:

> Thus rit this duc, thus rit this conquerour,
> And in his hoost of chivalrie the flour,
> Til that he came to Thebes and alighte,
> Faire in a feeld, ther as he thoughte to fighte.
>
> (*KT*, 981–84)

But when the vulgar Sir Thopas rides forth, Chaucer describes the movement in far more lively detail:

> Sir Thopas fil in love-longynge
> Al whan he herde the thrustel synge,
> And pryked as he were wood.
> His faire steede in his prikynge
> So swatte that men myghte him wrynge;
> His sydes were al blood.
>
> (*Sir Thop*, 772–77)

The first two lines of this passage describe an aristocratic figure, for Thopas' title, his love-longing, and the singing bird are all accessories of a courtly hero. It is the violence to which his love-longing leads, the precise insistence on the physical action, and the aimless vigor of that action ("and pryked as he were wood") that immediately places him in a properly comic perspective.

When Bercilak appears as the host, he, like Thopas, has some of the accessories of a courtier—a title, a castle, a lovely lady, and a taste for the aristocratic pleasures of the hunt. But he also shouts, rushes about, and like Dangier, Thopas, and the challenger (v. 2289), he behaves "As wyȝ þat wolde of his wyte, ne wyst quat he myȝt" (v. 1087). Gawain raises his voice only once in the poem, at the Green Chapel where he "con calle ful hyȝe" for the Green Knight (v. 2212). The rest of the time he usually "quoth" his speeches, whereas his challenger and host shout and roar their words. When Gawain moves from one place to another, he usually "gotȝ" or "boȝeȝ," "walkeȝ," and "romeȝ," as he does at the Green Chapel. When the Green Knight enters that scene, he comes characteristically "whyrlande out of a wro wyth a felle weppen," and he "stalked" to the stream, "hypped ouer on hys ax, and orpedly strydeȝ" (vv. 2222–32). Likewise, at Bercilak's castle Gawain sits quietly with the ladies while his host leaps aloft, calls for mirth, snatches off his hood and hangs it on a spear (vv. 981–83).

The poet takes care that his audience will not miss the

significance of this ceaseless activity, for he repeatedly
stresses the contrast between the inactive, passive courtier
and his churlishly energetic opponent. At Bercilak's castle
this becomes a source of comedy when the decorous,
elaborately ceremonious Gawain is pulled and pushed
about by his enthusiastically shouting and laughing host.
When Gawain first arrives,

> Gawan glydeʒ ful gay and gos þeder sone;
> Þe lorde laches hym by þe lappe and ledeʒ him to sytte,
> And couþly hym knoweʒ and calleʒ hym his nome.
>
> (vv. 935–37)

The unaggressive, and probably startled, Sir Gawain does
not even ask his host's name. When he attempts to leave,
Bercilak simply grabs him—"þe god mon hym lachcheʒ"
(v. 1029)—and forcefully questions him about his journey.
When he sees that there is no reason for his guest to leave
the castle until New Year's, he is so delighted he lapses
into his one use, as host, of the impolite singular pronoun
—"Þenne laʒande quoth þe lorde, 'Now lenge þe byhoues'"
(v. 1068), and he presses his advantage with such excited
vigor that the courtier can only submit. He grabs Gawain
again—"Þenne sesed hym þe syre and set hym bysyde" (v.
1083)—and speaks with merriment and force:

> Þenne he carped to þe knyʒt, criande loude,
> "ʒe han demed to do þe dede þat I bidde;
> Wyl ʒe halde þis hes here at þys oneʒ?"
> "ʒe, sir, for soþe," sayd þe segge trwe.
>
> (vv. 1088–91)

One is reminded of Chaucer and the forceful eagle in *The
House of Fame*. Later, in the bedroom scenes, there is a
trace of the same contrast. The lady becomes the pursuer,
Gawain the pursued, and when she wins her kisses, it is

she who must embrace and kiss the passive and submissive courtier.

In the Green Knight this aggressive, churlish energy is threatening rather than amusing. In some ways the Green Knight is even more threatening and more churlish than Dangier, for he appears in a royal court where he disdains to dismount or even to greet anyone. His entry is in the tradition of wild men like the young Perceval in the English romance: "Þare made he no lett/ At ȝate, dore ne wykett. . . . His mere witt-owtten faylynge/ Kyste þe forhevede of þe kyng,/ So nerehand he rade" (vv. 489–91, 494–96). It is even more similar to the entry of the churlish Guinehot, Macaire's messenger in *Aiol:*

> Tant par fu fel li mès que ne daigne desendre,
> Ains s'apoie as arçons, si desploie s'ensenge.
> Fierement en apelle le rice roi de Franche.
>
> (vv. 8818–20)
>
> [The messenger was so fierce that he did not deign to dismount; rather he leans on his saddle-bow and vents his raillery; fiercely he calls to the noble king of France.]

The enmity implied by such an entry is unmistakable. When the skin-clad English Perceval rides suddenly into Arthur's court during a Christmas feast, the king recognizes him at once as a wild man.[50] Arthur's recognition of Bercilak's wildness is no less immediate, and he perceives that the stranger is a foe to the Round Table even before the challenge is delivered:

> And sayd, "Sir cortays knyȝt,
> If þou craue batayl bare,
> Here fayleȝ þou not to fyȝt."
>
> (vv. 276–78)

Since the Green Knight has just announced that he comes in peace (v. 266), some readers take this speech as evidence that Arthur has lost his self-control and is guilty both of a breach of manners and of unmotivated pugnacity.[51] The ironically elaborate form of address shows that Arthur, who later does lose his self-control, is here in full possession of both his manners and himself. The speech reveals not the king's pugnacity but his realization that the Green Knight is, partly at least, a wild man and thus the natural foe of Camelot and the knighthood it represents.

The greenness of the Green Knight

The Gawain-poet's audience probably recognized the green-man and wild-man aspects of Bercilak's character almost automatically, but his most striking characteristic —his strange green skin—must have been a good deal more puzzling, for it is not a conventional feature. Of course, the fourteenth-century hearer, accustomed to the marvels of romance, was probably not as startled by this aspect of Bercilak as the modern reader is. The medieval audience knew of a good many strangely colored knights, such as the Green Knight in *Valentine et Orson*, the White Knight (actually the disguised magician Gasozein) in *Diu Crône*, and the original of them all, the Felon Red Knight of *Perceval*, who appears in the English *Sir Perceval* completely clothed and equipped in red, mounted on a red horse, and associated with an old hag who has the power of restoring his life. Furthermore, the medieval audience expected the wild man to have a strange complexion, and although in literature it is customarily black, in painting it is often green.

Nevertheless, the green complexion is not a necessary, conventional feature of any of these figures. Even in painting, green skin is by no means common, and in literature

Bercilak's complexion has no exact analogue. Scholars have searched diligently for one, but even if they were able to find one or two green-skinned literary characters, they would probably shed little light on the poem.[52] The green skin is puzzling because that is what the poet intended it to be. This one unconventional element, the only one in the portrait of the Green Knight, casts the familiar parts of that character into a new and ambiguous context and lends him the novelty and mystery upon which the effect of a "ferly" depends.

Any strange color—red or blue or purple—would have had this effect, but green is especially suitable for this character. Not only is it a logical extension of the green man's conventional costume and the wild man's conventionally strange color, it is also a color that is rich in suggestions relevant to the theme of this romance. At the moment the green skin is first mentioned, one is at a complete loss as to which of the suggested meanings he should select. Green, he knows, is the color of fairies and sometimes of ghosts—and the courtiers believe at first that the Green Knight is "for fantoum and fayrye." [53] Green is also the color of death; "His rode was worþen grene" is a metaphor for death in one Middle English lyric, and the ambiguous word "fade" in "He ferde as freke were fade/ And oueral enker grene" does suggest that the Green Knight may represent death.[54] Green is also the color of otherworld creatures and sometimes of the "fiend," as Gawain calls his opponent.[55] No wonder then that Gawain leaves the court carrying charms to ward off phantoms and evil spirits—the Pentangle for evil spirits and the "brown" diamonds on his helm, which protect one against phantoms but are effective, the lapidaries warn, only so long as one preserves his chastity.[56]

Yet, as the medieval students of symbolism would put it, green has *bona* as well as *mala* significances.[57] It is the color of life as well as death, especially when it is an "enker" green instead of the pale green of death, and it is associated with spring and rebirth (in one later romance the hero is saved from death by a marvellous green liquor that leaves him with a green complexion [58]). It is difficult to take the substantial and merry challenger as a spectre of death, and the repeated association of his green color with nature and vegetation reminds us of his close connection with this world and of his pleasant as well as his threatening side.

The poet capitalizes on this ambiguity, and he takes care that his audience remains unsure of whether the green implies good or evil until the very end of the romance, when the green-skinned Bercilak leans on his axe and chuckles good-naturedly at the hero. If one did know immediately what the green represents, there would be no "ferly," no suspense, and no pleasure when we, with Gawain, finally discover that the man he thought was a fiend is actually his friend. It is the ambiguity of the greenness and the relevance of its ambiguous implications to the challenger's character that maintain the balance of attractiveness and fearfulness that the combined figures of the literary green man and wild man produce.

Bercilak's green skin also helped the poet solve his most difficult problem in the creation of the Green Knight, that of combining two such disparate figures as the wild man and the green man. They are such exact opposites that Henryson, who used the green man for his portrait of the young Jupiter in *The Testament of Criseyde*, draws upon the wild man for part of the antithetical portrait of Saturn, making him churlish and remarkably hairy as well as very old: "Ane busteous Churle on his maneir . . . atouir his belt his lyart lokkis lay" (vv. 153, 162). He is dressed in gray instead of green, he is associated with storms, and he frowns fiercely. In *Sir Gawain* the green skin, which occurs

at the exact center of the description, allows the poet to
unite the two antithetical figures in a single portrait. It
carries the green of the costume into the green of the hair
and beard, and it thus transfers some of the wild man's
frightening grotesquerie to the green man at the same time
as it brings some of the green man's pleasant implications
to the wild man. Furthermore, the color green, with its
suggestion of vegetation, allows the poet to develop the
unity of these two figures beyond the limits of description
by emphasizing the one characteristic they do have in
common, their association with nature.

The Green Knight's relation to the natural world is as
important as his churlishness, and the poet emphasizes this
relation throughout the poem, first by allusion in the initial
description of the challenger (the grass-green color, the
movements like lightning, the beard like a bush), then by
the accounts of Bercilak's joy in the hunt, and finally by
the Green Chapel, which, Gawain tells us, "Wel bisemeʒ
þe wyʒe wruxled in grene" (v. 2191). Like the Green
Knight, the chapel is "vgly, with erbeʒ ouergrowen," and it
is a frightening place, a chapel where, Gawain believes,
the Devil might well say his matins. But it is also a benevolent place, for here Gawain, like Caradoc at the isolated
chapel in the French tale, is finally brought to humility
and repentance. Most important, it is the opposite extreme
of Camelot, the place to which Gawain must come just as
the Green Knight came to Camelot the year before. It
thus shows us that the Green Knight does not, like Dangier, live within the garden of courtesy; he comes from
another world altogether, from the world of nature with
which both aspects of his appearance link him. He therefore assumes neither the validity nor even the existence of
the rules of courtesy. In *Le Roman de la rose* Dangier's
use of "tu" and "vassal" in addressing l'Amant simply re-

verses the roles proper to a gentleman and a *vilain,* and he thereby acknowledges the validity of courtly rules even as he violates them. The Green Knight grandly ignores them. His tone has none of Dangier's petulance, and his use of "sege" and "wyʒe" is uncourtly but not insulting; he calls himself "wyʒe." Consequently his manners impress us more with their energy than with their poor form, and the poet contrives to make this energy as attractive as it is natural and uncourtly.

He does this mainly through his characterization of the host. Bercilak reflects the same combination of features as appears in the Green Knight, though he is a somewhat simpler figure, since his wife embodies the beauty of the Green Knight's portrait, whereas he is almost completely grotesque. His passion for hunting and the churlish vigor of his action and speech reinforce this basic aspect of his character, but he has none of the vices his grotesque appearance leads us to expect. He is generous and hospitable despite his fierce red face and black beard, and though we know that so far as the plot is concerned he is a threatening character, we cannot feel that the threat is very serious as we watch the jolly host laughing and leaping for joy or as we admire his skill in the hunt. The long interlude at Bercilak's castle assures us of the humanity of the challenger just as it reveals the human weakness of the hero, and we are not completely surprised to learn that the Green Knight's threats were more comic bluster than tragic forewarning, for the challenger's forgiveness of the hero accords with our impression of the generous host. When the Green Knight reveals his identity, praises Gawain, and invites him back to the castle for a merry feast, the two aspects of his character as challenger and host are combined; he remains grotesque in appearance and he still ignores the rules of courtesy and addresses Gawain in the singular, but he is now as admirable and sympathetic as Gawain himself.

Gawain's perfection

Gawain is almost as difficult a character as Bercilak, and his relation to the romance tradition is even more complex, for whereas the poet had to create the Green Knight, Gawain came to him fully formed by the tradition, complete with a set of conventional characteristics so well known that the poet could play upon them, defining his hero through the interplay of the traditional Gawain and the Gawain of this poem. Yet, to the reader who does not know the tradition Gawain seems a very simple character. The narrator himself apparently explains Gawain to us, and when he pauses in the narrative to do so, there are no puzzling allusions, as in the description of the Green Knight; he tells us exactly what Gawain represents and precisely why the Pentangle suits him. The difficulty is that Gawain does not live up to this idealized characterization; he is presented as a knight of superhuman perfection, but he turns out to be human after all. Moreover, the knight of the Pentangle is not the Gawain the poet's readers knew from other romances. This audience no doubt did know Gawain very well, for he is the hero of more English romances than any other knight, including even Arthur.[59] They were aware that he is famed not for courtesy, chastity, and loyalty, but for courtesy, lechery, and treachery,[60] and they were probably puzzled to find the narrator ignoring these vices and presenting a hero closer to Galahad than to the Gawain of most romances.

But then Gawain moves from Camelot to Bercilak's castle, and he begins to act a bit more like the Gawain of tradition than the ideal knight of the Pentangle. He lays aside the rich armor that symbolizes his knightly perfection, dons the robes that Bercilak's attendants offer him, and reveals himself as an imperfect, slightly comic figure, with a weakness for women and the capability of betraying his host. At the Green Chapel Gawain changes again, for there he is both human and admirable, less perfect than the knight who undertook the adventure at Camelot but braver and more noble than the man who hid beneath the bedclothes from a woman at Bercilak's castle. The developments in Gawain's character are so well motivated by the situations in which he finds himself that we accept them without difficulty, yet each new development is somewhat different from what we have been led to expect. The basis for these changes is not the narrator's characterization of Gawain in the description of the Pentangle but the familiar tradition that constantly functions as a lightly ironic backdrop for the untraditional Gawain whom the poet keeps in the foreground.

Gawain does not come into that foreground until well after the poem has begun, for he is not introduced until after the long characterization of the court and king that he represents. Like Gawain, Arthur and Camelot are presented as models of courtesy, untouched by any of their traditional vices or even by any traditional virtues that are not consonant with their kind of perfect courtliness. This is not what the opening two stanzas of the poem lead us to expect. They are cast in an elevated epic style, and they create an impression of fierce and violent activity that encompasses all from the eponymous founders of the kingdoms of Europe to the strong men who were Arthur's immediate predecessors and "In mony turned tyme tene þat wroʒten." Such an introduction seems to be leading to a great war chief like the Arthur of the alliterative *Morte Arthure*, who conquered "kyngryke thorowe craftys of armes." Instead, we read,

Bot of alle þat here bult of Bretaygne kynges
Ay watȝ Arthur þe hendest, as I haf herde telle.

(vv. 25-26)

From the kings of conquest we pass to the king of courtesy, not the boldest but the "hendest," and the poet emphasizes the weakness and finality of even this anticlimactic epithet by the avowal of hearsay that abruptly checks the forward movement of the verses—"as I haf herde telle."

The introduction thus functions as a means of isolating Arthur far in the past, before the decline of manners that the romancers so often lament, and as a way of isolating the king from his own past by contrasting him to the fierce line of warriors who preceded him. Their world of vigorous activity is the world that the Green Knight brings into the court. Arthur, on the other hand, is above all a courtier whose every action is governed by ceremony. He will not eat until he sees or hears of some adventure (it is noteworthy that he wishes only to see or hear of, not take part in, some adventure) because of the custom that he through "nobleness" has acquired. When the Green Knight enters, Arthur's first thought is that the proper ceremony be observed, that the intruder dismount, join the feast, and then afterwards turn to business. Arthur is a good knight (v. 104), and when he is taunted by the challenger, his headstrong youth overcomes his courtesy, but this is only a temporary departure from his customary mode of conduct, as shown by the elaborate, ceremonial manner in which he transfers the adventure to Gawain. This is not quite the Arthur of tradition. This is a young Arthur, "sumquat childgered," [61] and though Arthur is usually the ideal courtly king, this is an Arthur whose only virtue is courtesy, known to Bercilak's courtiers as "Arthur þe hende," a famous courtier rather than a powerful king.

Nor is the court that Arthur rules a traditional Arthurian court.[62] Like Gawain and the king, it is idealized and purified of all its usual vices. There is no hint of the adultery, incest, and treachery that finally brought ruin to the Round Table, and familiar characters whose names might serve as allusions to these vices are carefully omitted. There is no Mordred in this Camelot, Lancelot is only a name in a list of knights (and that list does not appear until after the departure of the Green Knight), and even Sir Kay is missing. The omission of Kay is significant, for he played a major role in *Caradoc* and inevitably appears in most Arthurian romances.[63] The author of *The Grene Knight* was evidently disturbed by Kay's absence, for he brings him back into the court and assigns him the part he usually has in such scenes.[64] Yet, traditional as Kay was and important as he had been in *Caradoc*, he could not appear in the Camelot of *Sir Gawain* without marring the tone of courtly perfection that the poet is building. Guillaume de Lorris shows us why in the well-known passage in *Le Roman de la rose* where he uses Gawain as the model of courtesy ("Par sa cortoisie ot de pris") and Kay as his opposite, universally blamed for being "of word dispitous and cruell" ("Par ce qu'il fu fel e crueus," v. 2096). In this idyllic court Kay's courtly sin of discourtesy would have been as jarring a note as Mordred's real sin of treachery.

Unusual as the Gawain-poet's omissions are, the reader has no difficulty in accepting them. Partly this is because the poet assures us that this is a Camelot in its "first age," the time before it acquired the villainies that mar its perfection. Mainly it is because this Camelot has a familiar tone, one that the poet works carefully to establish in the unusually long description, over a hundred lines, that he devotes to the court before the Green Knight appears. The tone is that of the *premerain vers* of the courtly lyric, of the more sophisticated romances, and, most important, of *Le Roman de la rose.* As Bezzola writes, "This *premerain vers*—joyful, sun-filled, spring-like—is followed by pains and sorrows, by all that is serious in the love of the troubadours or in the adventure of the romance." [65] In most romances this is reserved for the hero, for the young knight about to begin the chivalric life. In *Sir Gawain,* as in *Le Roman,* it is extended to the entire court:

> With all þe wele of þe worlde þay woned þer samen,
> Þe most kyd knyȝteȝ vnder Krystes seluen,
> And þe louelokkest ladies þat euer lif haden,
> And he þe comlokest kyng þat þe court haldes;
> For al watȝ þis fayre folk in her first age,
>> on sille;
> Þe hapnest vnder heuen.
>
>> (vv. 50–56)

Superlative youth, beauty, and mirth prevail in this first age. The courtiers carol, tourney, and feast, and "Ladies laȝed ful loude þoȝ þay lost haden," in refreshing contrast to the usual Arthurian court, in which the competitive spirit of the ladies so often caused trouble. Camelot has no troubles; it is like the walled Garden of the Rose or the Heaven of *Pearl* (another ideal court of youth, beauty, riches, mirth, and courtesy), for it is isolated completely from the world of nature outside its confines. The time is the middle of winter, but we are never conscious of this fact at Arthur's court, where the tone is more like spring than a cold January and where the narrator calls the New Year the "young year," emphasizing the season's youth. The world outside does not matter here; courtesy and ceremony are the most important concerns, and even the democratic Round Table survives only as a name for a brotherhood of knights who take their places at the feast with due attention to degree.

The Green Knight emphasizes this concern when he tells the courtiers that he has heard of their "kydde cortaysye,"

"And þat haʒ wayned me hider, iwyis, at þis tyme."

(v. 264)

One hardly expects a fierce challenger to be interested in the courtesy of Arthur's court; it is usually the prowess of the Round Table that attracts adventure. Yet, though the knights of this court are also known as warriors (v. 260), they are primarily courtiers, and when a chance does come for them to prove their prowess, they are overcome with a word (v. 314) and sit helpless and silent before the Green Knight, "Not al for doute," the poet adds, "Bot sum for cortaysye" (vv. 246–47). These refined gentlemen, more used to dances and jousts than to real fighting, do not quite know how to deal with the vigorous world of adventure that the Green Knight represents. This joyous Camelot is the Arthurian court as it was viewed by Guillaume de Lorris, to whom it was a type of courtly virtue, rather than as it was viewed by the poet's fellow romancers, to whom it was a home of warriors or, especially in the fourteenth century, a scene of sin and tragedy. That other Camelot, the flawed Camelot of tradition, hovers always in the background and lends ironic depth to this Camelot, the idealized seat of courtesy.

Bercilak's castle reinforces the irony, for it contains much of what was missing in the court at the beginning of the poem. There are riches, beauty, and mirth at Bercilak's castle, too, but there we are never allowed to forget the world outside, and the blazing fires remind us of the winter even as the company feasts. The old lady personifies all the age, ugliness, and villainy that Camelot lacks, and, as we later learn, she also embodies the treachery, hate, and deceit of which Arthur's court is innocent.

Her presence alongside Bercilak's lady shows us that a romance castle can be a more complex place than the idyllic Camelot, and she, along with the warm fires and the consciousness of a world larger than the court, makes Bercilak's castle, the home of disguise and magic, a more "realistic" place than Camelot.

After the departure of the Green Knight Camelot also becomes more realistic. He has brought the world of nature and violence into the court, and when he departs, the innocent mirth of the Round Table is gone. When Gawain prepares to leave on his adventure, there is another rich feast, but all are "joyless" now (v. 542). It is at this point that the name of Lancelot appears (v. 553), and the discord he faintly implies becomes explicit when the courtiers weep at Gawain's departure and complain bitterly about the king who has allowed him to take on the challenge (vv. 672–83). These hints suggest the traditional Camelot, and Bercilak's castle reinforces the suggestions, and then finally, with the appearance of Morgan la Fay at the end of the adventure, the traditional flaws of Camelot are brought forcibly to the foreground.[66] However, all these developments come later. At the beginning of the poem Camelot's unalloyed joy and youthfulness establish a tone of superlative youth and courtesy that prepares the audience for the perfect courtier who is its champion.

The poet explicitly disrupts his narrative—"þof tary hyt me schulde" (v. 624) in order to explain Gawain's character to his audience. He gives him the armor appropriate to the ideal knight,[67] and he even provides him with a new heraldic device, as if by changing his usual arms he could also change some of his usual characteristics, and he emphasizes the novelty of that device by calling it the "pentangle *nwe*," because it is new to Gawain even though, the narrator explains, it is an old symbol, invented by Solomon. Later the reference to Solomon acquires an

ironic cast when we are reminded that the inventor of the
Pentangle was himself a "fole made" and brought to sorrow by the wiles of a woman (v. 2417), but at this point
there is no obvious irony. The poet capitalizes on the interest the unusual heraldic symbol arouses (late medieval
audiences had a passion for heraldry, even the fictional variety [68]), and he directs that interest to Gawain. The hero
wears the Pentangle, we are told, because it is the token
of "trawþe," and it fits him because he is devoid of faults
and adorned with virtues, a "tulk of tale most trwe/ And
gentylest knyȝt of lote" (vv. 638–39). In the next stanzas
the poet explains that Gawain is faultless in every way (so
that, as we later learn, a single flaw will break the whole of
the endless knot)—in his five fingers, in his faith in the Five
Wounds of Christ, in his fortitude derived from the Five
Joys of Mary, and, most important, in his perfect courtliness:

> Þe fyft fyue þat I finde þat þe frek vsed
> Watȝ fraunchyse and felaȝschyp forbe al þyng,
> His clannes and his cortaysye croked were neuer,
> And pité, þat passeȝ alle poynteȝ, þyse pure fyue
> Were harder happed on þat haþel þen on any oþer.
>
> (vv. 651–55)

The qualities asserted in these lines are repeatedly emphasized in the poem, and Gawain's actions are clearly
governed by the "pure five" courtly virtues. When the lady
attacks his "clannes" at Bercilak's castle, she capitalizes on
the "felaȝschyp" that led to the bargain with the host, and
she plays upon the "fraunchyse," "pité," and "cortaysye"
that he must display if he is to remain the "gentylest knyȝt
of lote." [69] Gawain is keenly aware of the importance of his
courtly virtues, and he scrupulously avoids "vylanye" even
when a "lodly" refusal would remove him from a difficult
and dangerous situation (v. 1772).

It is not difficult to accept Gawain as a model knight, for in many romances, especially the early verse romances, he was indeed a model of knighthood. It is only in the later works, the prose romances and poems like the stanzaic *Le Morte Arthur*, that we encounter the treacherous Gawain of Malory and Tennyson, "Light in life and light in death." [70] With his model knighthood defined mainly as perfect courtesy it is even easier to accept the Gawain-poet's characterization, for both in early and in late romance Gawain was so well known for his courtesy that Chaucer needed only mention "Gawayn, with his olde curteisye" (*SqT*, 95) to evoke the superlative courtliness he had come to represent. However, the Gawain-poet insists that his hero is not only a perfect courtier, he is a perfect Christian knight. He is presented as Mary's knight, and his famous courtesy is explicitly linked with "clannes," making it a spiritual quality of the sort one finds in *Pearl*, where Mary is Queen of Courtesy.

In this initial characterization there is no trace of the traditional Gawain, whose notorious weakness for the things of the world prevented him from attaining the Grail and whose courtesy was conventionally linked with love-making rather than "clannes." Even in the First Continuation of *Perceval*, in which Gawain is generally a model of chivalric virtue, he is guilty of two characteristic crimes, lechery and rape.[71] Rape was seldom necessary, for Gawain is one of the most accomplished lovers in medieval literature. He was not, like Tristan or Lancelot, famous for his attachment to any one partner; rather he enthusiastically distributed his attentions among a large number of ladies. Gawain was "Cortois d'amour," sadly wrote the moral Gower, "mais il fuist trop volage" (*Traitié*, xii, 2). His reputation for being "trop volage," too fickle, is probably what led the author of *The Weddynge of Syr Gawen* to assure his readers, somewhat charitably, that "Gawen was wedded ful oft in his dayes" (v. 832). But it was not marriage for which this hero was famed. He was a master of the casual amour of the sort that Bercilak's lady seems so eagerly to desire, and, as his adventure with Sir Pelleas shows, he was hardly the sort that could be trusted alone with one's wife or mistress.[72]

Gawain's traditional imperfections

In the description of the Pentangle the narrator is so positive in his statements and he so carefully invokes the force of religion to account for Gawain's virtue that the reader is inclined to overlook Gawain's traditional character and accept this hero in his "first age," free from his conventional fault of lechery. But the poet does not allow us to overlook it, for when Gawain arrives at Bercilak's castle his conventional character as a lover is repeatedly stressed. Bercilak's attendants make as much of Gawain's courtesy as the narrator does, but they link it with "luf-talkyng" (v. 927) rather than chastity, and they regard Gawain not as Mary's knight but as a famous and experienced lover. So does Bercilak's lady, as she pleads again and again that he, who is so "cortays," is obliged to teach a young thing "sum tokeneȝ of trweluf craftes" (v. 1527). When the temptation begins, Gawain remains true to the character that the narrator has given him, and he tells the lady "I be not now he þat ȝe of speken" (v. 1242). But he cannot long maintain this perfect detachment from the flesh, and by the last day of the temptation he is passionately involved; "Wiȝt wallande joye" warms his heart when his beautiful seductress appears.

The Gawain of tradition could seldom resist such an opportunity. In *Le Chevalier à l'épée*, when the "perilous bed" prevents his profiting from a similar opportunity, his first thought is for his reputation as a lover; he fears that his fame will be tarnished and that he will become a butt of ridicule; in *Hunbaut* and *The Carl of Carlisle*, which contain chastity tests of a sort, Gawain fails without hesitation.[73] When Gawain is commanded to kiss the Carl's wife, he brings matters to a critical point so quickly that the Carl must hastily intervene: "Whoo ther," he cries, "That game I þe forbede" (vv. 467–68). On the rare occasions when Gawain does resist temptation, as in *Perlesvaus*, the ladies concerned can barely believe that he is Gawain.[74] Bercilak's lady expresses the same sentiment (v. 1293), but there is no doubt that her guest is indeed Gawain. In *Perlesvaus* he resists mainly because the presence of a suspicious-looking dwarf has forewarned him, and in *Sir Gawain* he very nearly falls. The lady "nurned hym so neʒe þe þred" (v. 1771) that it takes Mary, his concern for his courtesy, and his fear of sin and disloyalty to save him, and even then it is a pretty close thing.

In medieval literature the knight who overcomes temptation is seldom really tempted. Yder merely kicks his temptress in the belly, and in *Perlesvaus* Gawain simply refuses to speak to the ladies. The perfect knight of the Pentangle would have reacted in the same way, but not the Gawain of romance tradition, and it is this traditional character that makes the bedroom scenes so difficult for the hero of *Sir Gawain*.

Perhaps this is why the poet chose to add a sexual temptation to the beheading. As we have noted, he needed some means of testing the hero's courtly qualities as well as his bravery and loyalty. He might easily have found some other test, but only a sexual temptation would so completely fit Gawain's conventional character, and only a test of this sort would provide the rich but delicate comedy that one finds in the bedroom scenes. Gawain's problem is that he will lose his reputation for courtesy, the "clean courtesy" defined by the narrator, if he makes love to the lady, and just as surely he will lose his traditional fame for courtesy, love-making, if he does not. Gawain is torn by the contradictory demands of his courtliness, and he cannot help becoming ridiculous as he pretends to misunderstand, coyly grants the kisses, and is finally "al for-wondered" by this charming antagonist whose most dangerous weapon is his own traditional character.

In Gawain's last interview with the lady the darker aspect of his traditional character is briefly and lightly invoked, and the "tulk of tale most trwe" accepts the girdle and agrees to conceal the fact from his host. There is a suggestion here of the treachery that mars Gawain's character in the later romances and of the trickery, the willingness to accept a compromise in battle, that is one of his conventional characteristics throughout romance.[75] The perfect knight of the Pentangle would have scorned such aid; the Five Wounds of Christ are in his mind "Quere-so-euer þys mon in melly watȝ stad" (v. 644), but the Gawain of tradition knows the value of a ruse; he thinks the charm would be "a juel for þe jopardé," and that if he can escape death "þe sleȝt were noble" (vv. 1856–58). His use of "noble" shows his awareness of the claims of chivalric virtue, but he employs the ruse not because of his nobility but because of his conventional faults. He later recognizes that his error has led to "vylany and vyse þat vertue disstryeȝ," and he laments,

> "Now I am fawty and falce, and ferde haf ben euer
> Of trecherye and vntrawþe."
>
> (vv. 2382–83)

Of course, the fault is slight, and the suggestion of the treachery that is his blackest sin in romance tradition is very light. Yet the fact that he does succumb to the temptation of the lace and does acquire a touch of treachery reminds us finally that his traditional character exactly suits the plot that the poet created, for Gawain is the one hero in romance who is as famous for his conventional faults as for his virtues and who comes near perfection but never attains it.

When it later becomes clear that he has partially failed the beheading test, Gawain's first concern is for the "vylanye" that he has acquired, for in the description of the Pentangle he was characterized as "voyded of vche vylany." Courtesy untouched by churlishness is the essential quality of Gawain's perfect knighthood, and his main concern is always his manners. Caradoc does not bother with ceremony when he leaps suddenly forward and fiercely seizes the axe, but Gawain is of a later, more refined generation, and when he accepts the challenge, it is with a long, ceremonial speech, in which he takes care that Guenevere and the king will permit him to rise from the table "wythoute vylanye" (v. 345). In that scene his main problem is to accept the challenge in the correct courtly manner, and at the heart of the poem, the scenes at Bercilak's castle, his greatest difficulty is the delicate matter of courtesy posed by the lady's advances.

Gawain consequently impresses us more as an ideal courtier than as an ideal knight, for though all romance knights are courteous none is so exclusively preoccupied with that virtue as the Gawain of this poem. Chaucer's ideal knight, for example, is as courtly as Gawain, for he is "meek as is a mayde" and "nevere yet no vileynye ne sayde" (*GenPro,* vv. 69–70), but he has the full complement of chivalric virtues, and in the well-known description in *The General Prologue* the main emphasis is on his many campaigns and his fifteen "mortal battles." He is a seasoned warrior, content to wear a battle-stained "gypon." Gawain, on the other hand, has little of the warrior about him, and when he arrives at Bercilak's castle, he changes out of his travel-stained garments as soon as possible. He has more in common with Chaucer's Squire than with his Knight.

Of course, this is a matter of emphasis. Gawain is brave, for he accepts the challenge; he is strong, for his mighty blow sends the challenger's head flying; and he is a skilled warrior who fights many wild beasts on his way to Bercilak's castle. Yet the poet barely mentions these aspects of Gawain's knighthood. His strength and bravery are only indirectly stated in the list of virtues that accompanies the description of the Pentangle,[76] and his battles are quickly passed over in the narrative, whereas his courtly deeds are narrated at great length and his courtesy is mentioned again and again. Gawain finds only hardship on his journey instead of the high adventure that most romance knights prized, and when he arrives at Bercilak's castle "þenne his cher mended" among the courtly amenities that he prefers. Once within the castle this perfect courtier can lie abed for three days in succession while his more vigorous host energetically hunts in the woods. Such conduct is dangerous for one's morals, since long lying in bed, Chaucer's Parson informs us, is conducive to lechery.[77] It is also unbecoming to a knight of the older school. When Chrétien's Erec remained in his bower while the rest of the court hunted, Enide reproached him bitterly—and justly in Chrétien's view—for unchivalric sloth.[78] Yet what was shameful for Erec seems suitable to the Gawain of this poem. He is, as the Green Knight mockingly calls him, a "Sir swete," famed not for warlike deeds but for "sleʒteʒ of þewes" and "luf-talkyng," and his knighthood is more clearly related to the pattern of chivalry in *Le Roman de la rose* than to that of the older Arthurian romances.

To a certain degree this was made inevitable by the nature of the plot and by the kind of challenger the poet created for it. In the action of the beheading tale Gawain is called upon to display only his moral qualities. Strength and skill are of no avail to the hero who must meekly bow for the return-blow, and in the temptation, should Gawain use his strength as the lady suggests ("ʒe ar stif innoghe to constrayne wyth strenkþe, ʒif yow lykeʒ," v. 1496), he would fail the test. Restraint and fortitude are the virtues necessary to the hero of this poem. Furthermore, Gawain's opponent is partly a wild *vilain*, who is conventionally a mighty hunter and fighter, the equal and sometimes the superior of the knight in brute strength and ferocity. Certainly the Green Knight, who survives even a beheading, is more than a match for Gawain. When, after the return-blow, Gawain leaps back and draws his sword, the Green Knight merely leans on his axe and laughs, and we cannot help feeling the futility of Gawain's gesture. Compared to Bercilak, Gawain is indeed a beardless child. It is only in courtesy that Gawain can be shown to be the Green Knight's superior, and it is only in manners that a sure distinction between the knight and a churl can be drawn, for though a *vilain* may hunt and fight as well as the chevalier, he can never be *cortois* without ceasing to be a *vilain*. Gawain does have some military prowess and Bercilak some courtesy, but in general the two are opposites, with Gawain essentially a courtier and his opponent a *vilain* with traces of churlishness in his conduct and appearance even when he appears as lord of a fine castle. To understand how the poet uses this opposition we must next learn something of his style and literary techniques.

The Style

The literary relations of *Sir Gawain* are complicated by
the fact that it is both a romance and an alliterative poem.
We have seen how much the poet owes to the French tradition for his materials, and certainly in tone *Sir Gawain*
is the most continental of English romances; but England
provided the poet with his style, and the art of *Sir Gawain*
is essentially the art of the alliterative tradition. Yet critics
have paid little attention to this style,[1] and consequently
it is often misunderstood. Few readers repeat the errors of
those nineteenth-century critics who read the poem with
Chaucerian metrical expectations and then condemned it
for its "harshness"[2] or of those moderns who, on the same
basis, extravagantly praise it for its "native vigor." Yet
fewer still recognize that an alliterative poem differs from
a nonalliterative work in more than vocabulary and meter,
that this style is a mode of discourse which in generations
of use had developed its own way of designating objects
and concepts, of describing places and events, and of
building a narrative. Consequently, one must read *Sir Ga-*

wain not only with a sympathetic awareness of its traditional meter and diction but with a set of syntactic, semantic, and even structural expectations much different from those one brings to the works of Chaucer and Gower.

This is not easy, for now we are all "Southren men" who "kan nat geeste, 'rum, ram, ruf,' by lettre," [3] and we have forgotten the aesthetic grammar of poets who can. Try as we will, we can never again hear the alliterative line as it must have sounded when it was a normal, common meter "in londe so hatȝ ben longe," just as we can never again hear the pentameter couplet as it sounded when the inventive Chaucer first used it. We can, however, discover the basic stylistic traits of *Sir Gawain* and define the dominant tendency of its style, relating it to the tradition in which the poet wrote and examining his uses of it. [4] If we achieve only this much, we will have come a long way toward understanding the poem, for the artistic syntax that a style provides affects every part of a good poem, from the words and sentences to the structure of the work as a whole. This is not to agree with the Gestalt psychologists or Ben Jonson that "oratio imago animi," though that is good medieval doctrine. [5] It is simply that the form in which a poet, or any speaker, casts his statements reflects the way in which he expects his audience to perceive them, the way, indeed, that they must perceive them if they are to understand what is being said. To understand the form of *Sir Gawain* and the genius with which the poet endowed it, we must know more exactly what this alliterative style is, how it came into being, and how it affected his poem.

The development of the Middle English alliterative line

The general facts of the meter and versification of Middle English alliterative poetry are well known, and they can be quickly summarized here. The Middle English line, like the Old English, consists of two half-lines, an "on-verse" (the first half-line) and an "off-verse" (the second). Each half-line contains a varying number of lightly stressed syllables and at least two heavily stressed ones.[6] Ordinarily both heavily stressed syllables alliterate in the first half-line and one of the two alliterates in the second. The usual rime scheme is thus aa/ax, with the on-verse slightly heavier in emphasis. This is the basic pattern of both Old and Middle English alliterative verse but, as most students are aware, the Middle English line differs from the Old English in a number of ways. In Middle English the meter is purely accentual, the alliterating syllables more frequent, and the rhythm predominantly rising, iambic and anapestic in movement (though an unstressed final syllable frequently appears) rather than falling, trochaic and dactylic, the usual movement of Old English verse. In the later period the verse is also more highly ornamented, and the lines are longer, more nearly equal in length and more often end-stopped. These changes are developments of features that had already appeared in late Old English poetry,[7] though the tendency toward excessive ornamentation is found in "classic" Old English poetry (such as the rimes in Cynewulf's *Elene*), whereas the longer, end-stopped lines seem to have been characteristic of "popular" Old English verse.

For Middle English poetry the most important change was the development of the predominantly end-stopped style. In both Old and Middle English verse the minimum metrical unit is the half-line (a single "foot" cannot stand alone), but in the classic "run-on" style of Old English the caesura that separates the two half-lines has far more weight. It can, and often does, mark a full stop, with the second half-line beginning a new clause that runs on to the next verse without a syntactic pause. This style involves what Malone calls a "plurilinear" mode of composition, in contrast to the "linear" style of popular verse, in which the end of the line marked a full stop.[8] Middle English verse seems to combine the two. As in popular Old English verse, the medial caesura marks a slight pause but almost never a full stop. Yet, as in the "plurilinear" style, the period usually runs on; sentences tend to be long, though each line is usually a major syntactic unit in itself and the end of the line is marked by a definite pause. Consequently, although Middle English, like Old English, still depends heavily on parallel constructions, the parallels are now often clausal rather than uniformly phrasal:

> Þay boȝen bi bonkkeȝ þer boȝeȝ ar bare,
> Þay clomben bi clyffeȝ þer clengeȝ þe colde.
>
> (vv. 2077–78)

The caesura does not have the weight of the end of the line, but the half-lines are still quite emphatic. They usually coincide with a syntactic unit and often, as in the verses quoted above, the major clause is completed within the first half-line. Since the caesura cannot ordinarily carry the weight of a full stop and one therefore cannot begin a new sentence in the second half-line, the Middle English poet had to fill out his verse by compounding some element of the first half-line or by using some formulaic filler or some parallel modifier. In Old English the first half-line commonly had more metrical weight than the second; in Middle English it often had more semantic weight as well.

These changes are due in large part to the changes that the language itself underwent in the shift from Old to Middle English.[9] The longer line became necessary once the language of poetry felt the general loss of the old inflectional endings and of the Old English habit of compounding, with the consequent shift from a relatively synthetic to a generally more analytic syntactic structure. Cynewulf could refer to God as "Rodera Wealdend"; to build a similar expression a Middle English poet had to use an article and a preposition—"þe kyng of heuen"—and his usual impulse was to analyze even further—"þe heiȝ kyng þat al heuen weldes." [10] The author of *Beowulf* could identify a ruler as "helm Scyldinga"; when a Middle English poet identified a king in the off-verse, he had to write "That lorde was of Rome" (*MA*, 23), or, at the very least, "The kynge of Cyprus" (*MA*, 596). As more function words, such as "the" and "of," must be added, the line necessarily becomes longer.

The rhythm of the line also changes as articles and prepositions increase in number, and it shifts from the naturally falling rhythm of the inflected language (Ródera Wéaldend) to the predominantly rising rhythm of Middle English (þe kýng of héuen). Furthermore, as the line becomes longer more alliteration is required to unify it. Three alliterating staves in the first half-line and two in the second are no longer so rare, and one finds verses, like those quoted on the previous page, in which every lift alliterates.

The heavier alliteration in Middle English and the tendencies toward greater regularity in the number of syllables and toward more verbal ornamentation are probably also partly due to changes in the conditions of composition and performance. Old English poetry was composed for the harp and performed to its accompaniment, Middle

English verse was evidently composed for readers as well as hearers, and it seems to have been delivered without musical accompaniment. Of course, it is almost impossible to be sure, for the practice was evidently not uniform. In *The Siege of Jerusalem* the author mentions "lered men" who sing the deeds of Joseph and Judas to the accompaniment of "sawters" (vv. 473 ff.), but the Middle English custom of alliterating unstressed syllables, such as "*bigyneʒ*" in *Sir Gawain* (vv. 112, 1571), shows that this verse was designed to appeal to the eye as well as the ear, and clearly such works as *The Wars of Alexander* and *The Destruction of Troy* were written primarily for readers.

When the verse was sung to the harp, a half-line of three accented syllables of which only two alliterate offered no problem. Without the aid of the harp's beat and melody, alliteration alone must unify the line and the more nearly isosyllabic structure of the verses must supply the regularity formerly provided by the musical accompaniment. The disappearance of the harp also meant a loss of the aural ornamentation it had provided. As in the case of the lyric, once the melody is removed, other, purely verbal ornamentation must be added. End-rime becomes more frequent, especially in the works of Northern poets, who generally write more of a "high style" than their Southern contemporaries, such as Langland (in the North the Norse influence may have been significant).[11] The alliterative patterns are often complex, and assonantal alliteration ("*brode* silken *bordeʒ*"), consonance ("*bereʒ* and *boreʒ*"), *adnominatio* ("*leder* of *ledeʒ*"), and ornamental repetition ("*to longe* lye or *to longe* sytte") become common. Strophic divisions of the line also become popular and frequently, as in the Gawain-poet's "bob and wheel" stanza, the alliterative line is used in combination with other metrical structures.

From the standpoint of the older poetry such changes appear to be a weakening of the tradition. Actually they are evidence of its continuing strength, vigorously adapting itself to the changing requirements of the language and to new conditions of composition and performance. Probably the late fourteenth-century writers were not even aware that the line they used represented a changing tradition. The Gawain-poet describes his line as one that "In londe so hatʒ ben longe" (v. 36), yet he places that description in the riming quatrain of a stanza that is unknown to the older tradition. So far as one can judge from the works that survive, the Gawain-poet's stanza is unique, but only because the long lines are unrimed and vary in number. Aside from that, the stanza is common in the later alliterative tradition. It appears in *Somer Soneday*, one of the earliest fourteenth-century alliterative poems, and it survives until long after the rest of the tradition is dead, even having a place among the few forms discussed by James VI (James II of England) in his treatise on Scots verse, where its presence bears final witness to the strength of the Middle English alliterative tradition.[12]

The changes in the tradition came about and won general acceptance because of the advantages they offered the poets who used them. The "bob and wheel" stanza is a good example. The long lines, varying in number and length, build to a narrative climax, signalled by the short "bob," which is often meaningless in itself but which is always aurally significant in its abrupt shift in meter. Then follows the four-line "wheel" with its insistent rimes and tight meter. The sudden change from the long line to the short lends the bobs and wheels an emphasis that the Gawain-poet exploits to build narrative units in which "the sting is in the tail." When the Green Knight first appears, for example, the narrator does not mention the most amazing aspect of the intruder until the bob and wheel:

And alle his fetures folȝande, in forme þat he hade,
      ful clene;
   For wonder of his hwe men hade,
   Set in his semblaunt sene;
   He ferde as freke were fade,
   And oueral enker grene.

                              (vv. 145–50)

In the next stanza, which describes the Green Knight's equipment, the poet again waits until the bob and wheel to introduce the most amazing piece of equipment, the green horse. Likewise, when Bercilak's lady offers herself to Gawain, the blunt proposition occurs in the bob and wheel. So regularly does the poet employ the emphasis his stanza provides that, as Gustav Plessow recognized, the quatrains alone provide a kind of outline of the poem's action.[13] The Middle English stanza prevents a poet from developing the long sweeps of narrative possible in the older poetry or in fourteenth-century works such as the *Morte Arthure*, but the Gawain-poet's use of the form shows that this development, like so many of the others, opened as many possibilities for the Middle English poets as it closed to them.

Traditional formulas and the new "high style"

Until quite recently scholars spoke more often of "survivals" than of "developments" in the Middle English alliterative tradition, for it seemed as if this later poetry was a consciously archaic revival of a tradition that had been fixed in pre-conquest times and survived only piecemeal into the fourteenth century. J. P. Oakden did demonstrate the continuing development of the tradition by isolating some of the stylistic peculiarities of Middle English verse that have no counterpart in the older poetry (such as the formulaic "fillers" in the second half-lines) but that appear in a fully developed state in the earliest fourteenth-century works.[14] Yet even Oakden believed that the main tradition survived rather than grew and that it was to be traced in the few alliterative poems left to us from the twelfth and thirteenth centuries, even though those few, such as Laȝamon's *Brut,* seem to point more clearly to the dissolution of the tradition than to its continuity. Then about a decade ago F. P. Magoun applied to Old English poetry the techniques of analysis developed by Milman Parry and Albert Lord, whose investigations of classical and modern oral traditions established what oral poetry is and how it is made, and he was able to show the close relation of Old English verse to an oral-formulaic tradition.[15] Shortly thereafter, R. A. Waldron, using the same methods, demonstrated the oral-formulaic basis of Middle English alliterative verse.[16] He concentrated on but one poem, the *Morte Arthure,* and obviously more study of this problem is needed, but even this beginning is enough to prove that a continuous oral tradition accounts for both the survival and the continuing development of alliterative verse in Middle English.

The fourteenth-century poets were aware of their debt to their oral predecessors. In the "prologue" to *Wynnere and Wastoure* we read:

> Whylome were lordes in londe þat louid in thaire hertis
> To here makers of myrthes, þat matirs couthe fynde,
> [And now es no frenchipe in fere bot fayntnesse of hert;]
> Wyse wordes with-inn þat wroghte were neuer
> Ne redde in no Romance þat euer renke herde.[17]

> (vv. 20–24)

This passage is part of the narrator's general complaint about the new entertainers now replacing the older kind of poets, who produced wise words that were never before composed ("wroghte") and never written down in books. The narrator identifies himself with this older school, in which the poet is both composer and performer and does not depend on books, and his claim is the more convincing, since this passage follows a catalogue of "monsters" of the sort that were frequent in popular prophecies—"And hares appon herthe-stones schall hurcle in hire fourme." Yet, we must not take the passage at its full face value, for throughout this prologue the narrator characterizes himself as a provincial, old-fashioned man, suspicious of London and out of step with his own time. Then in the body of the poem he proves how cosmopolitan and contemporary he really is. The passage is clearly not autobiographical, but it is at once a valuable testimony to the existence of the older, oral tradition and a suggestion of the sophisticated, rather playful attitude that a fourteenth-century poet could adopt toward it.

There is something of this even in *Sir Gawain*, for the Gawain-poet also pays the older tradition the compliment of identifying himself with it. His matter has obviously been "read in romance"—"þe Brutus bokeȝ þerof beres wyttenesse" (v. 2523)—and his subject is more likely to have been heard in court than "in toun." Yet he claims,

> I schal tell hit astit, as I in toun herde,
> > with tonge,
> > As hit is stad and stoken
> > In stori stif and stronge,
> > With lel letteres loken,
> > In londe so hatȝ ben longe.

(vv. 31–36)

The Gawain-poet obviously considers alliterative verse a written form of poetry—"*letteres* loken"—but his insistence on oral transmission—"with tonge"—seems to reflect at least a transitional stage of the sort A. C. Baugh discovered in the metrical romances, the stage of literary composition and oral transmission, a situation that accounts for the survival and spread of oral formulas even after the introduction of written literature.[18] That tradition must have been very weak by the Gawain-poet's time, just as the minstrel tradition survived in the Elizabethan period only in a few singers like Sidney's blind "crowder," but it was still strong enough and respectable enough when *Sir Gawain* was written that the poet claims to be a part of it.

The claim was justified, for despite the obvious literacy of these poets and despite the lightly humorous stance which so clearly shows that they were not interested simply in imitating the oral poets, that older tradition provided them with their style. This is true even of the Gawain-poet, the most literary of these writers, for *Sir Gawain*, though less formulaic than works such as *Morte Arthure* or *The Destruction of Troy*, is deeply indebted to the tradition of oral verse. In the poem's opening stanza, for example, there is hardly a line without some trace of a formula (underlined) or formulaic expression (broken underlining):

> Siþen þe sege and þe assaut watȝ sesed at Troye,
> Þe borȝ brittened and brent to brondeȝ and askeȝ,
> Þe tulk þat þe trammes of tresoun þer wroȝt
> Watȝ tried for his tricherie, þe trewest on erþe;
> Hit watȝ Ennias þe athel and his highe kynde,
> Þat siþen depreced prouinces and patrounes bicome
> Welneȝe of al þe wel in þe West Iles.
> Fro riche Romulus to Rome ricchis hym swyþe,
> With gret bobbaunce þat burȝe he biges vpon fyrst,
> And neuenes hit his aune nome, as hit nou hat;
> Ticius to Tuskan and teldes bigynnes,
> Langaberde in Lumbardie lyftes vp homes,
> And fer ouer þe French flod Felix Brutus
> On mony bonnkes ful brode Bretayn he setteȝ.[19]

(vv. 1–14)

A phrase like "brittened and brent" is a formula, a fixed phrase occurring with the same words (or nearly the same) in similar contexts and in the same metrical position in a number of other poems (e.g., "I be bretenet and brent in baret to byde" (*Pistill,* 147). A phrase like "To bronde3 and aske3" is a formulaic phrase—a fixed verbal pattern that appears under the same metrical and semantic conditions with one principal word invariable and the other words varied to suit the context. Here the system is composed of a preposition at the beginning of a second half-line and "aske3" at its end, the formulaic phrase used to complete a line with brent in the first half: "Betyn and brent doun vnto bare askes" (*DT,* 5007). Finally, a phrase such as "þe trewest on erþe" is a syntactically formulaic phrase; that is, a metrical unit in which the verbal content varies though the metrical and syntactic pattern remains the same. Here the formulaic pattern is a second half-line composed of an absolute superlative adjective plus a prepositional phrase, a very common pattern in alliterative poetry: "The first was Sir Ector and aldeste of tyme" (*Parl,* 300). It is in such formulas and formulaic phrases and patterns that the ancient tradition was transmitted to the poets of the Revival. On that tradition, its diction and its syntax, the Gawain-poet formed his style.

The existence of an oral tradition and the obvious debt owed it by the poets of the Alliterative Revival do not solve all the problems raised by their style, for though there is no doubt that an oral tradition existed, it is equally obvious that there was a sudden literary revival and that the poets who participated in it had more sophisticated goals than merely reducing to paper what once existed in song. Even after we have made a generous allowance for the manuscripts that have been lost, we must conclude that in the twelfth and thirteenth centuries very few alliterative poems were written down. Then in the fourteenth century a great many writers turned to this style and the literary tradition was revived. The reasons for this rebirth of interest have never been clear, and scholars have searched for some specific cause, such as the "baronial opposition" to the royal court that Hulbert believed provided the impetus for the Revival.[20]

However, we cannot even be sure that the Alliterative Revival began in any one specific place or time. Indeed, the marked stylistic differences between poems like *Piers Plowman* and *Sir Gawain* probably indicate that there were two traditions of alliterative verse, a Southern and a Northern, which were not very closely related. Moreover, the Alliterative Revival is not an isolated phenomenon. It seems to have no immediate literary forebears, but neither does Chaucer. The same can be said for any sophisticated poet or group of poets in the fourteenth century, for there is little in what survives from the twelfth and thirteenth centuries to prepare us for the amazing production of the fourteenth, a period of sudden flowering in every genre save possibly that of the religious lyric. Only a dozen or so secular lyrics and five romances (all popular in subject matter and treatment) survive from the thirteenth century, as compared to the great number of fourteenth-century works in these genres. If one were to calculate the ratio of fourteenth- and fifteenth-century works to twelfth- and thirteenth-century works in every genre, he would find that the ratio for alliterative poems differs little from that for other forms.

The reasons for a poet's decision to adopt this style must therefore be sought along with the causes for the general rise in the cultural status of English in the fourteenth century, when the native language was used once again in schools, in Parliament, and in literature throughout the country.[21] We cannot even explain the choice solely on regional grounds, for nonalliterative verse was composed throughout the country, and the influence of alliterative verse is likewise to be found throughout England. The lyrics, dramas, and rimed romances of the fourteenth and fifteenth centuries abound with alliterative phrases and formulas.[22] Chaucer himself occasionally uses one, such as "holt and heeth," and when he wishes he can produce a flawless alliterative line—"Ther shyveren shaftes upon sheeldes thikke." [23] Nor can we explain that poets chose this style because they lived in what J. D. Bruce called "cultural backwaters" or because alliterative verse was somehow closer to the "folk" than rimed verse.[24] *Piers Plowman,* with its involved theological discussions, is not the sort of poem that could hold the attention of back-country peasants or culturally underprivileged country gentlemen.[25] It is unlikely that the refined Humphrey de Bohun, with his appreciation for French and Italian literature, would have had *William of Palerne* written for his household if he had considered alliterative verse a merely popular form, or that its author could have maintained the fine social distinctions in his use of the second person pronoun (with a rare consistency this early in the century) if he had been a "backward" poet.[26] What truly popular English verse survives from the late Middle Ages is not alliterative. John Ball's letter to the peasants is rimed verse; Mirk's *Layfolk's Massbook* is in couplets; and early in the century Robert Mannyng, who professedly wrote for the "lewd," chose the octosyllabic couplet and carefully avoided the language of "seggers" and "harpours" who used a diction too difficult for "symple men/ þat strange Inglis can not ken." [27]

Robert's words partly explain why the alliterative style attracted the efforts of poets who were, as a group, the most sophisticated in fourteenth-century England; he reminds us that even as an oral tradition alliterative verse was a sophisticated medium, demanding an experienced audience that could understand its specialized diction and syntax, its "strange Inglis" unknown to "symple men." But probably an even more important part of its appeal for cultivated poets is the paradoxical fact that this archaic stylistic tradition was exactly suited to the most recent and fashionable standards of English literary taste. The fourteenth century was the age in which poets and audiences discovered English rhetorical verse, poetry adorned with all the "colors of rhetoric" taught by critics like John of Garland and Geoffrey of Vinsauf, Chaucer's "Gaufred, deere maister soverayn." [28] These doctrines were not new in the fourteenth century; Geoffrey's *Poetria Nova* was two centuries old by the Gawain-poet's time, and Geoffrey himself, despite his title, drew on Horace and the Pseudo-Ciceronian *Rhetorica ad Herennium*. What did seem very new and exciting was the discovery that English too could be treated in the high style of medieval rhetoric. How exciting it seemed is apparent from the enthusiastic comments, and excesses, of Chaucer's followers. To them he was not the author of the first psychological novel or an early master of realism; he was the "noble rhetor Poete" who, as Lydgate wrote, "made firste to distille and reyne/ The golde dewe droppis of speche and eloquence." [29]

Chaucer was the best of the "rhetor poetes," but he was not, as his disciples claimed, the first. The alliterative poets who were his predecessors and contemporaries shared his admiration for the teachings of the rhetoricians, and they found in the alliterative line a style that tended almost naturally toward a heavily adorned verse of the sort that the rhetoricians recommended. From the beginning the basis of both the diction and the syntax of alliterative verse was "variation," the "double or multiple statement of the same concept or idea in different words, with a more or less perceptible shift in stress." [30] The basis of the rhetorical style was also a kind of variation—*expolitio*,[31] which

Geoffrey of Vinsauf both exemplifies and defines in the *Poetria Nova* when he advises his students,

> . . . multiplice forma
> Dissimiletur idem; varius sis et tamen idem.
>
> (vv. 224–25)
>
> [. . . let the same thing be concealed in a variety of forms; be varied yet always the same.]

The amplified periods, periphrases, and repetitions of the traditional alliterative style are exactly the methods the rhetoricians advised for being "varied yet always the same." Perhaps that is why those poets who are the most traditional and formulaic in their style, such as the authors of the *Morte Arthure* and *The Parlement of the Thre Ages,* are also the most rhetorical.[32] Why one should find this similarity between the alliterative and Latin rhetorical styles (a similarity that has led some critics to believe that the works of Virgil directly influenced the authors of *Beowulf* and *Sir Gawain* [33]) is another question with no sure answer. Perhaps it is because the stylistic ideal of the rhetoricians was the classical epic, which, like alliterative verse, is ultimately derived from oral tradition.

However that may be, to a sophisticated fourteenth-century audience the opening stanza of *Sir Gawain* would seem not an exercise in an archaic verse form but an astonishing display of the author's command of the most fashionable poetic idiom. Along with the formulas and formulaic expressions that we noted in this stanza, one finds the *interpretatio* of "borʒ" and "Troye," the *contentio* of "tricherie, þe trewest on erthe," the *compar* of the balanced clauses in the first two lines, the *dissolutio* in the juxtaposition of the first two verses, the *circuitio* of "þe tulk þat þe trammes of tresoun þer wroʒt," the *adnominatio* and chiasmus of "Riche Romulus to Rome ricchis," the *similiter cadens* of "brondeʒ and askeʒ," the *disjunctio* of "teldes bigynnes" and "lyftes vp homes," the *adjunctio* of "Ticius to Tuskan," the possible *nominatio* in "Ticius," and the admirable *commoratio* of the whole.

We need not assume that the poet knew he was using all these *colores rhetorici*, for the rhetoricians were descriptive as well as prescriptive, and it is only in the larger aspects of a poet's style (such as the Gawain-poet's descriptions) that we can surely detect their influence. Yet the fact that the opening stanza of *Sir Gawain* can be so fully analyzed both from the standpoint of traditional formulas and from that of medieval rhetoric shows how well the traditional style suited the literary fashions of the fourteenth century and helps explain why the alliterative poets were, until the coming of the fifteenth-century Chaucerians, the most rhetorical poets in Middle English; for a poet interested in cultivating the new high style the alliterative line was at hand with all the advantages of a fully developed tradition, especially for those poets in the North and West, where the oral tradition evidently survived for so long. There are, of course, exceptions; Langland and his followers show little interest in rhetorical adornments—and relatively few traditional formulas. In most cases, however, alliterative verse and a taste for the rhetorical high style seem to coincide. Even a century and more later Dunbar, the most "aureate" of Chaucer's followers, found the alliterative style congenial and produced one of the last and most delightful products of the Revival in his *Twa Mariit Wemen and the Wedo*.

Variation: the synonyms

The most obvious feature of this style, and one of the most difficult to appreciate for us "simple men" outside the tradition, is the remarkably heavy use of synonyms. The redesignation of objects, concepts, and characters by varied synonyms is part of the technique of composition that was originally developed to meet the needs of oral poets, and a certain amount of variation is characteristic of all oral poetry; but in the English tradition variation became the dominant stylistic feature, "the soul of Old English poetry," as Klaeber called it,[34] and it remained so even after the tradition had become literate, providing the poets not only with an easy means of ornamentation but with a subtle and analytical method of defining concepts and making statements. We are apt to recognize only the ornamental function of the technique, dismissing the varied synonyms as merely "elegant variation," a stylistic fault in our view, but this is only because variation and its related traits are so foreign to the styles to which we are accustomed in modern fiction and nonalliterative verse.

In nonalliterative works—Chaucer's poems, for example —relatively few synonyms are used, and a very small vocabulary is employed for purposes such as the designation of characters. A proper noun and perhaps as many as three or four synonyms appropriate to the character's station in life are all that is needed. In the whole of *The Knight's Tale* only four nouns are used for Theseus: "Theseus," "duc," "knyght," "counquerour." Palamon and Arcite are designated in the same restrained manner, and Emelye is invariably "Emelye." This is the usual style of designating characters in all of Chaucer's work, whether romantic, like *The Knight's Tale*, or "realistic," like the fabliaux. In *The Shipman's Tale* the cuckold is designated only by "husband," "merchant," and "good man." He shares no common noun with the lover, who is consistently "Daun John" and "monk." The name and station complete the designation of a Chaucerian character, and the designation seldom varies even when it leads to considerable repetition —"Palamoun, this woful prisoner" (v. 1063), "This sorweful prisoner, this Palamoun" (v. 1070). The Gawain-poet, on the other hand, uses a larger vocabulary for Gawain in but two stanzas (vv. 536–89) than Chaucer uses for any of his characters in the whole of *The Knight's Tale;* in these few lines Gawain is *lede, þat ientyle, knyȝt, Wawan, mon, sege,* and *wyȝe.* This is the style of designating characters in all of the Cotton Nero poems.[35] Even in *Pearl,* which is not a strictly alliterative poem, the poet uses nine different synonyms for Pearl in the first seven stanzas in which she appears (vv. 157–240).

Elaboration, not simplicity, is the ideal of such poetry, and its aesthetic has little relation to the modern assumptions that a good style consists in brevity—"so many things in so many words"—and that the best style is one that reflects colloquial speech. Certainly the Gawain-poet could sound colloquial when he so chose, as we can hear in the marvellously idiomatic voice of the lady when she wonders why Gawain has not asked for a kiss, "Bi sum towch of summe tryfle at sum taleȝ ende" (v. 1301). Likewise, he knows the uses of brevity and simplicity; the description of Gawain's reaction to the Green Knight's explanation of the adventure catches the whole movement of the hero's mind in three short lines, as he stood "in study," "gryed withinne," and "Alle þe blode of his brest blende in his face" (vv. 2369–71). The Gawain-poet is a master of his medium, and he can put his line to a great variety of uses. But, like most alliterative poets, he prefers elaboration to simplicity. He likes to have a great many more words than things (and he does; he uses about 2,690 words in 2,530 lines [36]). His accounts of hunts and banquets sparkle with as much sheer joy in the play of words as in the actions represented, and he employs a special poetic vocabulary that shows that most of the time he was no more interested in approximating the diction and rhythm of speech than was Virgil, the author of *Beowulf,* or Milton. A good poem in this view of poetry is not one that breaks with tradition in order to return to common speech but one that flaunts and capitalizes on its traditionalism, its distance from ordinary speech. Therefore, when Gawain's host is described (vv. 842–49), he is not simply "host" or "lord"; he is "gome," "burne," "haþel," elegantly redesignated with words drawn from a poetic diction that shows the poem's relation to *Beowulf* (*guman, beorn, æþeling*) rather than fourteenth-century life.

Yet the vocabulary inherited from Old English times could not possibly supply a fourteenth-century romancer with all the words he needed to maintain this heavily varied style. As old subject matters fell into disuse, part of the old vocabulary was lost; as new subjects came into fashion, new words had to be found. French borrowings supplied some of the needed words, and the large proportions of romance words in the vocabularies of most alliterative poems show how frequently the poets drew on this source. Specific dialectal forms, usually Norse in origin, were also useful. However, neither French nor the English dialects could supply much more than a doublet for an already existing word—*rouncé* along with *hors, dame* with *lady*. For most purposes, notably for designating characters, the poets turned to the tradition itself, which offered them the needed words not in the vocabulary but in conventionalized means of inventing new synonyms: the use of the absolute adjective and of periphrastic phrases and clauses. These are more noteworthy than the Old English survivals, for they show the vitality of the tradition. Change was built into it, and the poets could adapt it to new subject matters, lending their vocabularies freshness even as they observed the ancient conventions.

The absolute adjective ("þat ientyle") is perhaps the most distinctive means of inventing synonyms. Of course, this construction has always been possible in English, and

it occasionally appears both in Old English and nonalliterative Middle English verse. However, in the poetry of
the Revival it is so common that Oakden regards it as one
of the distinguishing traits of the tradition, and it appears
so frequently in the work of the Gawain-poet that it was
once considered a distinctive mark of his style.[37] Some adjectives, such as "þe hende" (meaning "well-mannered person"), are used as nouns so often that one could consider
them simply nouns, even though they never take nominal
inflections. However, the pattern of usage that "hende"
exemplifies also extends to a great number of undoubted
adjectives whose implied substantives shift with the context. When "þat shene" appears in one context in *Pearl*
(v. 166), it refers to a person, in another in *Sir Gawain* it
refers to a sword (v. 2268), and in yet another context in
Patience it means the "bright sun" (v. 440). In every case
the word retains its adjectival force, emphasizing not the
person, sword, or sun, but the brightness common to all
three. This is usually true of the absolute adjective; it oper-
ates as a kind of metonymy that, like the rare synecdoches
in the poem ("þe scharp," "þe schaft"), identifies the whole
by one of its constituent elements—a quality ("þe scharp")
or a part ("þe schaft"). It thus gives directness and force to
the vocabulary; when the Gawain-poet varies his designation of the lady with "þat fre" or "þat lufsum," he not only
creates an elegant variation of the sort the tradition requires, he also specifies for his audience the quality of the
lady that he wishes to emphasize at each stage in the
action.

The Gawain-poet, like all alliterative writers, uses the
absolute adjective for everything from objects ("þe coolde"
for "the ground"), to animals ("þe broun" for "the deer"),
to persons. This last category is by far the most important,
not only because the qualities of persons are most significant to the action but also because this use of the absolute

adjective provided the means of filling one important gap in the traditional vocabulary. A romancer needs a large number of words for "woman" if he is to handle his materials in the traditionally varied style of alliterative verse. Yet none of the variations that the older poets had used for a Judith or a Wealhþeow survived into the Middle English period, and French borrowings supplied little more than "dame" and the proper names. The absolute adjective provided the necessary synonyms. Thus, when Olympias and Anectanabus meet in *The Wars of Alexander* (vv. 220 ff.), Olympias is designated both as "lady" and "quene" and as "þat mylde," "þat hend," and "þat dere." The Gawain-poet uses the same technique; of the nine synonyms used for Pearl when she first appears (vv. 157–240), four are adjectives used substantively—"þat schene," "þat gracious gay," "þat fresch," "þat swete." Of the twenty-three different synonyms used for Bercilak's lady, fourteen are absolute adjectives.[38] The adjective used as a substantive also provides a means of designating romance knights. Alliterative poetry is rich in a traditional stock of nouns meaning "man" or "warrior," but poor in nouns appropriate to the gentlemen of late medieval romance. The absolute adjective allows the poet to build the necessary vocabulary, and Gawain is "þat comly," "þat semly," and "þe hende." Such constructions enable the poet to maintain the traditional style even in the courtly temptation scenes, which, so far as subject matter is concerned, seem far removed from the alliterative tradition.

The Old English poetic words that the later alliterative poets did have at hand were probably transmitted to them in alliterative formulas and formulaic phrases, which themselves supplied an even more important source of synonyms for the Middle English alliterative poets—the periphrasis. The phrases "men vpon molde" (v. 914) and "freke vpon folde" (v. 1275), for example, are formulas that the poet inherited from the oral alliterative tradition. Such phrases are valuable in themselves and for the words, such as "freke," that they helped transmit, but they are even more valuable because they also supply the pattern— noun (or absolute adjective) plus prepositional phrase—on which similar periphrases could be built. The construction is a useful one to an alliterative poet, for it is built upon the metrical pattern of the alliterative line. When both nouns alliterate, one need only add an unstressed syllable at the beginning of the phrase to make a full half-line; when only one noun alliterates, the phrase makes a full second half-line as it stands:

> Þenne *þe lorde of þe lede* louteӡ fro his chambre
> For to mete wyth menske *þe mon on þe flor.*
>
> (vv. 833–34)

Of course, the construction of noun plus prepositional phrase is very common; I have just written one—*construction of noun.* What makes it formulaic in alliterative verse is the frequency of its occurrence, its relation to formulas (such as "men vpon molde"), and its metrical character. Chaucer, like any other English writer, uses the noun plus prepositional phrase, but in his works the construction can occur anywhere in the line.[39] In *Sir Gawain* it almost always occurs in the same metrical position. This is true even when the first half-line has three alliterating syllables, as is so frequently the case in Middle English alliterative verse; in such a line the phrase invariably occurs next to the caesura:

> "Now, lege *lord of my lyf,* leue I yow ask;
> ӡe knowe *þe cost of þis cace,* kepe I no more
> To telle yow teneӡ þerof, neuer bot trifel;
> Bot I am *boun to þe bur* barely to-morne
> To sech *þe gome of þe grene,* as God wyl me wysse."
> Þenne *þe best of þe burӡ* boӡed togeder.
>
> (vv. 545–50)

I have quoted this entire passage in order to show how profoundly this simple formulaic pattern affected the poet's style. Only "lord of my lyf," "gome of þe grene," and "best of þe burȝ" are formulas, but the formulaic pattern they embody appears in the same metrical position in every line but the third, and each of these phrases has the same metrical structure—"lórd of my lýf."

The variety of ways in which the Gawain-poet uses this simple formulaic pattern is not extraordinary, for though "formula" itself sounds rigid and inflexible and though metrically these formulas are often rigidly fixed, the tradition itself is more free than one might think. The phrase "of þe best," for example, is used in *Sir Gawain* only at the end of the second half-line—"ledeȝ of þe best" (v. 38), "sesounde of þe best" (v. 889). The phrase "vpon molde" appears only at the end of the first half-line, whether the entire formula ("men vpon molde") is used or not—"Byfore alle men vpon molde his menske is þe most" (v. 914), "I may mourne vpon molde, as may þat much louyes" (v. 1795). Yet even within these rigid patterns, as these examples also show, great freedom is possible. The tradition can be reshaped and new formulas invented to meet the changing needs of the poets; a formulaic pattern may become a formula, which in turn yields new formulaic patterns and new formulas. The phrase "of pris," for example, usually occurs, like "vpon molde," only at the end of the first half-line:

Þat myȝt be preued of prys wyth penyes to bye.

(*SG*, 79)

And mare passand of prisse þan al þi proude rewmes.

(*WA*, 4242)

Was a prouynse of pris & praty men in.

(*DT*, 10815)

The related formula is "prynces of pris":

> For þat pryncece of pris depresed hym so þikke.
> > (*SG*, 1770)

> Among prynces of prys, and þis a pure token.
> > (*SG*, 2398)

> Sone as þis prynces of pris þis pistill had deuysid.
> > (*WA*, 5099)

> And his prynces of price prestlich he quelde
> > (*Alex A*, 925)

The formula, in which "prynces" is now the most important element, can be altered to fit other semantic conditions by changing the second alliterating syllable:

> Vnder a prince of parage of paynymes laghe.
> > (*Erk*, 202)

Once another noun is substituted as an object of the preposition the formulaic pattern is simply "prynce" plus prepositional phrase, so that now it can appear in the second half-line:

> In presence of þat precious, prynce of alle other.
> > (*MA*, 3806)

The new formulaic pattern can also yield new formulas:

> To þe prynce of paradise, and parten ryȝt þere.
> > (*SG*, 2473)

> "Be þe prince of paradis!" quaþ piers þo in wraþþe.
> > (*PP*, A, vii, 109)

The order of development implied in this series is, of course, purely conjectural. One can only be sure that the pattern used is an old one in the alliterative tradition, as phrases such as "men vpon molde" show, but that the formulas we have been discussing developed in the Middle English period, since almost all the words involved are romance words. The pattern supplied by the oral formula is permanent, but within its limits each poet is free to alter the formula to suit his own needs.

The clausal periphrasis composed of a noun or pronoun plus a relative clause is another common English construction that became formulaic in Middle English alliterative verse. When it is used in the works of nonalliterative poets like Chaucer it has no special metrical or syntactic peculiarities, and it can appear anywhere in the line. In alliterative poems like *Sir Gawain* it almost invariably occurs within the half-line.[40]

> Alle þat euer ber bugle blowed at ones,
> And alle þise oþer halowed þat hade no hornes;
> Hit watʒ þe myriest mute þat euer men herde,
> Þe rich rurd þat þer watʒ raysed for Renaude saule.
>
> (vv. 1913–16)

The head-word may be separated from the modifying *þat*-clause, which may appear in the preceding half-line, as in vv. 1913–14 above, or even in the preceding full line:

> Þat aþel Arthur þe hende haldeʒ hym one,
> Þat is þe ryche ryal kyng of þe Rounde Table.
>
> (vv. 904–05)

The separation of the relative clause from its head-word seems to show that the poets regarded it as an appositive, since in Middle English an appositive need not immediately follow the noun it modifies. But it is an expanded appositive, and it thus allowed a poet to expand and link together lines and half-lines even in this predominantly end-stopped style at the same time it provided a source of new and more elegant synonyms.

The Gawain-poet is especially fond of this kind of synonym for designating God, and he uses it so frequently that the periphrasis for "God" was once considered a peculiarity of his style. However, such periphrases were common in the alliterative tradition,[41] and aesthetics rather than piety determines their use. When the Gawain-poet writes "He þat spedeȝ vche speche" (v. 1292), he at once manages to designate God in an elaborate manner, to emphasize the aspect of the Deity that is relevant in this context (the line occurs in the conversation between Gawain and the lady), and to complete a half-line.

The metrical usefulness of all the verbal devices I have discussed thus far—the archaic poetic diction, the absolute adjectives, the phrasal and clausal periphrases—obviously accounts in large part for their survival and widespread use in the poetry of the alliterative tradition. The style is basically the style of oral poetry, in which the poet is simultaneously composer and performer. Such a poet needs a vocabulary of words and phrases and a ready stock of syntactic patterns that will fit his meter, and he has little concern with the very fine shades of meaning important in written verse. The literate poet who uses this style is also influenced by the metrical requirements of the line. In *Sir Gawain* there is no doubt that the meter often determines whether a periphrasis composed of a noun plus a prepositional phrase or a noun plus a relative clause will be used in any one line, and it is clear that the alliterative scheme often determines the particular noun that may be chosen. Obviously in a line alliterating on /t/ the word "tulk" will appear rather than "freke" or "burne," for the semantic distinctions between such words had long since disappeared, leaving a large number of synonyms for "man" so neutral in meaning that they could easily be interchanged to meet the need of any one particular line. (Note that despite the large number of these words no two begin with the same sound and none begins with a vowel, since vocalic alliteration is relatively less important in the later tradition than consonantal alliteration.[42] In *Sir Gawain* the word "wyӡe" is used indifferently for Gawain, the Green Knight, a minor character, and even God Himself, for it means merely "person" or "being" without any limiting modification. Likewise, whether the poet refers to Bercilak's lady as "þe cortays" or "þat fre" depends not on any difference in meaning but on whether the line alliterates on /k/ or /f/, for the words are so neutral that they can fit a great number of females, from Pearl to Bercilak's lady to the Virgin Mary. In such cases any one of a large number of synonyms could be used so long as it fits the general context. The Green Knight could hardly be "þe cortays" and Gawain would not be "þe sturne," but aside from this limitation the choice of any particular variation is a matter of meter rather than meaning.

The aesthetic function of the synonyms

This fact is very easily misunderstood if one forgets the important qualification that the kind of synonym chosen must fit the context. The difference between "tulk" and "freke" is a matter of sound, but these two words and others of the same class differ considerably from words such as "prynce" and "knyӡt"—a difference, as we shall see, that the Gawain-poet fully exploits. Moreover, the difference between a simple designation such as "lorde" or "haþel" and an extended periphrastic designation is a difference in emphasis as well as meter. If we miss these differences in reading the poem, that is not because they are insignificant. It is only because our ears are not attuned to the kind of distinctions that could be drawn in this basically oral style.

The distinctions could be drawn because, important as metrical necessity is, it is not the only reason for the use of variation. Some poets completely avoided the frequent use of synonyms in designating their main characters. They maintained the traditional style by applying the variation to objects and minor characters, designating the main characters with a stock of synonyms as small as Chaucer's and providing for the alliteration merely by varying the adjectives. *Piers Plowman* is an obvious example. It is not in the high and traditional style of alliterative romance, and in this poem, in contrast to *The Destruction of Troy* or *The Siege of Jerusalem*, the main characters are designated by a very small number of synonyms. In the account of Mede that lady is almost invariably "Mede," only occasionally "woman" or "wyf," and only once "burde." [43] God, Who is "Haþel" and "Tulk" in *Wynnere and Wastoure* and *Cleanness*, is never designated by such varying nouns in *Piers Plowman*. There He is almost always "God," "Christ," or "Lorde." The only exceptions are the occasional periphrases, but even in them the head-word is usually restricted to words such as "Fader" or "Kyng" instead of the common alliterative synonyms for "man" used in this position by writers such as the Gawain-poet.

A desire for ornamentation must have been as strong an influence on variation as the need to alliterate, for in general those poets who use varying synonyms most freely are the northerly poets who, in contrast to Langland and his followers, also wrote an ornate, highly rhetorical style. For them the periphrasis was a *circuitio*, one of the admired *ornates difficiles*, as well as a traditional formulaic variation, just as the absolute adjective was a *pronominatio* when applied to a person, a *denominatio* when applied to a thing, as well as a convenient means of securing a metrically useful synonym.

Obviously some poets found the ornamental and metrical function of the synonyms sufficient reason for their frequent use of them. However, for the best alliterative writers these incidental advantages opened new possibilities of expression and variation became a mode of defining a character. A phrase such as "þe comlokest to descrye," a synonym for Guenevere in *Sir Gawain*, obviously satisfies the demands of both meter and ornamentation. It also defines Guenevere more effectively and even more briefly than any other method of designation would have allowed. Another poet might have written "þe comlokest Guenevere," but this would have shifted the emphasis, which is not upon Guenevere herself but on the particular quality of beauty that she represents at this stage of the action. Likewise, when the poet refers to Bercilak as "þe tolke þat þat telde aȝt," he is not merely designating the host in a circumlocutory fashion; he is emphasizing the one aspect of the character that is directly relevant to the narrative at this moment, when Gawain is considering his obligation to his host. The Gawain-poet's characters are not simple and one-dimensional, and they cannot be defined by abstract names like "Bercilak" or by any one of their qualities. They have a variety of aspects, any one of which the poet's use of variation allows him to stress to the momentary exclusion of the others, and they are constantly redefined by the synonyms applied to them.

This is clear enough in the use of periphrases. It is more difficult to recognize when simpler variations are used. The author of the *Morte Arthure*, for example, usually avoids this sort of variation. His hero is no ordinary man, and he is almost always "Arthur," "conqueror," or "kyng." [44] His nobility is unwavering, and he has nothing in common, not so much as a noun, with a churlish character like the giant of St. Michael's Mount. When Arthur encounters that giant (vv. 1041–1151), the poet uses only three synonyms in the thirteen times he refers to the king—"that hende" once, "Arthur" three times, and "kyng" nine times. The giant, on the other hand, is designated by a new synonym almost every time he is mentioned; the poet uses twelve different synonyms in the fifteen times he designates him by a noun—reke, segge, sott, renke, gloton, hulk, bierne, schalk, lede, carl, warlowe, theef. Some of these nouns, such as "theef," are pejorative, but five of them are the alliterative synonyms for "man." The difference between the king and the giant is thus established not simply by the words but by the mode of designation, in which the restrained, decorous manner of designating the king is sharply contrasted to the freely varying mode of designating the giant, a character with none of the unchanging nobility of Arthur. To modern readers, unaccustomed to variation, this seems a very subtle technique; to medieval hearers, for whom variation was as much a part of poetry as the alliterative meter itself, it was probably both obvious and effective.

Such an audience would have had no difficulty in following the Gawain-poet's use of variation, for his technique of juxtaposing modes of designation is the same as we find in *Morte Arthure,* even though the Gawain-poet uses it for different ends. The use of varying synonyms is the rule rather than the exception in *Sir Gawain,* where the poet's point seems to be that even opposites are not irreconcilable. Arthur's courtiers, for example, are both "kniȝteȝ"—a word suitable only to the nobility—and "tulkeȝ," a word that the poet uses for all classes, from "þe tulk þat þe trammes of tresoun þer wroȝt" to God Himself:

> Þer tournayed tulkeȝ by tymeȝ ful mony
> Justed ful jolilé þise gentyle kniȝteȝ.

> (vv. 41–42)

Even noblemen, the vocabulary implies, are no more than men.

This, of course, is the lesson that Gawain learns at the end of his adventure. The poet establishes this fact by manipulating his vocabulary as carefully as does the author of the *Morte Arthure*. At the beginning of *Sir Gawain* the hero is the perfect knight, conscious of his station and obligations and, so far as he shows, immune both from the fears that deter the other courtiers from accepting the challenge and from the rage that Arthur betrays when he takes it up. He is emphatically "Gawain þe hende," and though the poet applies a great number of synonyms to the other courtiers and to the Green Knight the hero is invariably "Gawain" or "knyȝt" throughout the first fit.[45] His knighthood rather than his common humanity is emphasized.

After the Green Knight has destroyed the festive joy of the court, the tone of the poem shifts. The seasons pass, and with the approaching winter Gawain, who was at first undismayed by the Green Knight, now begins to be troubled by thoughts of the "anxious voyage" that he must face. The anxiety appears in v. 536, and the next time he is mentioned, in v. 540, he is no longer "Gawain" or "knight"; he is "lede." Throughout his journey to Bercilak's castle, his sojourn there, and his departure for the Green Chapel the poet uses a heavily varied mode of designating the hero, drawing both upon nouns suitable only to Gawain's knightly status and upon the common alliterative synonyms for "man" that he uses throughout the poem for the Green Knight. In this part of the poem, as appears most obviously in the bedroom scenes, Gawain is not the figure of perfection that he seemed to be in Arthur's court, where he was completely courteous, brave, and untouched by human emotions. He feels anxiety, cold, sexual temptation, and fear. But after the guide tempts him to give up the quest and fails in his temptation, the poet returns to the technique he used in the opening scenes, and he concentrates solely upon "Gawain þe knyȝt" throughout the almost two hundred lines from the moment Gawain refuses the guide's offer (v. 2126) to the point at which he receives the return-blow (v. 2312).

Then, precisely when he feels the axe and sees his own blood on the snow, the narrator shifts from the particular, knightly mode of designation to the more general word, "burne":

> And quen þe burne seȝ þe blode blenk on þe snawe.
>
> (v. 2315)

Five lines later, when the poet next refers to Gawain, he again uses "burne":

> Neuer syn þat he watȝ burne borne of his moder.
>
> (v. 2320)

This use of "burne" twice within five lines temporarily fixes the identification of Gawain with the common synonym. It is thus significant that in the first line Gawain speaks, only two verses later, "burne" again appears; only this time it refers to the Green Knight:

> "Blynne, burne, of þy bur, bede me no mo!"
>
> (v. 2322)

The word is used yet again, this time referring to Gawain, in the first line of the Green Knight's reply:

> "Bolde burne, on þis bent be not so gryndel."
>
> (v. 2338)

Previously whenever Gawain and the Green Knight appeared together, the poet had used the same technique employed in the *Morte Arthure* for Arthur and the giant; Gawain was always the knight, his antagonist an "aghlich mayster" who could be designated by a great variety of synonyms. Now, as the insistent use of "burne" shows, they have arrived at a basic equality; Gawain lowers himself and the Green Knight raises himself to the level of common humanity, and the poet establishes this fact not by explicit statement but by the synonyms he uses. Throughout the rest of the episode he draws upon common nouns for both men.[46] Gawain, like Arthur's courtiers at the beginning of the work, is now both a knight and one who shares the common lot of humanity. Basically this kind of variation is a device of oral poetry, metrically necessary and often with little semantic force even after it passed into written alliterative verse. In the hands of sophisticated poets such as the authors of *Morte Arthure* and *Sir Gawain* it became a delicate and expressive part of the poetic technique.

Variation: the syntax

"Inner variation," the redesignation of concepts within the sentence and the multiplication of its constituent elements, allows the poet the same analytical method of defining concepts as the elegant—"outer"—variation of synonyms discussed in the previous section. This is perhaps more characteristic of the alliterative tradition as a whole than elegant variation, for even those poets who avoided designating characters by a large number of synonyms wrote periods in which variation of the constituent elements is a basic stylistic feature. The typical period in alliterative poetry, as we have noted, is a short statement extended from a single half-line throughout a series of verses by amplification (the *dilatatio* of the rhetoricians), the sense thus "variously drawn out from line to line," [47] as in Mordred's lament for Gawain in the *Morte Arthure:*

> This was Sir Gawayne the gude, the gladdeste of othire,
> And the graciouseste gome that vndire God lyffede,
> Mane hardyeste of hande, happyeste in armes,
> And the hendeste in hawle vndire heuene riche. . . .
>
> (vv. 3876–79)

The period begins with a complete clause in the first half-line—"This was Sir Gawayne the gude"—to which the poet adds a long series of coordinate appositives that define the good qualities of Gawain and extend the original clause from a single half-line to eleven full lines (I have quoted only the beginning of the period). The half-lines, we may note, are all based on common formulaic patterns, beginning with a fixed formula, "Gawayne the gude," and extended by the use of the formulaic patterns that we have already seen in the alliterative periphrases. The absolute adjective plus prepositional phrase provides the first appositive—"the gladdeste of othire." The noun plus relative clause supplies the next—"gome that vndire God lyffede" —which is extended to fill out the line by the modifying "And the graciouseste," suggested to the poet by the common pattern of superlative-noun-relative clause. The next three appositives are all built on the same phrasal pattern as the first, although in the third line "mane" is added to complete the line and in the final verse the phrasal formula is extended by the addition of another formulaic phrase— "vndire heuene riche" (cf. "vndire God lyffede").

The same patterns appear in *Sir Gawain,* and they account for the syntax of some of the poet's best passages:

> Bot þen hyȝes heruest, and hardenes hym sone,
> Warneȝ hym for þe wynter to wax ful rype;
> He dryues wyth droȝt þe dust for to ryse,
> Fro þe face of þe folde to flyȝe ful hyȝe;

Wroþe wynde of þe welkyn wrasteleȝ with þe sunne,
Þe leueȝ lancen fro þe lynde and lyȝten on þe grounde,
And al grayes þe gres þat grene watȝ ere;
Þenne al rypeȝ and roteȝ þat ros vpon fyrst.

(vv. 521–28)

These lines are often taken for the "most original" in the
poem, and certainly no other poet of the fourteenth century could have written them. Yet their style is completely
traditional. The formulaic patterns used in "þe dust for to
ryse" and "to wax ful rype" are two of the most common
in Middle English alliterative verse, and "þe gres þat
grene watȝ ere" is built on the noun-relative clause structure that we have seen so often before. The rest of the
passage is built upon the parallel repetition of the constituent elements of the period: "Warneȝ hym" in the second line repeats the form of "hardenes hym" in the first,
just as "of þe folde" in the fourth verse is parallel to "of
þe welkyn" in the third, and the rest of the third line,
"wrasteleȝ with þe sunne," provides the pattern for
"lancen fro þe lynde" and "lyȝten on þe grounde" in the
next. The two final lines are almost identical in structure.

In the lines quoted from the *Morte Arthure*, as in many
passages in *Sir Gawain*, the varied sentence elements repeat both form and content, and the result is a series of
appositives. Verbs and verbal phrases can be varied in the
same manner—"And *rimed hym* ful richely and *ryȝt hym*
to speke" (v. 308). However, the repetition of form with a
slight shift in content is the more common method, and
even in the passage from the *Morte Arthure* the repeated
elements are sometimes enumerations ("Happyeste in
armes,/ And the hendeste in hawle") rather than simple
appositives. In the passage quoted from *Sir Gawain* the
repeated verbs form progressions, as in "hyȝes," "hardenes," "warneȝ," and in the final two lines, as so often in
the poem, the repeated elements are whole clauses, paral-

lel in form, enumerative or progressive in function. Whether form, content, or both are repeated, the basic stylistic trait is the same, and variation of one sort or another is apparent in every alliterative line.

The structure of the Middle English alliterative line made such variations both easy and dangerous for the poets who used them. In Old English verse a clause is seldom contained within a half-line, and the variations therefore are usually included within the clause itself, "with a disruption of [normal prose] syntactic relations," in Paetzel's words.[48] In Middle English verse the first half-line usually contains the main clause, and the variations are simply added at the end. The semantic interest of the sentence therefore tends to lie in the first half-line, with the succeeding half-lines of the clause often merely redundant. The author of *Alexander and Dindimus*, for example, usually translated his Latin text in his first half-lines and then filled out the second halves with variations.[49] Moreover, with parallel constructions so useful and so easy to create, the line is always in danger of becoming merely monotonous and falling into the excessively long series of parallel syntactic units that mar much of *The Destruction of Troy*. The dangers of meaningless addition and monotonous parallelism are increased by the medieval poets' fondness for *amplificationes*, since the rhetorical *amplificatio* is often simply a catalogue limited only by the author's sense of tact. One recalls such notable failures of tact as the catalogue of birds in *The Squire of Low Degree*, in which the period does not end until the author has listed twenty-three different varieties. In alliterative poetry the fondness for the catalogue joined to the cumulative method of constructing a period can be disastrous; the alliterative *Morte Arthure* has one sentence that wanders on for over thirty lines before it is completed.[50]

Yet most alliterative poets, including even the author of

the *Morte Arthure,* seem to have been aware of the weakness of such constructions, and they developed a number of techniques for controlling the variations. The simplest method is to impose a climactic structure on the period and thus limit the amount of variation and retain the full force of the main statement by a simple reversal of the usual order, placing the varied elements first and the main clause last:

> In a summer seson when soft was the sun
> I shop me in shroudes . . .
>
> > (*PP*, B, I, 1–2)

> Wyth alle maner of mete and mynstralcie boþe,
> Wyth wele walt þay þat day . . .
>
> > (*SG*, 484–85)

Or one could use the variations rather than the main clause for conveying the most important information:

> Þe fole þat he ferkkes on fyn of þat ilke,
> > sertayn,
> > A grene hors gret and þikke,
> > A stede ful stif to strayne.
>
> > (vv. 173–76)

Hors is merely a synonym for *fole* and *grene* a restatement of *þat ilke,* but the variation *grene hors* carries the most amazing and important information in the sentence.

Or, finally, one could build sentences in which the variations are bracketed within other structures. In a complex sentence the dependent clause could be placed first, with the variations bracketed between the subordinating connective at the beginning of the period and the independent clause at its end. In a sentence with no subordinate clause one could bracket the variations within parallel elements. Both methods are used in this passage:

If any *so hardy in þis hous* holdeȝ hymseluen,
Be *so bolde in his blod, brayn in his hede,*
Þat dar stifly strike a strok for an oþer,
I schal gif hym of my gyft *þys giserne ryche,*
Þis axe, þat is heué innogh, to hondele as hym lykeȝ,
And I schal bide þe fyrst bur as bare as I sitte.

(vv. 285–90)

The first set of italicized variations is enclosed with the *so . . . þat* construction, which is itself bracketed within the conditional "if" and the result clause. The second set has no such enclosure, since they are extensions of the result. By adding a final clause, parallel to the first result (both begin with "I schal"), the poet provides a limiting framework, and by saving the most astonishing part of Bercilak's proposal until the final half-line ("as bare as I sitte") he maintains the semantic interest of the period throughout its entire length.

To counteract the excessive regularity that such parallels threaten to impose on the line the alliterative poets had constantly to exploit another, somewhat less obvious tendency of this style toward the establishment of contrasts. The tension between the movement toward parallelisms and that toward contrasts lends the alliterative line much of its strength. In that passage quoted above from the *Morte Arthure* the poet works to vary his structure even as he builds his parallels. He writes "Mane hardyeste of hande" instead of "*the* hardyeste of hande," even though "the" is more common in this formulaic structure and would have satisfied the metrical needs of the line and maintained the exact parallel with "the gladdiste of othire." Yet "mane" obviously makes a better line, partly because of the assonance with "hande," partly because of the additional elegant variation it provides, but mainly because it slightly varies the structure of the phrase. Certainly the casual reader or hearer does not notice this shift, for it merely changes the structure from an absolute adjective plus prepositional phrase to a noun plus absolute adjective plus prepositional phrase. Yet such slight contrasts in structure, like that created by the omission of any word at all before the adjective in the following line, are as important to the verse as the parallels. All poetry requires some such contrast along with its regularity. Perhaps when alliterative verse was still sung to the harp, the varying meter of the line contrasting with the regularity of the accompaniment supplied the necessary variety. In Middle English times, when the verse was ordinarily read rather than sung, the line itself had to provide both the regularity and the contrast.

Most alliterative poets were content with simple structural contrasts such as appear in the passage from the *Morte Arthure,* but the Gawain-poet also works frequently with the more complex contrasts provided by chiasmus and antithesis. The concluding lines of the description of the seasons, for example, are almost exactly parallel in construction and concept:

> And al grayes þe gres þat grene watȝ ere;
> Þenne al rypeȝ and roteȝ þat ros vpon fyrst.
>
> (vv. 527–28)

In each verse the first half-line contrasts with an antithetical off-verse—*grayes* as opposed to *grene, rypeȝ and roteȝ* as opposed to *ros.* In addition to these antitheses, the structure of each full line is delicately contrasted to the other. The two lines seem nearly exact parallels; each first half-line begins with the pattern of connective plus *al* plus verb, and each second half-line is a relative clause. Yet a closer examination shows that the substitution of *roteȝ,* a verb, in the position a noun (*gres*) occupied in the previous line shifts the structure completely. The *al* of the second line becomes the subject of the clause rather than its modifier. Within the apparent parallel there is a chiasmic reversal, a shift from a verb-subject order—*al grayes þe gres*—to subject-verb—*al rypeȝ*.

Even more complicated patterns of chiasmus appear when the metrical structure supplies the contrast, as in this quatrain:

> He tened quen he schulde telle,
> He groned for gref and grame;
> Þe blod in his face con melle,
> When he hit schulde schewe, for schame.
>
> (vv. 2501–04)

In the first two lines the caesurae fall after the verbs. In the second two the metrical structure is exactly reversed, and the caesurae fall after "face" and "schewe." The passage is a complex of parallel repetitions within these contrasting metrical structures; the adverbial clause of the first line—"quen he schulde telle"—is repeated with only minor differences in the fourth line—"When he hit schulde schewe"—yet the shift of the caesura creates a metrical contrast that strengthens the passage by the slight structural tension it creates.

Antithesis is somewhat less frequent than chiasmus. It does appear, as Adrien Bonjour noted, in such contrasting pairs as "blysse and blunder," and it is also evident in lines such as "þat is grattest in grene when greueȝ ar bare" (v. 207).[51] Usually, however, the antithetical elements are larger units, such as the contrast between summer and winter in the passing of the seasons or, the most notable antithesis in the poem, the contrasting descriptions of the beautiful and ugly ladies at Bercilak's court:

> For if þe ȝong watȝ ȝep, ȝolȝe watȝ þat oþer;
> Riche red on þat on rayled ayquere,
> Rugh ronkled chekeȝ þat oþer on rolled.
>
> (vv. 951–53)

Contrast is a common device in medieval literature, especially the contrasts of youth and age or the beautiful and the grotesque, but usually they are established by describing first one figure and then the other or, more rarely, by uniting the two in the same figure, as in the *puer senex* of classical tradition.[52] In *Sir Gawain* the characteristic form of statement allows the poet to bring the two contrasting figures into the same sentence, shifting from one to another and defining each by its contrast. Even fixed formulas are altered to establish the antithesis: "ȝonge and ȝep" is a common formula for describing youthful beauty ("And ther-to ȝonge and ȝape, and ȝouthe was his name," *Parl*, 134; "þat so ȝong and ȝepe as ȝe ar at þis tyme," *SG*, 1510). It becomes the first member of a markedly untraditional antithesis when the line is completed by "ȝolȝe watȝ þat oþer."

The analytic function of the syntax

The potential disadvantages of this alliterative syntax—its tendencies toward mere repetition of form and content—are far outweighed by its advantages. Like the varied synonyms, this syntax is less an ornament than a tool of analysis, a method of defining concepts at the same time it presents them, and it leads to a style that depends upon particulars and implies rather than states the generalizations. This is apparent even in the traditional formulas, for most of them are analytical, formulized enumerations and progressions that provide a ready means of defining a concept by the parallel juxtaposition of its parts. The solid texture of *Sir Gawain* is largely due to the poet's development of this analytical syntax. For example, the common full-line formula for expressing the general idea that a city has been destroyed is that which appears in the *Destruc-*

tion of Troy: "Betyn and brent doun vnto bare askes" (v. 5007). The formula is naturally analytical; it defines the destruction by the events—first the city broken down (by siege engines) and then the burning—and by their result —"vnto bare askes." The Gawain-poet extends the analysis even further when he writes "þe borȝ brittened and brent to brondeȝ and askeȝ" (v. 2). The substitution of "brondeȝ" for a modifier of "askeȝ" extends the analysis to the result, and by coupling this with the preceding line, which is based on the formula used to report an attack on a town—"Sithen þe sege and þe assaut watȝ sesed at Troye"—the analysis is extended to a brief narrative: first there was the siege (the necessary bombardment of the walls) and then, when a breach was made, the assault itself, after which the city is first reduced to rubble and then put to the torch, leaving flaming brands and finally ashes.

The same technique, the same dependence on analysis and specification rather than generalization, is used throughout the poem, whether the events are as grand as the fall of Troy or as relatively simple as the Green Knight's mounting his horse. The usual full line formula for narrating this act is "Stridis into stele-bowe, stertis vpon lofte" (*WA*, 778); "He sterte tille his sterepe and stridez one lofte" (*MA*, 916). The Gawain-poet, as usual, extends the analysis the formula provides. The Green Knight turns,

> And syþen boȝeȝ to his blonk, þe brydel he cachcheȝ,
> Steppeȝ into stelbawe and strydeȝ alofte.
>
> (vv. 434–35)

The additional detail—"þe brydel he cachcheȝ"—is just enough to fill out the vivid little scene provided by the formula, and we see each stage of the action, as the Green

Knight seizes his bridle, steps into the stirrup, and swings himself onto his mount.

That the three verbs are stages of a single action is apparent from the "he" that governs them, for the poet introduces a new subject only when a new action begins. The lines preceding those quoted contain a different series of verbal variations ending with "Boȝeȝ to his blonk," and they describe the one smooth movement in which the challenger reaches out, snatches up the head, holds it aloft, and turns to his horse (vv. 432–35a). Mounting the horse is a new act and so it calls for a new subject, the "he" of the second half-line of the passage quoted above. In short, the introduction of a new subject rather than a new verb defines the major actions analytically presented by the variations.

This trait sometimes leads to apparently puzzling constructions:

> Þe burne blessed hym bilyue and þe bredeȝ passed—
> Prayses þe porter bifore þe prynce kneled,
> Gef hym God and goud day, þat Gawayn he saue—
> And went on his way with his wyȝe one.
>
> (vv. 2071–74)

Gawain's act of departing is not completed until he "went on his way." The poet therefore introduces no new subject for "went" even though the actions of the porter intervene between that verb and its subject. Likewise, modern usage does not allow constructions like this:

> Ȝet quyl Al-hal-day with Arþer he lenges;
> And he made a fare on þat fest for þe frekeȝ sake.
>
> (vv. 536–37)

The second "he" refers to Arthur, a faulty reference from our point of view. Yet the reference is clear within the context of the poet's style, for the new subject implies a new action rather than a continuation of "lenges."

As the pronouns show, alliterative verse has its own syntactic rules, quite different from ours, and because of this the analytical function of variation probably escapes many readers. It is a generally paratactic syntax, characterized by simple connectives such as "and" and by the frequent omission of connectives altogether. Within the sentence the relationships between the variations are thus implied by their position rather than by explicit statement, and ellipsis is as characteristic of the period as repetition.[53] The usual structure of variation begins with a first half-line that contains a complete clause followed by the other half-lines that vary only the significant element. In verbal variation the subjects are elided, so that the effect is of a series of compressed clauses rather than simply a compounding of verbs: "Mist mugged on þe mor, malt on þe mounteȝ" (v. 2080). In nominal variation the verbs are elided: "For hit is my wede þat þou wereȝ, þat ilke wouen girdel" (v. 2358). The varied elements are simply juxtaposed and the meaning depends on the context of the variation and the structure of the period. Consequently, the elliptical phrases are sometimes puzzling. A phrase like "Ticius to Tuskan" (v. 11), for example, is meaningless in itself, a fact that led Madden, the first editor of *Sir Gawain*, to emend it to "Ticius to Tuskan *turnes.*" As later editors recognized, "turnes" is unnecessary; in context the parallel "Romulus to Rome ricchis" clarifies its later variation in the elliptical "Ticius to Tuskan."

The meaning of whole sentences is also often a matter of position rather than explicit statement, and asyndeton is almost as common in the poem as ellipsis. When the poet analyzes Arthur's reaction to the Green Knight's taunt, he writes:

Wyth þis he laȝes so loude þat þe lorde greued;
Þe blod schot for scham into his schyre face
and lere;
He wex as wroth as wynde.

(vv. 316–19)

It is clear that first Arthur was annoyed, then he blushed
for shame, and finally he became enraged, and it is almost
equally obvious that the annoyance caused the shame,
which then led to the anger. Yet the poet states none of
these relations. He places the clauses side by side and allows their meaning to emerge from the juxtaposition. Nonalliterative writers occasionally used asyndeton in this
way, and it was a standard rhetorical tool (*dissolutio*) for
achieving brevity, but in *Sir Gawain* and most other alliterative poems it appears throughout the work. This is
hard on modern editors, who have to punctuate this verse,
and, as almost any printed alliterative poem will show,
dashes and semicolons are about the only solution they
have found. The hearer, however, has no such problem, for
the parallel structures themselves make the syntactic relations clear.

When a connective is used, it is most often the simple
and, which may smooth the transition from one clause to
another, but which, like asyndeton, leaves the relationship
undefined. The varied clauses are merely placed side by
side, in sharp contrast to the sometimes elaborate subordination characteristic of nonalliterative writers such as
Chaucer. For example, when the lady slips into Gawain's
room, the Gawain-poet writes:

Hit watȝ þe ladi, loflyest to beholde,
Þat droȝ þe dor after hir ful dernly and stylle,
And boȝed towarde þe bed; and þe burne schamed,
And layde hym doun lystyly, and let as he slepte;
And ho stepped stilly and stel to his bedde,

Kest vp þe cortyn and creped with-inne,
And set hir ful softly on þe bed-syde.

(vv. 1187–93)

But when Pandarus slips into Troilus' room, Chaucer
writes:

But Pandarus, that wel koude ech a deel
The olde daunce, and every point therinne,
Whan that he sey that alle thyng was wel,
He thought he wolde upon his werk bigynne,
And gan the stuwe doore al softe unpynne,
And stille as stoon, withouten lenger lette,
By Troilus adown right he hym sette.

(*Tr*, III, 694–700)

In the passage from *Sir Gawain* the position of the clauses
rather than the repeated "and" establishes the syntactic
relations; in the passage from *Troilus* each clause is explicitly related to the others, first by connectives such as
"Whan that" and then by the adverbial phrases that
cluster about the final clause and explain exactly the connection of "he hym sette" to the rest of the action.

Such a cluster of adverbial phrases is rare in *Sir Gawain*,
where the compounding of clauses rather than modifiers
prevails. Consequently, compared to Chaucer's nonalliterative style, even the Gawain-poet's grammatically complex
sentences seem to depend more on juxtaposition than on
subordination. For example, the well-known similarities
between the Green Knight's entry into Camelot and the
entry of the strange knight into Cambyuskan's court in
The Squire's Tale extend even to the periodic grammatical
structures that the poets use to emphasize the contrast
between the abrupt entry and the music and jollity of the
feast that it interrupts:

An oþer noyse ful newe neȝed biliue,
Þat þe lude myȝt half leue liflode to cach;

For vneþe watȝ þe noyce not a whyle sesed,
And þe fyrst cource in þe court kyndely serued,
Þer hales in at þe halle dor an aghlich mayster.

(*SG*, 132–36)

And so bifel that after the thridde cours,
Whil that this kyng sit thus in his nobleye,
Herknynge his mynstralles hir thynges pleye
Biforn hym at the bord deliciously,
In at the halle dore al sodeynly
Ther cam a knyght upon a steede of bras.

(*SqT*, 76–82)

The Gawain-poet's clauses are set out one after another
with a minimum of connectives, and each of his five lines
contains a clause, even the fourth with its elided "watȝ."
Chaucer's clauses, on the other hand, are carefully subor-
dinated in a pattern of elaborate modification.

The Chaucerian ease and fluency that later narrative
poets took as their ideal is dependent upon this careful
and explicit establishment of syntactic relations. However,
Chaucer's triumph should not obscure for us the merits of
the alliterative style. Perhaps there is less danger of this
today than there was forty or fifty years ago, since modern
poets, especially the Imagists with their insistence on presenting details rather than generalizations, have made us
more receptive to a style based on variation. The technique of Pound's little poem "In a Station of the Metro"
(which I quote in its entirety) is not much different from,
though more compressed than, the variation of alliterative
poetry:

The apparition of these faces in the crowd;
Petals on a wet, black bough.

Like the modern writer, the alliterative poet defines his
concepts by the juxtaposition of their parts, capitalizing on

the clash of perspectives that this technique allows. Such a style, in which the parts of an action, object, or concept are juxtaposed with a minimum of explicit explanation, leads at once to a multiplication of specific detail and to a structure that renders the details meaningful.

Variation: the narrative structure

The major importance of variation to the critic of *Sir Gawain* is the key it provides to the structure and meaning of the narrative, for the style of this poem is organic, and its basic stylistic trait affects every part of the work. The structure of the sentence, with its varied parallel constructions, its ellipses, its dependence on juxtaposition and analysis, is the model for the narrative as a whole. Because the style of the individual line and sentence has been so imperfectly understood, the structure and meaning of the poem have never been clear. It is no accident that the "unity" of the best alliterative poems has been a central problem for their critics, for the reader who approaches them with the same concept of structure that he brings to Chaucer or Gower is apt to find them badly constructed and poorly unified—a judgment that has been passed at some time or other on every good alliterative poem from *Beowulf* to *Sir Gawain*. Scenes and episodes in such works do not exist in the straightforward causal order of most narratives. Each forms part of a series of variations composed of other passages similar in form and content, and the meaning of each is modified and illuminated by its variations, even though, as in the sentence, their relation is implied rather than stated explicitly.

The Chaucerian style leads to a completely different kind of narrative. Chaucer designates his characters with a small, repetitive vocabulary. He elaborately insists upon the exact designation, and his apparent eagerness to avoid ambiguity even leads him to combine the demonstrative adjective with the proper noun—"Lo heere this Arcite and this Palamoun." [54] That construction never appears in the work of the Gawain-poet; he often designates his character by "the" plus a noun—"þe knyȝt"—a construction that Chaucer almost never uses. Chaucer's syntax is marked by the same insistence on clear and exact specification—"Bifil that in that seson on a day"—and his narrative technique as a whole is characterized by the same trait. In *The Knight's Tale,* for example, when the narrator shifts from one line of action to another, he emphatically signals the transition to his audience: [55]

> Now wol I stynte of Palamon a lite,
> And lete hym in his prisoun stille dwelle,
> And of Arcita forth I wol yow telle.
>
> (*KT,* 1334–36)

When the Gawain-poet shifts from one line of action to another, he does so within a single sentence:

> Þe lede with þe ladyeȝ layked alle day,
> Bot þe lorde ouer þe londeȝ launced ful ofte,
> Sweȝ his vncely swyn . . .
>
> (vv. 1560–62)

> And ȝe he lad hem bi lagmon, þe lorde and his meyny,
> On þis maner bi þe mountes quyle myd-ouer-under,
> Whyle þe hende knyȝt at home holsumly slepes,
> Withinne þe comly cortynes . . .
>
> (vv. 1729–32)

Chaucer avoids such abrupt transitions because as a narrator he is so eager to confide in us; he does not want us to miss his meaning. His *Knight's Tale* is built on parallels and contrasts as finely wrought as those in *Sir Gawain,* but he is not content to leave his tale without Theseus' explicit pointing of the moral. In the *Troilus* Chaucer himself draws the meaning out for us, standing apart from his story to address the "yonge fresshe folkes, he or she." In the Gawain-poet's narrative, as within the sentence, the variations are juxtaposed without comment and the meaning is allowed to emerge from the structure. Gawain and the Green Knight each have a last word, and the less personal voice of the narrator does not intrude to tell us which is right.

H. L. Savage's analysis of the relation between the hunting and temptation scenes is probably the best-known explanation of narrative variation in *Sir Gawain* (though Savage, of course, does not call it "variation").[56] Until his article appeared few critics understood the structure of the poem; indeed, one scholar argued for an English source on the basis of the apparent lack of skill with which the parts are joined together.[57] The two sets of scenes that Savage studied seem completely different. One takes place in a bedroom, the other in the forest. One concerns the niceties of courtship, the other the vigorous excitement of the chase, and one is almost pure action, the other almost pure dialogue. Yet, much as these two sets of scenes differ in content and emphasis, their form is the same. As Savage demonstrates, they are almost exactly parallel, providing different but parallel viewpoints on a situation whose meaning can be understood only in the light of both narratives. Taken alone, Bercilak's hunt is just an exciting account of the chase, the temptation scenes sophisticated bedroom comedy with a ludicrous reversal of roles. Together they are a set of variations that blend to point up the nature of Gawain's trial and the extent of Bercilak's involvement in it. The lady, we realize, is not merely attempting to enjoy her lord's absence. She is as intent upon her prey as Bercilak upon his. Bercilak's pursuit of his quarry becomes a commentary on the lady's pursuit of Gawain, and Gawain's skillful replies become meaningful as the desperate fox "trantes and tornayeȝ" in parallel fashion, finally attempting to escape through trickery only to run upon Bercilak's waiting sword.

The parallel series of scenes themselves have other parallel variations throughout the poem; Bercilak's capture of the fox is related to his final capture of Gawain, and its form is related to each of the previous hunts and to the lady's final victory. The lady's scene of triumph is related both to the hunts and previous temptations and to the other scenes in which bargains are made and broken, from the challenge itself, to the guide's temptation of the hero, to the final confrontation between Gawain and the Green Knight. The same principles that Savage discovered in the temptation scenes appear wherever one looks in the poem, for the parallel juxtaposition of apparently unrelated episodes is the basic characteristic of the narrative,[58] appearing even in the combination of the parallel but contrasting temptation and beheading tales, which posed the major problem of unity for the early critics.

Within the narrative one also finds the same sort of periodic, bracketing frameworks that contain and control the variations within the sentence. In the first fit, for example, each major stage of the action has its parallel variation, and each set of variations is bracketed within a limiting framework. The scene opens and closes with the feast that brackets the episode, which is indeed, as Arthur tells Guenevere, an "interlude" occurring between its courses. Within that framework is the Green Knight's amazing entrance and equally astonishing departure. When he enters, the action of his entry is suspended for the description of him and his equipment, which, as we have seen, is actually two descriptions juxtaposed by means of variation. Then the entry resumes and, once in the hall, the

Green Knight states his challenge; the conditions he states are repeated, with more sinister overtones, when he leaves. Then Arthur accepts the challenge, but Gawain interrupts the action as suddenly as the Green Knight had done, and he also makes a request of Arthur. The king grants his request, and he kneels to receive the axe, just as the Green Knight, after a restatement of the bargain, bows to receive Gawain's blow, which is, of course, parallel to the blow that Arthur begins to deliver. The beheading is the heart of the episode, surrounded by the parallel structures. And the whole episode, including the feast itself, is enclosed within yet another set of parallel passages, the catalogue of Arthur's ancestors and the narrator's characterization of the king at the beginning of the poem, followed by his new comments on the king at the end of the first fit and the catalogue of the seasons at the beginning of the next.

In its broad outlines the entire poem is constructed on the same principle. It begins with the Troy story and a scene of happy celebration. Then follow the challenge and the beheading, the arming and departure of Gawain, and his journey to Bercilak's castle. There, after more banqueting, he undergoes three days of temptation, each day parallel to the others and all three days paralleled by the hunting scenes. Then Gawain again arms and departs. There is another journey, the return-blow, and finally the journey back to Camelot, where there is yet another celebration at court and a final reference to the Troy legend at the poem's end. The beheading plot brackets the temptation within its parallel delivery and return-blows, and the temptation itself is composed on a complex of variations within that framework.

From the standpoint of Chaucerian verse, this seems a peculiar and subtle method of narration. However, it was common in the poet's own literary tradition. The best Old English poetry was also built on the principle of structural variation. Poems like *The Wanderer* and *Seafarer* depend for their effect on parallel, secular and religious, restatements of the speakers' situations, and *Beowulf*, like *Sir Gawain*, is concentrated on a relatively small number of episodes that resemble one another in structure and content (Beowulf's three battles with the monsters) and that form significant parallel contrasts (Beowulf's initial triumph and final tragic death). The structure of the narrative is concentrated and appositional, enclosed within the framework of the burials at the beginning and end.[59] Evidently some of the Old English narrative techniques survived even in Middle English alliterative poetry, since one finds the same concern with parallels, contrasts, and variations in the narrative structure of poems such as *Morte Arthure*, *Golagros and Gawane*, and the *Awntyrs of Arthur* (all, like *Sir Gawain*, Arthurian poems of the northern, heavily ornamented and formulaic tradition of alliterative verse).[60]

So ancient a technique could be used in the fourteenth century, because the general aesthetic of the period was especially favorable to this kind of structural variation; the juxtaposition of parallel, opposing elements without an explicit statement of their relation is basically the technique of "dramatic conflict" that, as Hauser writes, dominates "the whole relation of Gothic art to nature and the inner structure of its composition." [61] When the contrast is between the courtly and the churlish or the sacred and the profane—between such completely contrasting characters as Gawain and the Green Knight—the dramatic conflict is late Gothic *par excellence*. We more decorous moderns are sometimes apt to overlook this principle, considering (as museums and photographs sometimes force us to do) only the marvellous statue of the Virgin and overlooking the equally marvellous grotesquerie that exists alongside it, reading the *Inferno* without the *Paradiso* or the tales of the Miller and Reeve without those of the Knight and Man of Law.

Perhaps the one surviving genre of medieval art in which such selective distortion is impossible is that of the illuminated book, the magnificent psalters and books of hours produced by English scribes, mainly of the so-called "East Anglian school," in the late thirteenth and four-teenth centuries.[62] The illuminated page has a fixed form. On the left side or at the top appears the illustration of the religious text. The figures are frontally portrayed, often stiffly hieratic in style. The background is conventionalized (usually diapered), and the whole is enclosed within the frame provided by the letter. Surrounding this and the text is the lush foliage characteristic of the East Anglian school. Here the lines are twisting and naturalistic, though the color is not always natural green; blue, purple, and silver may replace the green (as in the Windmill Psalter). At the bottom of the page, competing, as it were, for the reader's attention, is the grotesque—strange, twisted beasts or naturalistically drawn peasants, wild men, or animals frolicking in a natural setting, unconfined by any framing letter. They are almost always in a forest setting, far re-moved from the decorous scene in which the religious figures appear. They are usually humorous, sometimes in-decent, and invariably irreverent or at least unconcerned with the reverent topic at the top of the page. In the good-humored tension between the decorous portrait that illus-trates the religious text and the lively grotesqueries one sees the same principle that underlies the contrast between the hunting and temptation scenes or the more obvious contrast in which the grotesque Green Knight holds aloft his bleeding head and whirls to turn upon the shocked and motionless court. Here we have not only the "deux civilisa-tions littéraires" that Pons detected in *Sir Gawain* but also the characteristically Gothic "interplay between the

epideictic style of knightly ceremony and the starkly crea-
tural realism that does not shun but actually savors crass
effects." [63]

In *Sir Gawain* the juxtapositions are used not only for
their local, sometimes crass effects but also as the principal
method of communicating meaning. This is what distin-
guishes structural variation from the use of parallels and
contrasts that is essential to any work of art and from apparently similar narrative techniques, such as the *en-
trelacement* of French romance. In alliterative narratives
form has an immediate semantic function that enables a
poet to imply his generalizations and allow his narrative
to communicate its meaning without the explicit comments that Chaucer employs. Consequently, when the Gawain-poet thought about the meaning of a text, he thought
in terms of formal criticism. This sounds more like a
modern than a medieval idea, but the Gawain-poet's one
surviving exercise in critical interpretation is an analysis
of form.

This is the "Prologue" to *Patience*. The poet first quotes
the Beatitudes from the Gospel of St. Matthew. He then
argues for a close relation between poverty and the virtue
of patience. This was, of course, a very common idea in the
Middle Ages, but the poet's method of proving it was not
so common, at least among literary men. When Chaucer's
Parson wants to make the point that one should be patient
though impoverished, he cites the example of Christ:

> That oother grevance outward is to have damage of thy
> catel. Theragayns suffred Crist ful paciently, when he was
> despoyled of al that he hadde in this lyf, and that nas but
> his clothes.
>
> (*ParsT*, 664)

When Langland wants to make a similar point, he appeals
to authority:

And patriarkes and prophetes and poetes bothe
Wryten to wissen vs to wilne no ricchesse
And preyseden pouerte with pacience; the apostles bereth
 witnesse,
That thei han heritage in heuene and bi trewe riȝte.
(PP, B, X, 340–43)

The Gawain-poet appeals neither to examples nor to authority. Instead, he derives his interpretation from a close
analysis of the structure of the passage, displaying the
keen awareness of the semantic function of form that we
might expect from one so imbued with the alliterative tradition as the Gawain-poet but that we so seldom find in
medieval criticism:

Bot syn I am put to a poynt þat Pouerte hatte
I schal me poruay Pacyence, & play me with boþe;
For in þe tyxte þere þyse two arn in teme layde,
Hit arn fettled in on forme, þe forme & þe laste,
& by quest of her quoyntyse enquylen on mede.
(Pat, 35–39)

The critic of *Sir Gawain* must acquire the same sensitivity
to "forme" as the poet displays in this interpretation of a
text, carefully noting what elements "arn in teme layde"
and taking account of the meaning this "quoyntyse" pro-
duces.

But before we consider that problem we must examine
the poet's style in the narrower sense of the word, the particular devices that he uses for conveying meanings in particular contexts, especially his techniques of description
and narration—the "rhetoric" rather than the "syntax" of
his art.

The Narrative and
Descriptive Techniques

The qualities that one prizes most in *Sir Gawain* are those which set it apart from the general run of medieval poetry rather than those more traditional elements discussed in the previous chapters. This work has a freshness and vigor, a "sense of felt life," in James' phrase, that one rarely encounters in the works of the poet's fellow romancers. The dramatic vividness of its action, its sharp and unforgettable imagery, and its rich psychological insight so invigorate the conventional Gawain, green man, and wild man of tradition that even the most jaded scholar, steeped in the conventions of romance, cannot avoid the feeling that here the old materials are being used for the first time. As he reads he almost believes that the hero may yet escape the lady's snares.

It is rare that critics can agree on what qualities compose a poem's individual texture, much less on what techniques produce it, for in any good poem this is largely a matter beyond the reach of art and even further beyond the cruder grasp of criticism. *Sir Gawain* is apparently an exception. Certainly it has its full share of indefinable beauties, yet its critics, who disagree about almost everything else, almost unanimously agree on what makes this poem an artistic triumph: the poet's technique of concrete, specific description and narration—"his remarkable visualization of the action and setting of the story," [1] and his effective use of this visual detail in the closely observed "series of slight movements" that bring the action to life in the dramatic fashion that students have so long admired.[2] Lately critics have even begun, again with a remarkable unanimity, to isolate the techniques that the poet used to organize and present his richly detailed descriptions and narrations. Dorothy Everett and Werner Habicht have both noted how "the poet describes things as they appeared to the hero," and, more recently, Alain Renoir has justly compared this technique to that of the modern cinema.[3]

It is so seldom that critics agree on the more subtle aspects of a poet's art that one begins to fear for the poem, lest by overwhelming vote criticism should reduce *Sir Gawain* to a mere mechanical construct. A rereading of the work is enough to assure us that there is no danger of this and that a closer understanding of the poet's individual techniques can only enhance our enjoyment of the poem. It can also refine our understanding of the poet's art in relation to fourteenth-century literature, for though this individual technique is a matter of genius rather than tradition, it is genius working with the tools of tradition, with the techniques of narration and description that had been developed in the romance and alliterative traditions. The poet's use of these devices along with his changes in the plot, his use of conventions, and his structure of variation enabled him to make the old materials at once "new" and poetically convincing, to sharpen and lend meaning to the contrast between the hero and the challenger, and to infuse the narrative itself with metaphoric significance.

The narrative orders in Sir Gawain

In the complex of descriptive and narrative techniques that compose the individual rhetoric of *Sir Gawain* the simplest element is also the most important. This is the manner in which the narrative is organized, not its structure of variation but the simple order in which the events are told. Like all well-made narratives, *Sir Gawain* is so skillfully constructed that the order of events seems perfectly natural and inevitable, and if we did not have the earlier *Caradoc* and the later *Grene Knight,* it would be difficult to imagine that the events in *Sir Gawain* could be related in any other way. For all three authors the challenge tale posed a basic problem of narration: There is a hero and a challenger, each of whom has his own personal history. There are thus two lines of action, necessarily separate until they coalesce in the encounter at Arthur's court. Of the two, the challenger's is the more important; the plot requires that he initiate the encounter by coming to the court, and his motives for this act are therefore crucial to the rest of the tale. Yet the Gawain-poet begins the poem with a history of the court that reaches all the way back to Troy, and then he introduces the challenger into this court without the slightest indication of the previous history that led to his sudden appearance at Camelot.

Neither *Caradoc* nor *The Grene Knight* is organized in this manner. Although in *Caradoc* the beheading tale itself is narrated in about the same way as in *Sir Gawain* (and thus may have provided the suggestion for the Gawain-poet's method of organizing his narrative), the chapters that include the tale are preceded by a chapter to Éliavres, which establishes his identity, his relation to the hero, and the source of his enmity for Arthur and the court. Only after this chapter is the author ready to introduce him into the action in the challenge tale proper. The author of *The Grene Knight,* having only the example of *Sir Gawain* before him, begins his poem with an account of the court. Then, where the Gawain-poet abruptly introduces the Green Knight, this poet feels it necessary to break off the scene at Camelot for a parallel account of Bredbeddle, explaining exactly who he is, how he got his strange disguise, and why he came to the court—the whole line of action (including even the presence of Morgan) that the Gawain-poet suppresses until the end of the poem.

The method of narrative adopted by the authors of *The Grene Knight* and *Caradoc* is what medieval critics called the *ordo naturalis.* According to rhetorical doctrine, a narrative can be ordered in two ways—"Natural [*naturalis*], that is, when the events are reported in the order in which they occurred, and artful [*artificialis*], that is, when what occurred first is told last." [4] The true artist, according to the medieval rhetoricians, "must love the artful order and spurn the natural," [5] but despite the precepts of these critics and the example of Virgil, most Arthurian romances are cast in the simple, chronological scheme used in *Caradoc* and *The Grene Knight.* Only the better romancers found a way to satisfy both art and tradition; they combined the natural and artful orders in the same work. [6] Such a romance usually begins with a scene at court, in which the hero is introduced by name, rank, and ancestry. The rest of the action, so far as the hero is concerned, follows in the natural, chronological order from that beginning until the end of the work. With the introduction of the antagonist—the felon knight or strange messenger who suddenly appears at court—an artful order of narrative is introduced. That antagonist, so far as his own history goes, enters *in medias res,* and the explanation of his appearance, of the motives and acts that precede his entry, is delayed until the mystery is unravelled at the end of the romance. This is the technique that the Gawain-poet adopted. Gawain's line of action begins *ab origine,* and it is narrated in a strictly natural order. Bercilak enters *in medias res,* so far as his own history is concerned, and his line of action is narrated in the artful order. Not until the end of the romance does the audience learn the challenger's name and rank or the actions that precede, and account for, his appearance at Camelot.

Obvious and simple as this juxtaposition of narrative orders may be, a comparison of *Sir Gawain* with *The Grene Knight* shows that it is highly effective. By casting both Bredbeddle's and Gawain's actions in the natural order the later poet creates a rather more logical narrative, and he escapes the necessity of saving all the explanation until the end, an awkward feature of many of the romances in which the two orders are combined.[7] Furthermore, the simpler narrative organization of *The Grene Knight* allows the audience to share the narrator's omniscience and to enjoy from the standpoint of their superior knowledge the predicament in which the hero finds himself. To achieve this, however, the poet had to sacrifice both the surprise generated by Bercilak's sudden entry and the continuing tension and ambiguity created by that character in the poem. In *The Grene Knight* Arthur's courtiers are amazed when Bredbeddle enters, but the poet's audience, who know exactly the intruder's identity and purpose, can share none of this emotion. In *Sir Gawain,* on the other hand, the consistent use of the natural order for Gawain and the artful order for the challenger establishes a significant contrast between the familiar Gawain and the unknown Green Knight and allows the audience to become emotionally involved in the action to a degree impossible in either *Caradoc* or *The Grene Knight.*

This effect depends upon a more subtle technique, which few romancers were capable of using. The two narrative orders make possible—even require, if they are to be effective—two distinctly different narrative points of view, the omniscient in the natural order, and a limited, objective and dramatic, viewpoint in the artful. Omniscience is almost inevitable in the natural order of narration. One begins *ab origine,* and he must account for everything, even the events that he cannot possibly narrate, since the natural flow of time must not be disturbed. The narrator must therefore have the omniscient power to move quickly through time and space, compressing the unimportant events and dilating the significant ones, freely employing the *occupatio* ("þat were to tor for to telle"), the *conclusio* ("þe fest watȝ ylyche ful fiften dayes"), the *transitio* ("þis day wyth þis ilk dede þay dryuen on þis wyse/Whyle oure luflych lede lys in his bedde"), and all the other devices necessary to keep the action moving without disrupting its continuous flow from beginning to end. If the narrative is an Arthurian romance, omniscience is unavoidable, for Arthur's court is a subject about which a narrator could not possibly pretend ignorance. Not only must his supposed source be an "old book," his audience is apt to be almost as well informed about this court and its heroes as the narrator is. Only occasionally can he plead ignorance of some event (where his sources are silent) or artfully imply that the outcome is in doubt, as the Gawain-poet does when he warns his hero to keep the bargain (vv. 487–89); the over-all technique must remain omniscient.

In the artful order a much different narrative technique is possible. The action begins *in medias res,* and there is no need to account for the previous events until the end of the adventure. Indeed, one must take care not to account for them if he is to maintain the mystery inherent in this narrative order. The main line of action remains with the hero; he provides the continuity for the plot. The antagonist need not appear except when he is acting on the hero, and the narrator can adopt and maintain the stance of an eyewitness, with the audience learning no more about that antagonist than his appearance, actions, and speech reveal to the hero. This is true even in Arthurian romance. Arthur's knights are well known and one must handle them omnisciently, but their antagonists, the felon Red or Green Knights, are ostensibly "unheard of" marvels, as strange to the audience as to the hero. And they are unpredictable, even in well-known plots, for the romancers customarily altered the role of the villain more freely than that of the hero. Of course, the villain is always a stock character, and the romance audience easily recognizes the type, but the individual and his particular history remain unknown. The poet can adopt a limited point of view without fear of the audience's own knowledge intruding.

Concrete description in the alliterative tradition

This use of a limited viewpoint is successful only if a poet has a fully developed command of the concrete, visual mode of description that it requires. Few earlier romancers had either this skill or the concern with the physical texture of experience that it implies, and consequently when the two narrative points of view are combined, as in parts of *Caradoc*, the effect is seldom striking. When the author of *Caradoc* narrates the first beheading, he tells us only that a blow has been struck: the hero "haulsa l'espee qu'il tenoit de laquelle en donna au chevalier telle coulee qu'elle coulla jusque au doigtz." In *Sir Gawain* this brief statement is extended through seven richly detailed lines (vv. 421–27), and we see Gawain raise the axe, place his left foot a bit before his right, and deliver a blow that is described with almost surgical accuracy. Even when an early romancer is able to use specific detail effectively, he is apt to use it in a symbolic rather than a representational manner. For example, that celebrated passage in *Perceval*, in which Chrétien's hero sees the three drops of blood on the snow, is presented with unusual vividness (vv. 4164–4215). The account of the birds' flight is circumstantially presented, and the image of Perceval leaning on his lance to study the contrasting red and white is as representational as anything in *Sir Gawain*. Yet this detail is only incidental, for the emphasis in this episode is not on the objects but on the meditation that begins when Perceval sees the blood.[8] Narrative time speeds up for the account of the physical actions and objects—only two lines are devoted to Perceval's leaning on his lance—and it slows down for his thoughts of Blancheflor, which occupy seventeen lines.

The proportion is reversed when Gawain sees his blood on the snow. Here the psychological events are reported in only two lines (the last two), whereas the physical events are carefully and lengthily specified:

> He lyftes lyȝtly his lome, and lette hit doun fayre
> With þe barbe of þe bitte bi þe bare nek;
> Þaȝ he homered heterly, hurt hym no more,
> Bot snyrt hym on þat on syde, þat seuered þe hyde.
> Þe scharp schrank to þe flesche þurȝ þe schyre grece,
> Þat þe schene blod ouer his schulderes schot to þe erþe;
> And quen þe burne seȝ þe blode blenk on þe snawe,
> He sprit forth spenne-fote more þen a spere lenþe.

Braydeʒ out a bryʒt sworde, and bremely he spekeʒ—
Neuer syn þat he watʒ burne borne of his moder
Watʒ he neuer in þis worlde wyʒe half so blyþe.

(vv. 2309–16, 2319–21)

This passage is no less symbolic than that in *Perceval,* but it is symbolic in the representational manner of the later Middle Ages, which delighted in giving each spiritual entity a palpable, physical form.[9] The fact that the axe "schrank to þe flesche þurʒ þe schyre grece" of the hero's neck is unmistakably related to the first scene, where Gawain's axe also "schrank þurʒ þe schyire grece" of the Green Knight's neck (v. 425), but such details are allowed to speak for themselves, unaided by any explicit interpretation such as Perceval's meditation.

The success of a passage like this is only partly dependent on the details themselves; more important is their organization, which lends such passages the "dramatic" quality for which they have so often been admired. The details are presented to our attention in a sequence that is more than merely temporal or causal, for they are organized by a process that focuses our attention first on the movement of the axe, next shifts to its edge, and then, when the edge touches, moves to the neck and from there to the blood that falls on the earth. Then, turning on a visual act ("þe burne seʒ"), the focus shifts to Gawain, and his reaction is narrated with the same careful attention to the process involved. The processes, first of movement and the transfer of energy from one object to another, and then of reaction to this movement, account both for the organization of the details and for their selection. Nothing is admitted into the passage that does not fit into the scheme provided by the process, and no detail is mentioned until its proper place in the process has arrived. The poet's descriptions are organized in the same manner. Even the *descriptio* of Gawain, traditionally a static portrait, is rendered dramatic by the process of arming him, for the poet's use of an organizing process leads him almost always to coalesce narration and description. Sometimes he is led to an even more subtle technique of description, and the process involves not the movement of some character or object but the movement of the viewer's eyes. "Things are described as they appear to the hero," [10] and the act of perception itself informs the objects perceived.

Stated so abstractly, this seems a highly sophisticated and individual technique, yet it is one that the Gawain-poet shares with the best of his alliterative peers. Their varied style provided them with the necessary concern with details, for their tendency was always to analyze, to suppress the generalization and present instead the parts of the object described or the stages of the action narrated. From this basic tendency evolved a method of narration and description built upon the use of an organizing process to order the details. This is clearest in the alliterative poets' best and most characteristic passages, their descriptions of nature, which have often been admired for their apparent "realism," so unusual in this period. "Verisimilitude" is a better word for them than "realism," for although these landscapes seem "real" they are as conventional within the alliterative tradition as the *locus amoenus* or *gaste forest* of continental romance.[11] In the alliterative *Destruction of Troy*, for example, the coming of winter is communicated by a marvellously detailed description of a storm:

> Trees, thurgh tempestes, tynde hade þere leues;
> And briddes abatid of hor brem songe;
> The wynde of the west wackenet aboue,
> Blowyng ful bremly o the brode ythes;
> The clere aire ouercast with cloudys full thicke,
> With mystes full merke mynget with showres;

fflodes were felle thurgh fallyng of Rayne,
And wyntur vp wacknet with his wete aire.

(vv. 12467–74)

The function of this passage is symbolic, for not only
does one storm represent the whole coming of winter, the
change in the seasons also represents a change in the for-
tunes of the armies. Yet the passage seems realistic, for the
poet describes not just the storm but the coming of the
storm, with each detail in its proper place in the temporal
and causal sequence, although, as usual in the alliterative
style, these relations are implied rather than stated. First
there are the leafless trees and silent birds, then the rising
of the wind; it blows over the waves and brings with it the
thick clouds, then the showers, and finally the full force of
the autumn rain that swells the rivers and announces that
winter has come. In all this there is a close attention to
exact spatial relations that indicates that the process involves more than a temporal order. The wind does not
merely begin; "The wind *of þe west* wackenet *aboue*." The
narrator seems to be standing in a definite physical location that supplies the viewpoint from which the events are
observed. He becomes an observer, an eyewitness to the
storm as it dramatically unfolds before his eyes. By his
power to focus our attention on the action from the same
point of view, he also manages to involve us in the process,
and we see the events of the storm in the order we would
perceive them if we were physically present at the moment
it breaks.

One finds the same technique in almost all the descriptions of nature in alliterative poetry; the direction of movement and the spatial relations of objects are carefully specified, and the details themselves are reported from a fixed
viewpoint in a strict, though usually unstated, temporal
and causal order.[12] In *Patience*, for example, the source,
the Book of Jonah, states only that the Lord sent a mighty

wind and raised a great storm on the sea—"Dominus autem misit ventum magnum in mare: et facta est tempestas magna in mare." [13] The Gawain-poet, in the customary manner of alliterative writers, seized the opportunity offered by this brief mention of a storm and expanded the one sentence into a long narration, in which he specifies exactly the direction of the wind, and tells how it blows over the water, bringing the clouds, raising the waves, and striking with full force on the sea:

> Anon out of þe norþ-est þe noys bigynes
> When boþe breþes con blowe vpon blo watteres.
> Roȝ rakkes þer ros, with rudnyng an-vnder;
> Þe see souȝed ful sore, gret selly to here;
> Þe wyndes on þe wonne water so wrastel togeder,
> Þat þe wawes ful wode waltered so hiȝe
> & eft busched to þe abyme. . . .
>
> (vv. 137–43)

The specification of the noise of the wind is the poet's own touch, since for him, as we shall see, violent noise and violent movement go together. Otherwise this fine description is perfectly conventional. The movement of the storm past the fixed point of observation provides the process by which the description is organized.

In a landscape in which there is no movement, the viewpoint itself can be put into motion. The narrative focuses on a character whose perceptions and movement provide the process by which the description is organized. Thus, in *William of Palerne* the conventional *plaisance* of romance comes charmingly to life when the child William is used to provide the viewpoint. Sleeping in a cave where the werewolf has taken him, he wakes when he hears the singing birds:

> What for melodye þat þei made in þe mey sesoun
> Þat litel child listely lorked out of his caue,

Faire floures forto fecche þat he bi-fore him seye,
& to gadere þe grases þat grene were & fayre,
& whan it was out went so wel hit him liked,
Þe savour of þe swete sesoun & song of þe briddes.

(vv. 24–29)

The same technique, even further refined, appears in *The Wars of Alexander*, when the poet describes the enchanted valley through which Alexander and his army must travel:

Þen metis he doun of þe mounte in-to a mirk vale,
A drere dale & a depe, a dym & a thestir,
Miȝt thare na saule vndire son see to a-nothire.
Þai were vmbe-thonrid in þat thede with slike a thike
    cloude,
Þat þai myȝt fele it with þaire fiste as flabband webbis.
With all the bothom full of bournes, briȝt as þe siluere,
And bery-bobis on the braes, brethand as mirre.

(vv. 4803–09)

Here the narrative not only focuses upon the characters and uses their physical position as the viewpoint for the description of this strange valley, it moves into their minds and uses their psychological point of view. The cloud is not just there; the men can feel it with their fists "as flabband webbis." The effect is reinforced a few lines later when the army emerges from the darkness as they climb back out of the valley into the daylight, its brightness blinding to their unaccustomed eyes:

Þai labourde vp a-gayn þe lift an elleuen dayes,
& quen þai couert to þe crest þen clerid þe welkyn,
Þe schaftis of þe schire son schirkind þe cloudis
And gods glorious gleme glent þam e-maunge.

(vv. 4814–17)

The sudden expansion of the imagery—"gods glorious gleme"—corresponds to the wonder and relief that Alexander's army feels at their first sight of the sun.

In *Sir Gawain* the same techniques are used. Storms, such as the snow on the night before Gawain's departure for the Green Chapel, are presented in the traditional manner that appears in *The Destruction of Troy* and *Patience*.[14] For static landscapes, such as the country through which Gawain travels, the poet, like the authors of *William of Palerne* and *The Wars of Alexander*, focuses on the main character and uses his movements and perceptions as the organizing process, and in these landscapes, as in the one in *The Wars of Alexander*, the character's psychological point of view becomes important.[15] However, in even the best alliterative poems the use of a process as an organizing principle of description was never more than an occasional feature, and the use of a character's viewpoint in narration was even more rare. The Gawain-poet alone extended these techniques beyond the landscapes and raised them from occasional or rare stylistic devices to consistently employed tools that enabled him to build sharply visualized scenes, and only he refined them so skillfully that he could use the movement of the hero's eye as the organizing process.

To accomplish this, the poet needed a better understanding of the limited, personal point of view than the alliterative tradition could provide. Perhaps he could have developed an awareness of the advantages and limitations of this technique without any tradition upon which to draw, but fortunately he did not have to make the experiment. Fourteenth-century literature included one genre in which a fully developed and consistently maintained personal, dramatic point of view was the traditional mode of narration.

This was the dream vision, a genre to which the Gawain-poet was indebted in many ways and in which, as *Pearl* shows, he himself excelled. In respect to narrative technique the dream vision is the exact opposite of romance. A romance always takes place in some remote past, and its narrator is always a clerk, depending on written authority and transmitting, ostensibly unchanged, the ancient story "as the book tells." The dream or vision, on the other hand, is always a contemporary event, a personal experience related by a narrator who, so he asserts, saw everything with his own eyes. Such a narrator is necessarily naïve rather than omniscient, for the "eyewitness" convention requires that he report only what he has personally seen or heard. His vision is not of an entire history *ab ovo* but of a limited segment of a history that he comes upon *in medias res*. How Winner and Waster came to be on the plain where the narrator observes them can only be inferred from their speeches, and what they will do in the future can only be guessed from what is dramatically revealed to the narrator and, through him, to us.

The poetic credibility of a dream vision, its authentication, therefore depends to a great extent on the credibility that the poet is able to create for his narrator. Chaucer achieves this by a circumstantial characterization of his dreamer; he places him firmly in real space and time in the prologues to his visions. It is no accident that we learn, or seem to learn, so much about Chaucer from his dream visions. The Gawain-poet tells us little about his dreamer; he concentrates instead upon the experience of the vision itself, drawing upon the alliterative tradition's method of specification and its use of a process for organizing these details in order to make his dream seem for the moment a real experience.

Pearl shows how well these traditional alliterative techniques fit the dream vision. The poet strictly maintains the dramatic viewpoint that was conventional in this genre. No omniscient voice enters the poem to insist upon the reality of the vision or to explain exactly who or what Pearl represents, a fact that makes Pearl as puzzling a character in her way as the Green Knight is in his. Yet, despite its unearthly setting and the ambiguity of the main character, *Pearl* communicates a distinct and poetically credible experience. This results mainly from the poet's use of the process of visualization as the organizing principle of his narrative, a technique that allows the reader to experience the objects and actions of the vision along with the narrator. When we and the dreamer first glimpse the cliffs and forests of Paradise, our eyes are at once directed to the highest and thus most visually prominent feature of the landscape. Then they travel from that point to the ground at the observer's feet:

> Dubbed wern alle þo downeʒ sydeʒ
> Wyth crystal klyffeʒ so cler of kynde.
> Holtwodeʒ bryʒt aboute hem bydeʒ
> Of bolleʒ as blwe as ble of Ynde;
> As bornyst syluer þe lef on slydeʒ,
> Þat þike con trylle on vch a tynde.
> Quen glem of glodeʒ agaynʒ hem glydeʒ,
> Wyth schymeryng schene ful schrylle þay schynde
> Þe grauayl þat on grounde con grynde
> Wern precious perleʒ of oryente.
>
> (vv. 73–82)

As in *Sir Gawain,* "the experience is distinct because the landscape is distinct," [16] even so unrepresentational a landscape as this.

Pearl herself is presented in the same distinct manner, but our perception of the narrator's experience is deepened, because when Pearl appears, the poet uses not only the physical process of seeing but the psychological process of recognition. She is first seen at a distance, across a stream. The narrator's eyes have again been drawn to a high cliff, from which they travel slowly downward to the small object—the lady—at its base. Once the dreamer has noticed the lady, he focuses his attention on her, first noting the familiarity of her figure (v. 164), and then studying her more closely. He catches just a glimpse of her "fayre face" and "gladande glory con to me glace." Then she raises her head:

> Þenne vereȝ ho vp her fayre frount,
> Her vysayge whyt as playn yuore:
> Þat stonge myn hert ful stray atount,
> And euer þe lenger, þe more and more.
>
> (vv. 177–80)

It is the observation of the small, accurate movement— Pearl's raising her head—and the dramatic organization of the narrative from the dreamer's visual and psychological point of view—the sting in the heart at just this moment —that accounts for much of the power of *Pearl*.

In *Sir Gawain* one finds the same techniques used for presenting the strange experiences that Gawain encounters. The narrator focuses upon the hero, and, at significant points in the action, he uses Gawain in the same manner in which the narrator of *Pearl* is used. The viewpoints of the narrator and the hero coalesce, and scenes and characters are presented as they appear to Gawain, with his eye and emotions providing the process by which the details are organized. Thus, when Bercilak's castle is described, we see it from Gawain's point of view, as he looks through the boughs that frame it pictorially: [17]

> Er he watȝ war in þe wod of a won in a mote,
> Abof a launde, on a lawe, loken vnder boȝeȝ
> Of mony borelych bole aboute bi þe diches.
>
> (vv. 764–66)

At this distance the castle is the most prominent visual feature, and the description moves from it down to the surrounding forest:

A castel þe comlokest þat euer knyȝt aȝte,
Pyched on a prayere, a park al aboute,
With a pyked palays pyned ful þik,
Þat vmbeteȝe mony tre mo þen two myle.
Þat holde on þat on syde þe haþel auysed,
As hit schemered and schon þurȝ þe schyre okeȝ.

(vv. 767–72)

When Gawain approaches the castle, this order of description is reversed, and the eye moves from the bridge and
walls (v. 783), the dominant features to the vision of one
standing nearby, to the high towers (v. 800), which one
can see only after his eye has travelled up from the walls
to the battlements, to the tops of the buildings within,
with their roofs and chimneys.

However, in *Sir Gawain* the technique has a more complicated function than in *Pearl*, for here it is used in alternation with the omniscient point of view, thus allowing
the poet to manipulate two means of gaining credibility
—the omniscient authority of the "book" for Gawain and
the court and the personal testimony of the "eyewitness"
for the Green Knight. In the usual romance the combination of narrative orders is not accompanied by this combination of viewpoints and is therefore little more than a
trick, an easy means of concealing information from the
audience. The Gawain-poet plays that trick on us, but we
are not conscious of the trickery because he so carefully
differentiates the narrative viewpoints that he uses for his
two main characters. Moreover, his alternation between
the omniscient point of view used for Gawain and the
limited, dramatic viewpoint used for the unknown antagonist allows us to regard the action itself from significantly varied perspectives.

The alternating points of view

The poem begins with a completely omniscient account of Camelot. The narrator moves freely through time and space, compressing or expanding time as he chooses and explaining how Arthur's custom arose (vv. 90–102), who his ancestors were (vv. 1–26), and even how his mind works (vv. 85–89). Such a method suits this scene, for the poet works carefully to present a Camelot that seems familiar, and the passage is rich in allusions that invite the audience to share the narrator's omniscience. Should a hearer fail to recognize the conventional, familiar quality of Camelot, he will be reminded of it by the emphasis on fame—the knights are the "most kyd" under heaven (v. 51)—and by the catalogue of names that appears just before the Green Knight's entry—Gawain, Agravain, Yvain, Baldwin (vv. 109–13). Except for Gawain, none of these knights has any part in the action. Their names, like the catalogue of knights that appears just before Gawain departs on his journey (vv. 550–55), serve only as allusions, reminders of the familiar, courtly quality of Camelot.

The careful omission of any allusions to the court's vices invites the audience to admire and sympathize with this familiar place. The narrator is unreserved in asserting his complete knowledge of Camelot and its admirable qualities—"þat may ȝe wel trawe" (v. 70), "Vch wyȝe may wel wit no wont þat þer were" (v. 131)—and he seems enthusiastically to share its ideals, admiring without qualification each of its superlative aspects. Of course, the audience knows that this scene is only a prelude to adventure, for the narrator has promised an "outtrage awenture," and Arthur's custom must be observed. Yet the suspense is slight and the over-all impression is of a flawless romance court, one whose values the audience is invited to admire and accept for the moment as their own. Then, just after the first course is served—the usual time for such entries —in rides the wonder that Arthur requires and the audience expects.

With the entry of the Green Knight the narrative technique completely changes. The viewpoint becomes limited and dramatic, and the audience must now view the intruder from the standpoint of a spectator actually present in the court. The narrator does not give the challenger's name, he only supposes ("I hope") that he is "half etayn" (v. 140), and he must even infer the Green Knight's strength from his external appearance—"Hit *semed* as no mon myʒt/ Vnder his dyntteʒ dryʒe" (vv. 201–02). In the language of medieval poetics the description itself is all *effictio* (a catalogue of external appearances) with no *notatio* (the list of internal qualities that usually accompanies the *effictio*, as in the description of Gawain), for the dramatic point of view allows the poet to report only the visual facts. The psychological effect of this sudden change in viewpoint is enhanced by the equally drastic change in narrative pace. Time passes swiftly in an omniscient narrative. Verses 37–135, which describe Camelot, cover fifteen days in rapid summary, and verses 1–26 cover more than as many centuries even more quickly, but when the Green Knight bursts onto the scene at verse 136—"þer hales in at þe halle dor"—narrative time stops altogether, and it remains suspended for over one hundred lines, until verse 221, when it takes up again with the Green Knight still moving into the hall—"and þe halle entres," a half-line that could almost serve as the second half of verse 136.

During this long interval, while the previously laughing and bustling court sits stone-still and gazes at the challenger and while the point of view focuses unwaveringly upon him, the poet's audience is forced to look as long and as carefully at the Green Knight as Arthur's courtiers do. The audience must look carefully, for the narrator offers no explanation of the challenger. He maintains his dramatic stance and merely allows the audience to over-hear the courtiers' speculations. By having the obviously puzzled knights suggest that Bercilak is "for fantoum and fayryʒe," the troubled Arthur attempt to dismiss him as an "interlude" suitable to the Christmas season, and later the deluded Gawain try to explain him away as a devil, the poet denies his audience even these solutions. The hearer or reader, who began by admiring the familiar scene at Camelot and who has now been brought to share its visual and psychological experience of its unknown challenger, feels almost as uncomfortable in the face of this mystery as Arthur and his courtiers.

This limited, objective viewpoint is maintained for Ber-cilak whenever he appears. Once Gawain enters the poem, the viewpoint is narrowed even further, for now Gawain himself is the spectator through whose eyes we gaze at the challenger. Thus, when Bercilak appears as the host, he is introduced in the dramatic manner established for the Green Knight in the opening scene. The castle, as we have already noted, is viewed entirely through Gawain's eyes. When the host enters, we must again depend entirely on what Gawain sees, and Gawain's judgment, based purely on his limited perspective, is our only guide to the quali-ties of the characters and objects he sees:

> Gawayn glyʒt on þe gome þat godly hym gret,
> And *þuʒt hit* a bolde burne. . . .
>
> And wel *hym semed,* for soþe, as þe segge *þuʒt,*
> To lede a lortschyp. . . .
>
> (vv. 842–43, 848–49)

Gawain's thoughts neatly bracket the description of Ber-cilak, and they reappear throughout the scene, emphasiz-

ing the use of Gawain's viewpoint and suggesting the contrast between appearance and reality that is one of the
basic themes of this episode. Even the lady's beauty is
judged by Gawain alone. At Camelot Guenevere's beauty
was flatly stated by the narrator—"A semloker þat euer he
syȝe/ Soth moȝt no mon say" (vv. 83–84). The beauty of
Bercilak's lady is rendered strictly from Gawain's point
of view:

> And wener þen Wenore, *as þe wyȝe þoȝt.*
>
> (v. 945)

The narrator does not even reveal the host's name, and all
we know of Bercilak is what he himself reveals in his
speeches and actions.

At the Green Chapel the point of view is limited in the
same manner. Nothing is explained, and only the visual
facts, the guide's words, and Gawain's thoughts provide
our information about this strange place and its master.
When the Green Knight appears, we first hear the sound
of the axe, then the shout, and then, in a richly detailed
description of his action, the challenger comes vaulting
over the stream. Not until the blow has been delivered,
when the Green Knight is about to reveal his identity,
does the narrator enter his mind in the way he freely enters the minds of Arthur and Gawain (v. 2335b). Though
Bercilak's viewpoint is sometimes used in the poem, this
half-line is the only touch of omniscience in the narrator's
treatment of the Green Knight. Even when we do learn
the challenger's name, social position, and motivation for
the action, these facts are presented dramatically by Bercilak's speech, and when he finally departs, it is for an unknown destination—"Whiderwarde-so-euer he wolde"—beyond the limited viewpoint of Gawain and the narrator.

The emotional power of these dramatically rendered
scenes is enhanced by the omniscience of the rest of the

narrative, and the poet's method of shifting from one point of view to the other emphasizes the tension created by the limited viewpoint and its contrast with the omniscient scenes. Each time Bercilak is about to appear there is a gradual narrowing of the temporal and spatial focus with a consequent loss of omniscience. Our view first takes in a broad expanse of time and space—the history of Troy that precedes the Green Knight's appearance at Camelot, the passage of the seasons and the long journey to Bercilak's castle, the winter storm and the journey to the Green Chapel. Then the viewpoint narrows temporally to a specific day—New Year's, Christmas, New Year's again—and spatially to a specific scene—the courtiers feasting at the high table, Gawain and Gringolet seeking the castle, Gawain rejecting the guide's advice. At these points the narrative becomes nearly dramatic, and the emphasis is upon the specific actions of the characters. Consequently we have also lost some of our omniscience. We know the general pattern of Gawain's noble actions or of the traditional feast at Camelot, but we do not know the details within these patterns, how exactly the courtiers are seated on this particular occasion. Next, an object or a character appears to the characters we have been viewing, and when they look toward this new object of attention, we look with them. Their point of view is adopted, the narrative becomes completely dramatic, and our omniscience is entirely gone. In the scene at Camelot the audience, like the courtiers themselves, can only gaze in puzzled wonder at the strange intruder.

When the Green Knight leaves, the process is reversed. He rushes suddenly out of Camelot, and we move back to a dramatically rendered scene between Arthur, Guenevere, and Gawain. Then the viewpoint moves a bit farther back for a summary of the rest of the feast. Finally, the viewpoint, and the audience with it, moves all the way back to complete omniscient detachment, and the narrator apostrophizes the hero and turns to a panoramic account of the passing of the seasons. This restoration of omniscience (throughout the poem, the farther we are from the Green Knight the more omniscient the viewpoint) is the beginning of another slow movement back to drama. The narrative next concentrates more narrowly upon Gawain and his grieving friends, focusing only on Gawain while he is being armed, but moving freely from him ("He sperred þe sted," v. 670) to the courtiers ("Al þat seȝ þat semly," v. 672) as he departs. When he leaves the court (v. 691), the focus narrows only slightly. Although Gawain is its only subject, it remains omniscient, panoramically surveying the journey and its hardships, now concentrating on a dramatic description (the stormy weather), now moving back for a broader view. As Christmas Eve approaches, the tempo decreases, the tone intensifies, and the narrator no longer summarizes, as he did in the previous, purely omniscient stanzas. He concentrates entirely on Gawain's present situation. With Gawain's first glimpse of the castle, the narrative becomes completely dramatic and his viewpoint is adopted.

This almost cinematic technique of slowly narrowing the focus to a scene which is presented completely in "close up," using the hero as the camera's eye, is not entirely unknown in fourteenth-century literature. Froissart uses a similar "eyewitness," almost "documentary" technique in his chronicles. This is a significant testimony to the age's interest in visual representation, since Froissart adopts this technique for events he himself did not witness, whereas de Joinville, who lived a century earlier and who was actually an eyewitness to the events in his history, writes in the style of *causerie*, emphasizing the moral rather than the physical qualities of the events.[18] Froissart likewise employs the slowly narrowing focus as a means of shifting from the omniscient account of the preparations for a significant event to the dramatic viewpoint of a specific observer, from which the event itself is narrated. This is the technique he uses for the account of Poitiers, which opens with a panoramic view, narrows to the English troops, and then narrows even further to the Black Prince, who provides the viewpoint from which the battle itself is reported.

Yet the Gawain-poet's use of this technique is quite different from Froissart's. He is writing romance rather than factual chronicle, and he fuses this late-medieval, representational method of narration with the older, psychological and symbolic method developed in romance. The dramatic scenes reveal as much about Gawain as about the things he sees, for those objects and actions that are described with the most circumstantial detail are those that loom largest not in life but in Gawain's own mind, and the apparently realistic scenes are actually finely wrought objective correlatives for Gawain's own emotions.[19] For example, the foes that the hero encounters on his way to Bercilak's castle are quickly dismissed from the narrative, but the storms—which annoy him most—are described at length with a richness of detail that Werner Habicht compares to Giotto's landscapes.[20] Moreover, at exactly the point that the account of the journey becomes most circumstantial the poet enters Gawain's mind to show him "Carande for his costes, lest he ne keuer schulde/ To se þe seruyse of þat syre" (vv. 750–51).

Throughout the poem the more detailed and dramatic the narrative becomes, the more psychological and symbolic it is, and concrete descriptions of what Gawain experiences are almost always accompanied by detailed accounts of his thoughts. On the first day of the temptation, for example, Gawain is lying uneasily in his bed. In his anxiety he perceives each movement of his unannounced visitor, even the "littel dyn" at the door. Her every action is carefully described as she moves from the door to the bed (vv. 1180–94) while Gawain anxiously watches. His mental state is reported with equal detail as Gawain, immediately after the narration of the lady's entry, wonders whether or not he should speak to her (vv. 1196–99). On the second day Gawain thinks he has nothing to fear from his visitor. He is not apprehensive when she enters, and her entry is described with corresponding brevity and almost no detail. It takes but one line—"Ho commes to þe cortyn and at þe knyȝt totes"—to the first day's twelve. Throughout the second day's interview Gawain is assured and victorious, and there is almost no detailed rendering of actions and objects. The temptation is presented by almost pure quotation of Gawain's and the lady's speeches, and not once does the poet report Gawain's thoughts. However, the lady is not defeated. That night at supper she returns to the attack and presses Gawain so closely that he is "at his wits' end." The next day his assurance is gone, and he fears that his power of resistance will fail him. The narrative of that day's interview is correspondingly rich in concrete description and narration and in lengthy accounts of Gawain's disturbed mental state—his dreams (vv. 1750–54), his determination not to fail (vv. 1771–75), and his decision to accept the lace (vv. 1855–58).

It is the same technique as we noted in *Pearl*, where the dreamer's dawning recognition of his Pearl leads to a slower movement of his eye, a more detailed description, and an attention to even the slight movements that are psychologically important to him (vv. 177–79). However, in *Sir Gawain* the relation of action to psychology is even more marked, for the whole movement of the narrative reflects the hero's mind. Even the Green Knight seems to change as Gawain's attitude toward him changes. In the opening scene, before his purpose is clear, he is partially attractive; at his own castle, where his purpose is hidden, he is completely attractive; and at the Green Chapel, where Gawain expects death, he is completely grotesque and frightening. The pace of the narrative itself depends on the hero's psychological state. As the fatal day of the return-blow comes nearer and Gawain's fear and anxiety increase, the focus tightens, the tempo slows, and the detailed descriptions increase. Eight lines were enough for the entire history of Aeneas at the poem's beginning, for the whole harvest season at Gawain's departure from Camelot (vv. 521–28), but in the brief panorama that precedes his departure for the Green Chapel eight lines serve only to tell of one winter night (vv. 1998–2005). Time becomes more precious to the hero and the outside world more threatening. The narrative slows accordingly until at the Green Chapel time almost stops again, as the preparations for the blow, the feints, and the fall of the axe are described with all the painful circumstantiality with which they appeared to Gawain.

In such scenes we share rather than judge Gawain's experience. The main disadvantage of the limited viewpoint is that it makes it difficult for the audience to see the action in a larger perspective. Of course, an audience always has its own moral sense against which fictional acts can be scaled, but in a romance or dream vision the scale of everyday life is not easily applied and the ironies of representational fiction are not readily available. We need a guide, Dante's Beatrice or the Gawain-poet's Pearl, to help us see the hero in the proper perspective (especially in *Pearl*, which makes the point that men are deceived by visual appearance). If Gawain's viewpoint were used exclusively, if his emotions and judgments were our only perspective on the action, we would be as discomfited as the hero at the court's amused reception of him at the conclusion. But Gawain is not a trustworthy guide, and his judgment of the adventure's meaning—the "couardise and couetyse þat I haf caȝt þare" (v. 2508)—is as mistaken as his failure to recognize the lady's real intentions. The other viewpoints in the poem are the guides we need; they provide the larger perspectives that reveal the limitations of Gawain's point of view. The most important of these are established at the beginning of the second fit and in the varying points of view employed at Bercilak's castle.

The method used to establish the varying viewpoints in the temptation episode is the same as the poet uses in narrating the hunting scenes. The hunts are, as we have remarked, variations that provide a perspective on the actions within the castle. The transitions from the fields to the bedroom are effected by an abrupt "montage" technique rather than by the narrowing focus used for the other changes of scene. In the hunts themselves the narrative point of view shifts from the hunter to the hunted; it is always dramatic but it is not limited to any one character. Thus, the third day's hunt begins from the point of view of Bercilak and his men, and the narration continues from this viewpoint until the fox is sighted:

> And quen þay seghe hym with syȝt þay sued hym fast,
> Wreȝande hym ful weterly with a wroth noyse;
> And he trantes and tornayeeȝ . . .
>
> (vv. 1705–07)

When the hunters' attention falls on the fox, so does ours, and the viewpoint is smoothly shifted to Reynard. From this moment forward we experience the hunt from his point of view. The discovery of the hounds that lie in wait at the "tryster" is therefore as surprising to the reader, who sees only what Reynard can see, as it is to the fox:

> Þenne watȝ he went, er he wyst, to a wale tryster,
> Þer þre þro at a þrich þrat hym at ones,
> al graye.

He blenched aȝayn bilyue
And stifly start on-stray,
With all þe wo on lyue
To þe wod he went away.

(vv. 1712–18)

We even know the fox's emotional state at this point—
"With all þe wo on lyue"—as we do Gawain's in the parallel
account of the temptation, for which the account of the
hunt is here interrupted.

When it is resumed, Bercilak supplies the point of view,
and when the fox stumbles into an ambush this time, we
see the action through the eyes of the waiting hunter:

Þe wyȝe watȝ war of þe wylde, and warly abideȝ,
And braydeȝ out þe bryȝt bronde, and at þe best casteȝ.
And he schunt for þe scharp, and schulde haf arered;
A rach rapes hym to, ryȝt er he myȝt,
And ryȝt bifore þe hors fete þay fel on hym alle,
And woried me þis wyly wyth a wroth noyse.

(vv. 1900–05)

Our sympathies for Reynard are tempered by this new
point of view. When we see the hunt from the fox's viewpoint, we share his experience. From Bercilak's point of
view we can judge the fox as well as sympathize with him,
and we can perhaps find him guilty of the one unforgiv-
able offense for this "wyly" fox—falling prey to superior
cunning (the "wyȝe watȝ war" and "warly abideȝ").

Gawain's case is the same. We can sympathize with him
when we see the action from his point of view, but we are
enabled to judge him from the broader perspective provided by other viewpoints. In that third day's temptation
the viewpoint shifts from the hunter to the hunted, just
as it does in the hunt itself. The scene begins with a view
of the lady while Gawain still sleeps. We see her careful
preparations for the encounter, as she rises early, deter-

mined "Ne þe purpose to payre þat pyȝt in hir hert" (v.
1734). She dresses in the most provocative fashion, the
care of her toilet reflected in the details of her description.
Then she comes to the room and sets about her work in a
businesslike manner:

> Ho commeȝ withinne þe chambre dore, and closes hit
>   hir after,
> Wayueȝ vp a wyndow, and on þe wyȝe calleȝ.
>
> (vv. 1742–43)

When the point of view shifts to Gawain (by means of a
sensory perception—the sound of her voice), we, who know
of the lady's determined preparations, are able to understand the hero's emotions. We can therefore judge the
naïveté that is swayed by pure appearance:

> He seȝ hir so glorious and gayly atyred,
> So fautles of hir fetures and of so fyne hewes,
> Wiȝt wallande joye warmed his hert.
>
> (vv. 1760–62)

Gawain's emotions and actions are thus placed in a larger
perspective than that of which he can be aware.

Likewise, when Bercilak returns to the castle after this
crucial third day, we see the hero from the host's point of
view. With Bercilak we carefully scrutinize Gawain's
handsome, courtly attire (vv. 1925–31) and watch him rush
forward to pay the kisses (he had waited patiently until
Bercilak had delivered up the game on the previous days).
The betrayal is seen clearly from the knowledgeable eyes
of the host. At the end of the adventure, when Gawain,
like the fox, shunts to avoid the blow, then submits, and
then leaps back to shout his defiance, the sudden shift to
the Green Knight's point of view, here even his psychological viewpoint, provides a new perspective on the whole
action:

The haþel heldet hym fro, and on his ax rested,
Sette þe schaft vpon schore, and to þe scharp lened,
And loked to þe leude þat on þe launde ȝede,
How þat doȝty, dredles, deruely þer stondeȝ
Armed, ful aȝleȝ: in hert hit hym lykeȝ.

(vv. 2331–35)

Such shifts in the dramatic viewpoint, which remind us
that Gawain has judged experience only from its outward
appearance, lend metaphoric force to the narrative technique, linking it with the theme of appearance and reality
that hovers over the entire poem.

Narrative technique as characterization

The audience of *Sir Gawain* accepts the contrasting modes
of narrative, perhaps even considers them inevitable, because they so exactly suit the characters for which they
are used. In the opening scene and throughout the rest of
the poem Gawain is characterized as a cloistered, inactive
courtier whose forte is delicacy of speech and action, the
controlled action of the courtly knight rather than the violent activity of the churl. The narrative technique, which
requires that he often be a merely passive observer, fits
perfectly this kind of personality. The technique is equally
well suited to Bercilak. He is defined by allusion as a
churlishly vital character, the energetic opposite of the
courtier, and he thus fits the technique used to present
him, which requires that he be characterized almost entirely by action, by dramatically presented physical movements rather than psychological analysis. The poet is
therefore able to use the varying viewpoints to emphasize,
even to exaggerate the traditional distinction between the
violent energy of the churl and the dignified inaction of
the courtier.

In most romances this distinction can be shown only in isolated passages; in *Sir Gawain* the differing modes of narrative allow the poet to maintain the distinction each time the two characters appear, and Bercilak shouts, grimaces, rides, and leaps through the narrative, whereas Gawain seems inactive even when, so far as the plot is concerned, he is most energetic:

> Sumwhyle wyth wormeʒ he werreʒ, and with wolues als,
> Sumwhyle with wodwos, þat woned in þe knarreʒ,
> Boþe wyth bulleʒ and bereʒ, and boreʒ oþerquyle,
> And etayneʒ, þat hym anelede of þe heʒe felle.
>
> (vv. 720–23)

Evidently Gawain is a greater hunter than Bercilak. The host fights only one boar, but Gawain fights at least two and a number of other wild beasts as well. Yet our impression is not one of violent activity. Gawain's movement is expressed only by the general verb "werreʒ," and he seems as much acted upon ("hym anelede") as actor. The omniscient summary of Gawain's many actions thus leaves us with less of an impression of real movement than the dramatic presentation of the Green Knight's simple act of getting on his horse (vv. 430–36).

Likewise, the plot requires that Gawain and the Green Knight perform some of the same acts, but the contrasting narrative points of view lend them contrasting qualities, and even as we recognize the parallel we are reminded of the contrast. When the Green Knight bows to receive the blow, the dramatic viewpoint places the emphasis entirely upon his movements:

> The grene knyʒt vpon grounde grayþely hym dresses,
> A littel lut with þe hede, þe lere he discouereʒ,
> His longe louelych lokkeʒ layd ouer his croun,
> Let the naked nec to þe note schewe.
>
> (vv. 417–20)

When Gawain bows for the blow, his actions are the same, and the parallel is reinforced by the use of some of the same verbs. Yet the omniscient point of view allows the narrator to emphasize Gawain's emotions as much as his movements:

> He lened with þe nek, and lutte,
> And schewed þat schyre al bare,
> And lette as he noȝt dutte;
> For drede he wolde not dare.
>
> (vv. 2255–58)

The emphasis is less upon what Gawain does than upon what he fears will be done to him, and despite the parallel, we are left with the impression that Bercilak is purely active and Gawain almost purely passive.

This contrast is not only more consistently maintained in *Sir Gawain* than in most romances, it is also more significant, since the poet's technique allowed him to make it a part of a deeper distinction between the worlds of nature and the court. In romance the beautiful is characteristically static, and its only significant motion is the flashing and glimmering of light, the source of beauty to the medieval aesthetician.[21] This is most obvious in the ideal romance landscape, the *plaisance* or *locus amoenus* of the sort that greets the child in *William of Palerne*—a sun-filled garden with singing birds and gentle streams. The Gawain-poet treats his courtly characters and scenes in the same way most romancers treated the *plaisance*. Bercilak's castle, when it appears to Gawain as if in answer to his prayer, has some of this quality; to reach it Gawain must pass through the "dark wood" that conventionally surrounds the *plaisance,* and when he sees it, it "schemered and schon þurȝ þe schyre okeȝ" and seems as still and white as a paper sculpture. Likewise, when Gawain is described, he stands without movement while the gleaming armor is put upon him, and even the feast at Camelot, which is filled with motion, is organized like those medieval miniatures in which the perspective is reversed and the courtiers sit larger than life, motionless at the high table while the lesser folk scurry about in front of them.[22] But the scenes that Gawain finds harsh and threatening, the dark woods through which he must pass to find his *plaisance* and in which he finds the Green Chapel, belong in another tradition altogether.

In some ways those threatening landscapes simply reverse the conventions of the *plaisance*. The well-tended orchard becomes a wild forest, the gentle stream a raging torrent, "þer as claterande fro þe crest þe colde borne renneӡ" (v. 731), and the birds, instead of singing, "pitously þer piped for pyne of þe colde" (v. 747). But the main characteristic of these landscapes is the violent movement of the traditional alliterative storm-scene, movement accompanied by the loud noise that the Gawain-poet usually associates with violence. The stream runs "claterande," that at the Green Chapel "blubbers," and the entire scene in that last, most threatening and least courtly, landscape rings with a "wonder breme noyse":

> Quat! hit clatered in þe clyff, as hit cleue schulde,
> As one vpon a gryndelston hade grounden a syþe.
> What! hit wharred and whette, as water at a mulne;
> What! hit rusched and ronge, rawþe to here.
>
> (vv. 2201–04)

Sound and movement coalesce in a vividly grotesque manner, and the noise not only rings, it moves—"rusched" and "whette, as water at a mulne."

The woods in which Bercilak engages in the courtly sport of hunting are not threatening, but, like himself, they are characterized by a noisy violence that sets them clearly apart from the courtly scenes in which Gawain appears while the hunt is in progress. The game rushes, the hunters shout—"Wylde wordeʒ hym warp wyth a wrast noyce" (v. 1423)—and the scenes reverberate with "Gret rurde in þat forest" (v. 1149). The narrator himself, as he does at the Green Chapel, adds his exclamations to the violent sound:

> What! þay brayen and bleden, bi bonkkeʒ þay deʒen.
>
> (vv. 1163)

> Þise oþer halowed hyghe! ful hyʒe, and hay! hay! cried.
>
> (v. 1445)

To us such scenes seem more lifelike than the static *plaisance* or motionless courtly *descriptio;* medieval audiences probably had the same impression, for they knew as well as we that "moving things are closer to life." [23] But, at least within the framework of romance assumptions, the lifelike and the admirable are not necessarily the same, and the main function of these scenes is to provide a basis for Bercilak's noise and activity that goes beyond churlishness to the indecorous vitality of the world of nature to which he is linked by the wild-man and green-man aspects of his character. The narrative technique itself thereby acquires an allusive value, and Bercilak and the vitality of the natural world are linked together and differentiated from Gawain by the techniques used to present them.

The narrator's voice

Such an artful use of the narrative viewpoints and so skilled a realization of the possibilities they offered would have evoked the approval of a Henry James, and certainly the vivid and dramatic narrative these devices help produce has called forth the admiration of generations of critics. However, a discussion of the poet's narrative technique is not complete without a consideration of some other passages that critics have not so greatly admired. The most important occurs at the end of the first fit, when the narrator intrudes upon the action in a heavily didactic manner. The Green Knight has just departed and the courtiers have returned to the feast when suddenly Gawain, who has behaved faultlessly, becomes the object of a stern, rather unsympathetic admonition:

> Now þenk wel, Sir Gawan,
> For woþe þat þou ne wonde
> Þis auenture for to frayn
> Þat þou hatȝ tan on honde.
>
> (vv. 487–90)

The apostrophe is notable not so much for its presence (*Caradoc* includes a similar one) as for the fact that it echoes the sentiments of the Green Knight. He too had warned the hero, "Loke, Gawan, þat þou be grayþe to go as þou hetteȝ." Furthermore, immediately after this apostrophe to Gawain, in the opening lines of the second fit, the narrator echoes the very taunt with which the Green Knight had attacked the court. The challenger asked "Where is now your sourquydrye . . . your grete words?" and he stated that the court's "reuel" and "renoun" had been overthrown with a single word (vv. 311–14). The narrator's tone is not taunting, as the challenger's was, but it has a touch of the same heavy-handed irony that characterizes the Green Knight's speech, and the narrator also implies that the court is guilty of "sourquydrye," the disparity between boastful word and actual deed that was the nobility's special failing in the eyes of medieval moralists:

> Thaȝ hym wordeȝ were wane when þay to sete wenten,
> Now ar þay stoken of sturne werk, stafful her hond.

For þaȝ men ben mery in mynde quen þay han
  mayn drynk,
A ȝere ȝernes ful ȝerne, and ȝeldeȝ neuer lyke,
Þe forme to þe fynisment foldeȝ ful selden.

(vv. 493–94, 497–99)

Gawain and Arthur, the narrator maintains, are like all men; they fail to see the consequences of their acts, not realizing how seldom the beginning ("þe forme") accords with the end. Yet the king and his knight have done exactly as they must do in a medieval romance. At the poem's beginning they are not like all men; they are superlative characters from romance whose destiny is to accept whatever adventure appears. Who ever knew a romance in which the knight did not eagerly accept the offered adventure, scorning an unknightly concern with consequences? Who ever knew the courtly Gawain to refuse to do what is "more seemly"—the motive that leads him both to rise to accept the challenge and to begin the conversation with the lady? How could Arthur choose but to yearn for some marvel? It is a custom that he through nobleness had acquired (v. 91). And how could he avoid taking his barons' advice and allowing Gawain to undertake the adventure? Yet only a few stanzas later the courtiers bitterly complain,

"Who knew euer any kyng such counsel to take
As knyȝtes in cauelaciounȝ on Crystmasse gomneȝ!"

(vv. 682–83)

And the narrator himself warns that though Gawain was happy to begin "þose gomneȝ" we should not be surprised "þaȝ þe ende be heuy" (vv. 495–96). From an ideal court of romance we have moved to a real court, whose members even complain about the government. From a sympathetic admirer of the court the narrator has become a stern moralist who can compare the beautiful creatures of Camelot to mere men befuddled by drink.

The narrator has cast his fictional creation into the context of the real world. He now judges the court not in terms of romance, in which one is obligated to take on impossible adventures, but in those of Christian morality, in which such an act is "surquidré," the sin of which the Green Knight accuses the court and which we later learn he has come to test. "Surquidré," explains Gower in the *Mirour de l'Omme,* is of such high pride that it believes it has no equal in this life:

> Mais neporquant par s'enticer
> Sovent as gens fait comencer
> Tieu chose que jammais nul jour
> Ne la pourront bien terminer;
> Dont en le fin leur falt ruer
> De sus en jus leur grant honour,
> Leur sen deschiet en grant folour,
> Et leur richesce en povre atour;
> Leur peas destourne en guerroier,
> Leur repos chiet en grant labour
> Tornent leur joyes en dolour:
> Vei la le fin de Surquider!
>
> (vv. 1477–88)

[Nevertheless, by its enticements men are often led to begin something they can never finish well; in the end their great honor is inevitably cast from high to low, their wisdom falls into folly, and their riches turn to poverty; their peace turns to war, their repose becomes hard labor, turning their joy into sadness: behold the end of the Overweening Man!]

This, as Gawain finally recognizes, is exactly what happened to him. He resolves that the green lace will guard him from this sin in the future:

> "And þus, quen pryde schal me pryk for prowes of armes,
> Þe loke to þis luf-lace schal leþe my hert."
>
> (vv. 2437–38)

When Gawain returns to Camelot, the whole court adopts this reminder of pride as its emblem. Arthur and his courtiers have also learned the lesson, although, as we shall see in the next chapter, their laughter shows that they have learned even more than Gawain.

The touch is light and Gawain's shame dissolves in good-natured laughter, but such didactic passages are as important to the poem as the more mimetic elements. They remind the audience of a larger world than a romance usually contains, and they thus provide as telling a perspective on Gawain's experiences as the reversals of the viewpoint at Bercilak's castle. Immediately after the narrator's intrusion at the beginning of the second fit appears the passing of the seasons, a powerful exemplum of the fact that a "ȝere ȝernes ful ȝerne," and when Gawain is next mentioned, thinking of his impending journey, the audience is prepared to regard him in the broader framework of nature and morality. Again when Gawain leaves Bercilak's castle, the narrator intrudes to remind us of his presence and of both his and our distance from the hero (vv. 1991–97). Finally, when the blow has been delivered, Gawain himself manages to step momentarily out of his knightly character. He thinks that he might be excused for being fooled by a woman. Adam, Solomon, Samson, and David, he says, all fell in the same way (vv. 2416–19). His precedents are entirely biblical, as untouched by romance as the ironic opening of the second fit. In each case the tone is drawn neither from romance nor the dream vision, but from the medieval sermon.

Such didactic intrusions may at first glance seem artless. They are actually touches of the most subtle art, showing us that Bercilak's and the narrator's views of the action are as important as Gawain's and that in this poem romance is only one part of the whole. Just as the poet's realistic techniques serve finally a psychological, symbolic end, so his skilled handling of the whole narrative has another, more important purpose. His shifting viewpoints and his didactic intrusions show that this purpose includes more than simply telling a tale in a vivid manner; he is scrutinizing Gawain's experience from all relevant angles. We must now consider the problem of what that experience is.

The Meaning

Sir Gawain and the Green Knight is so complex a poem
that it lends itself to many different interpretations, and
ultimately each reader must decide what particular meaning *Sir Gawain* has for him. Yet there is a common basis
for understanding even so rich a work as this, for whatever deeper implications a narrative contains, its readers
should be able to agree on answers to the more elementary
questions of meaning: "What is this work about?" "What
is its subject and main theme?" That readers of *Sir Ga-*
wain, who can agree on so much else about the poem, can
not yet agree on these simple matters is partly because they
have seldom taken them seriously; like those biblical
scholars whom Hugo of St. Victor reprimands for leaping
directly to the *sententia* without first studying the *littera*
and *sensus*, critics have so concerned themselves with this
poem's deeper meanings that they have overlooked and
sometimes obscured its simple subject and main theme.[1]
But principally this disagreement arises because the poem
has never been interpreted in the light of its literary con-

text. Read apart from other romances, it is indeed obscure, and one cannot be sure what *Sir Gawain* is about nor whether it is ritual, religious allegory, or simple adventure. Within that context its simplest meaning is quite clear: The subject of this romance is romance itself.

We have seen this demonstrated in each of the preceding chapters, for the poet's style, his characterizations, and his changes in the beheading and temptation tales have the immediate effect of making his materials more emphatically romantic. Everything becomes superlative; Arthur is the "hendest," Gawain the "best," the Green Knight both the "myriest" and the "worst," and even his chapel is the "corsedest." The result is an enthusiastic intensification of the traditional qualities of romance, with the hero more courtly, the challenger more sharply opposed to knighthood, the lady more irresistible, and the beheading more ghastly than in any work in the tradition. In itself this is not significant, for every romance is about romance and every hero in this genre is a representative of chivalric virtue who must overcome obstacles that test the ideal he maintains. Every romance is also, like *Sir Gawain,* cast in the superlative; such tests require the greatest of heroes and the most difficult of obstacles.

In this sense, the Gawain-poet's treatment of *Caradoc* is simply a development of the process that began when the author of *Caradoc* adapted the Irish tale to the conventions of romance. What does significantly differentiate *Sir Gawain* from *Caradoc* and from other romances is that alongside these exaggerated traditional elements the poet introduces equally emphatic untraditional materials, such as the surprising conclusion, and unromantic points of view, such as we noted in the previous chapter. They introduce another set of values, drawn from outside the framework of traditional assumptions within which the romance ideal is usually tested; the result is the testing of those assumptions themselves. When Gawain returns shamefaced to Camelot from an opponent who only laughs at him, we recognize that the poem has moved from pure romance to a gently satiric anti-romance, since even the reader cannot suppress a smile at the hero's expense, and comedy is not the stuff of which romance heroes are made.

The poem's theme, like its subject, is completely traditional, though significantly modified by the touch of comedy that places it in a new and nonromantic perspective. This is renown, the central ideal of chivalry and a universal topic of medieval romance, in which a concern for fame is the preoccupation of every good knight.[2] The poet carefully added this theme to each episode of the narrative, and the theme of fame more significantly than the bargains or the lace connects the beheading with the temptation and unifies the entire poem. It links the two most important subsidiary themes, the conflicts of courtesy with churlishness and of pride with humility, and unites with the plot even those episodes that the poet added to his sources and that seem to many to stand outside the essential structure of the work—Arthur's encounter with the challenger, the nonsexual elements of the bedroom scenes, the guide's temptation of Gawain, and the hero's return to the court.

Modern readers seldom recognize the importance of fame in *Sir Gawain* because that ideal and the vocabulary associated with it are no longer very meaningful. We are apt to associate fame with publicity rather than with virtue, thinking it an "infirmity of the noble mind," controlled by chance rather than deeds. This attitude is found even in the fourteenth century, in *The House of Fame,* where Fame is a capricious deity, and in *The Speculum Gy de Warewyke,* where the converted Guy is brought to realize the difference between Heaven's meed and knightly renown. But the fourteenth-century reader could still think of fame as an ethical force, and unless we also appreciate that attitude we remain unmoved by lines like Gerames' call to battle in *Huon de Bordeux*—"Let vs there do as good knyghtys ought to do, to the entente that good songes may be made of vs" [3]—and we find it puzzling that a knight like Lancelot (in Chrétien's *Lancelot*) should be so concerned about simply riding in a cart. Some of us even find it difficult to sympathize with Roland when he refuses to sound his horn because he fears the loss of his fame ("En dulce France en perdreie mun los," v. 1054).

To a medieval reader Roland's motive was credible and even admirable, despite its touch of foolhardy pride, because he knew that fame is more than mere reputation. One earns it by strenuous and virtuous deeds, as did Bevis of Hampton, who was widely known for a doughty knight "In yche lond, that he rideth and goos,/ For to wynne price and loos" (vv. 21–22). Having won his fame, a knight is obligated to maintain it by acting in the manner for which he is renowned. As the young Alexander explains at the beginning of *Cligés*, renown and inaction do not go well together ("Ne s'acordent pas bien ansanble,/ Repos et los," vv. 157–58),[4] and constant knightly effort is required of the good man. To lose one's fame by a failure to act—or worse, by an unchivalric action such as riding in a cart—is to acquire shame, for chivalric deeds are a religious duty and to fail in their performance is a sin to be avoided at all costs: "I had leuer be dismembered than to be shamed and blamed in this deed." [5]

Arthur and Gawain guard their fame as zealously as Roland and Alexander, but the nobility of their action is comically undercut by the relative triviality of the virtue for which they are famed, pure courtesy, and by the outcome of their conflict with the nameless churl who tests this fame, this pattern of noble conduct, and who finally demonstrates the limitations, even the slight absurdity of that ideal. Since this new theme was the Gawain-poet's most important modification of the tales he inherited, we can trace it most clearly in the passages he added to these tales in order to make their new function clear. So far we have only touched upon those additions; now that we know something of the poet's style and use of traditional materials we can reexamine the plot to define more clearly what the poem is about and why *Sir Gawain* is at once a brilliant affirmation and a comic rejection of the life that was romance.

Renown in the beheading episode

The poet's first thematic addition to the beheading tale is the Green Knight's speech explaining why he has come to Camelot. The challenger gave no such explanation in *Caradoc*, since his motive concerned the hero rather than the whole court. He therefore merely greeted the king and demanded a boon, though the later redactors added a few words of praise to the greeting: " 'Sire,' faict il, 'je vous sallue comme le meilleur et le plus hault roy qui pour ce jour sur terre regne.' " In *Sir Gawain* this is greatly expanded, and the expansions change it from a speech of praise to a statement of the court's renown, not its virtues but its reputation for them:

> "Bot for þe los of þe, lede, is lyft vp so hyȝe,
> And þy burȝ and þy burnes best ar holden,
> Stifest vnder stel-gere on stedes to ryde,
> Þe wyȝtest and þe worþyest of þe worldes kynde,
> Preue for to play wyth in oþer pure laykeȝ,
> And here is kydde cortaysye, as I haf herd carp."
> (vv. 258–63)

The virtues are neatly bracketed within the important qualification that they rest only on hearsay so far as the challenger is concerned—"los . . . lyft vp so hyʒe," "as I haf herd carp." Bercilak then requests his boon, not simply asking it, as Éliavres did, but capitalizing on the fame of Arthur and his court and using it as the basis for his demand:

> "Bot if þou be so bold as alle burneʒ tellen,
> Þou wyl grant me godly þe gomen þat I ask
>   bi ryʒt."
>
> (vv. 272–74)

Although neither Arthur nor Gawain realizes it, this speech rather than the challenge itself establishes the terms of the beheading test and the conditions for the action of the entire poem. The logic that the Green Knight employs here will reappear at crucial points throughout the adventure—when the lady wins her kisses and when the Green Knight urges Gawain to stand still and receive the return-blow. You are famous for bravery and courtesy, the Green Knight reminds Arthur. If that fame of which "alle burneʒ tellen" is deserved, you will act in the manner for which you are renowned. If you fail to live up to your reputation, your renown is but empty appearance, pride and "surquidré" rather than the virtuous substance of knighthood.

This is the issue in the whole adventure. The problem is not simply whether Gawain can keep the series of bargains he has made but whether he, the Round Table's representative, can live up to the fame of Arthur's court. The poet clearly states this essential fact in Bercilak's final explanation of Morgan's plot. There is no mention of the bargains; they were only the means:

> "Ho wayned me vpon þis wyse to your wynne halle
> For to assay þe surquidré, ʒif hit soth were
> Þat rennes of þe grete renoun of þe Rounde Table;

Ho wayned me þis wonder your wytteʒ to reue,
For to haf greued Gaynour and gart hir to dyʒe."
(vv. 2456–60)

We have already noted the weakness of Morgan's enmity
for Guenevere. It seems imposed upon the fabric of the
poem, suggested perhaps by Éliavres' words to the queen
in *Caradoc,* and it is probably here only to bring a completed cycle of action to the poem. The rest of the explanation is far more important, and *Caradoc* contains no suggestion for it; it grows from the logic of *Sir Gawain* itself,
and it is clearly not imposed on the poem. Furthermore,
Morgan is a good deal more successful in this part of her
plan. Her emissary does manage their "wytteʒ to reue"
when he comes to test the great renown of Camelot (for it
is "folly" to undertake the adventure, as Arthur himself
admits—v. 324), and he does find that this renown is mere
"surquidré," pride and boasting.

Therefore, when Bercilak taunts the Round Table with
its failure to live up to its reputation, he is emphasizing
the motive that underlies the entire action:

"What, is þis Arþureʒ hous," quoþ þe haþel þenne,
"þat al þe rous rennes of þurʒ ryalmes so mony?
Where is now your sourquydrye and your conquestes,
Your gryndellayk and your greme, and your grete wordes?
Now is þe reuel and þe renoun of þe Rounde Table
Ouerwalt wyth a worde of on wyʒes speche,
For al dares for drede wythoute dynt schewed!"
(vv. 309–15)

In *Caradoc* the briefer reference to fame in the challenger's taunt was merely an insult, though it moves
Arthur deeply to think that his reputation could be threatened. In *Sir Gawain* the reference to renown develops
logically from the challenger's opening speech and from
the assumptions of knighthood on which he had based it.

The taunt moves Arthur not only to grief but to shame, anger, and action.

He seizes the axe, swings it about, and is just about to strike when Gawain interrupts with the request that he be allowed to take on the adventure. When Arthur, so fierce the moment before, meekly surrenders the axe to Gawain, it is apparent that the king has failed, for to take up an adventure that one does not finish is "surquidré," especially when one takes it up with so boastful an announcement of his intentions as Arthur makes. Yet it is also clear that Arthur has somehow failed the test even before Gawain's interruption and that Gawain must step forward not only to show his loyalty to the king but also to save the integrity of the court. Critics have given relatively little attention to this episode, but we can be sure the poet's audience scrutinized it carefully because of both the great symbolic importance of Arthur in medieval romance and the rarity of a situation in which he undertakes and then fails an adventure.[6] This is the sort of action that one expects from Kay, not the king (and, as we have noted, the author of *The Grene Knight* replaces Arthur with Kay). The episode fully deserves the attention its novelty draws, for Arthur's failure foreshadows Gawain's fall and defines success and failure in this poem. It shows that the bargains are not as important as they seem; Arthur fails not because he cannot keep the bargain but because he does not live up to the fame of Camelot as it is defined in the Green Knight's opening speech.

In that speech we are told that there are two aspects of Camelot's fame, each of which its champion must display, its famous bravery and its "kydde cortaysye." The frightened courtiers quickly disqualify themselves. They are famed as the "stifest vnder stel-gere" (v. 260), but they are courtiers rather than warriors. They fail the test of bravery and look silently to Arthur, and the king, impelled by the rashness of his "young blood," accepts the challenge. He thus upholds Camelot's reputation for bravery, but in doing so he deserts what now becomes the most important aspect of its fame. He forgets that he is "þe hendest," and he becomes for the moment like the "methles" Green Knight, *démesuré* and churlish. This is the main point of this unusual episode. In it we are shown that in this poem manners are as important to the plot as the axe itself, for to live up to the reputation of Camelot, its champion must remain true to the courtesy that is central to that ideal. In it we are also shown the first of a series of varying scenes in which the knight and the churl face one another, each attempting to impose his own pattern of behavior on the other.

The episode begins with Arthur's elaborately courteous greeting:

> Þenn Arþour bifore þe hiȝ dece þat auenture byholdeȝ
> And rekenly hym reuerenced, for rad was he neuer,
> And sayde, "Wyȝe, welcum iwys to þis place,
> Þe hede of þis ostel Arthour I hat;
> Liȝt luflych adoun and lenge, I þe praye,
> And quat-so þy wylle is we schal wyt after."
>
> (vv. 250–55)

Despite the challenger's hostile and frightening appearance, the king is neither fearful nor hasty (*rad* can mean either [7]). He courteously invites the stranger to act in the proper courtly manner—to alight graciously ("luflych" from his mount, to be entertained, and then afterwards to state his business. This is exactly the course followed by the courteous Gawain when he arrives at Bercilak's castle and by the courtly Bredbeddle in *The Grene Knight*. However, our Green Knight abruptly refuses Arthur's invitation and delivers one of his own, demanding that the court's champion not only accept the challenge but that he do so

in the challenger's own fierce ("felle") and churlishly vigorous ("lepe lyȝtly") manner:

> "If any freke be so felle to fonde þat I telle
> Lepe lyȝtly me to, and lach þis weppen."
>
> (vv. 291–92)

Arthur's failure is that when he does take up the challenge he does so in exactly the churlish manner that the
Green Knight had demanded. His shame and anger lead
him to forget his famous courtesy entirely. He waxes "as
wroth as wynde" (v. 319)—a simile from nature that suggests the beginning of a resemblance between the king
and the churlish Green Knight. He surrenders to his natural impulse ("bi kynde"), and he moves away from the
dais and "stod þat stif mon nere" (v. 321):

> And sayde, "Haþel, by heuen, þyn askyng is nys,
> And as þou foly hatȝ frayst, fynde þe behoues.
> I know no gome þat is gast of þy grete wordes;
> Gif me now þy geserne, vpon Godeȝ halue,
> And I schal bayþen þy bone þat þou boden habbes."
>
> (vv. 323–27)

His speech, like his physical location, is now closer to that
of the Green Knight, rich in expletives ("by heuen," "vpon
Godeȝ halue"), insults ("þy grete wordes," "þou foly hatȝ
frayst"), and boasts ("I schal bayþen þy bone"). In the next
line he rushes forward to grasp the axe:

> Lyȝtly lepeȝ he hym to, and laȝt at his honde.
>
> (v. 328)

The challenger had demanded, "Lepe lyȝtly me to, and
lach þis weppen," and Arthur has done exactly that. But
whereas he has capitulated to the challenger's demand,
the Green Knight remains true to his own churlish self.

He alights not "luflych," as Arthur had asked, but in the "felle" manner he had proposed:

Þen feersly þat oþer freke vpon fote lyʒtis.

(v. 329)

The use of "þat oþer freke" and of "lyʒtis," echoing "lyʒtly" in the previous line describing Arthur's action, emphasizes the similarity between the king and the Green Knight. Arthur has become for the moment a churl. He seizes the weapon and,

Now hatʒ Arthure his axe, and þe halme grypeʒ,
And sturnely stureʒ hit aboute, þat stryke wyth hit þoʒt.

(vv. 330–31)

Prior to these lines and those immediately preceding, the poet had paid little attention to Arthur's movement. Closely described violent movement, like violent speech, is characteristic of churls rather than gentlemen. Yet here the poet describes Arthur's actions by the technique of exact specification that he usually reserves for the Green Knight. He emphasizes every movement as the king leaps fiercely forward, grasps the axe and sternly swings it about, as if he, like the Green Knight in the final scene, intends first to terrify his victim. The courteous Arthur, who was never before "rad," has given way to "la fretta/ que l'onestade ad ogni atto dismagha." The Green Knight, on the other hand, is silent and slow-moving for the first and almost the only time in the poem, his cool deliberation contrasting markedly with Arthur's churlish haste: "He stroked his berde,/ And wyth a countenaunce dryʒe he droʒ doun his cote" (vv. 334–35).

Arthur's action is so carefully justified by the dramatic situation (the shame and anger that he feels) and by the motivation that the poet provides in his characterization of the king ("his ȝonge blod and his brayn wylde") that we accept and perhaps even applaud this show of temper. But then Gawain interrupts with a long and ceremonial speech; it is a superlative display of the courtesy for which Camelot is famed, and it differs sharply from the manner that Arthur has adopted. Perhaps Gawain's speech reminds even the king of his obligation to courtesy, for his churlish ferocity immediately disappears. He now consults his barons and, with their consent, he delivers the axe with his formal blessing to the kneeling hero. The solemn and ceremonial tone of Arthur's surrender of the axe contrasts as markedly with the churlish haste in which he obtained it as Gawain's speech does with Arthur's angry words. The elaborate courtesy of this passage thus salvages some of Camelot's reputation at the same time it shows us that Arthur's failure in the challenge is a failure in manners. Then Gawain succeeds completely, and he saves the fame of Camelot by taking up the adventure with both the bravery and the courtesy for which it is renowned. Yet, since the king himself has failed, it is clear that the hero's triumph can only be temporary. The end will be heavy, Gawain will find himself unable to maintain his perfect character, and he too will desert his renowned courtesy to descend momentarily to the churlish level of his opponent.

The theme of identity and Gawain's failure

The theme of renown is even more important in the scenes at Bercilak's castle than it is at Arthur's court, and in them the theme is deepened and extended. *Yder* offered no suggestion for this. In that work the tempted knight is a young and unknown man whose only task is to avoid the queen's embraces. Gawain's problem, as we have seen, is considerably more complicated, and his greatest difficulty is caused by his own reputation. He has lived up to his fame at Camelot, and when he leaves that court he is still the perfect knight "for gode knawen." Here in Bercilak's castle the faultless Gawain acquires his touch of shame. When he leaves this court, his renown, his public character, is still intact, but beneath the armor that symbolized his perfection when he left Camelot he now wears the green lace, the concealed emblem of the villainy that will become public at the Green Chapel. Thus, at the end of the episode at Bercilak's castle, Gawain, like the Green Knight, disguises his true identity. He does not completely realize this, for his character changes slightly at Bercilak's castle and his very identity is brought into question by the lady.

Despite the many differences between this episode and the opening scene at Camelot, the temptation is a variation on that first scene, and its general outlines are the same. Here, as in Camelot, renown is the motive for the action of the knight who is confronted with an antagonist who demands that he desert his perfect courtesy and adopt a more churlish manner of conduct. Of course, the tone of these scenes is much different, since at Bercilak's castle renown is a source of comic misunderstanding rather than high adventure. We have already noted how much Bercilak's courtiers make of Gawain's fame. They are beside themselves with joy when they hear that the famous Gawain is their visitor. Now, they happily tell one another, we shall learn all about "love-talking." The lady is just as eager to learn from this "fyne fader of nurture," and she uses the pattern of conduct appropriate to the girl in *Brun de Branlant*, who loves Gawain for his reputation. However, she not only announces that Gawain's fame has won her love, she uses this fame in the same way that the Green Knight did, arguing first that it was his fame that attracted her to him, and then demanding that he act in

the way for which he is renowned: "Why! are ʒe lewed,
þat alle þe los weldeʒ? . . . I com hider sengel and sitte/
To lerne at yow sum game." (vv. 1528–32). Her argument
fails, even though it earns her kisses and makes Gawain
very uncomfortable, because she and he define his famous
courtesy in different ways. He attempts to remain true to
the "clean courtesy" of the Pentangle, while she invokes
the traditional courtesy of Gawain, the famous lover in
medieval romance. It is this ambivalence of Gawain's
fame that poses his comic dilemma.

It also provides the lady with grounds for a more powerful attack on Gawain. In our study of the temptation tale
we remarked that an important change in the nature of
the temptation occurs when Gawain refuses the lady's
blunt offer of her "cors." She turns to leave, admitting her
failure. Then she suddenly turns back, and the temptation
shifts from a simple trial of continence to a more complex
testing of Gawain's famous courtesy. At the same time the
theme of fame is subtly modulated, for when the lady
turns back she astonishes Gawain with a speech of "ful
stor wordeʒ"—"ful stor" not in quantity, since she speaks
only two lines, but in import:

> And as ho stod, ho stonyed hym wyth ful stor wordeʒ:
> "Now he þat spedeʒ vche spech þis disport ʒelde yow!
> Bot þat ʒe be Gawan, hit gotʒ in mynde."
>
> (vv. 1291–93)

Gawain betrays his astonishment by the haste ("freschly")
and unusual curtness of his reply:

> "Querefore?" quoþ þe freke, and freschly he askeʒ,
> Ferde lest he hade fayled in fourme of his castes.
>
> (vv. 1294–95)

Gawain is astonished, even frightened, at the thought
that his identity could be in doubt, and he knows immedi-

ately that only a failure in courtesy could be responsible ("fayled in fourme of his castes"). He realizes that a knight's reputation is a knight's identity and that he is the famous Gawain only so long as he acts in the way for which he is famed. The lady recognizes the advantage she has gained, and she insists that one so famous for courtesy,

> "Couth not lyʒtly haf lenged so long wyth a lady,
> Bot he had craued a cosse, bi his courtaysye."
>
> (vv. 1299–1300)

Gawain has no choice but to submit, for although the lady's tone is light her words have serious implications.

The situation is the same as that in which Gawain finds himself in Branch V of *Perlesvaus*.[8] He is riding through a wild forest when he comes upon a beautiful pavilion. In it are two lovely ladies who inform him that the place suffers from an "evil custom" that can be removed only if he selects one of them for his bed-partner that night. Gawain, whose continence rather than courtesy is on trial, merely thanks them and forestalls further conversation by going to sleep.

> "Par Dieu," fet l'une a l'autre, "se ce fust cil Gavains qui niés est le roi Artu, il parlast a nos autrement, e trovissions en lui plus de deduit que en cestui; mest cist est uns Gavains contrefez."
>
> (ll. 1813–16)
>
> ["By God," said the one to the other, "if that had been that Gawain who is nephew to King Arthur, he would have spoken to us differently, and we would have found more delight in him than this one. This is a counterfeit Gawain."]

The next day Gawain himself hears the charge that he is a "Gavains contrefez" when he has to fight two knights who meet him outside the pavilion. Only his victory proves his identity. In *Sir Gawain* the hero believes that there is an easier, more courteous way to prove that he is Gawain. He meekly allows the lady to kiss him. She is so satisfied with this stratagem that she uses it again on the second day, telling him at the very beginning of their conversation,

> "Sir, ȝif ȝe be Wawen, wonder me þynnkeȝ."
>
> (v. 1481)

She thereby earns her second kiss with far less delay than the first.

That both *Sir Gawain* and *Perlesvaus* should employ this concept of identity is not surprising, for in medieval romance one's fame, his "good name" (the survival of the idiom shows the tenacity of the ideal), and his identity are closely related. Since renown implies a pattern of conduct, to lose one's fame is to lose one's identity, to become a different person who acts in a different way. Thus a knight's name, which is at once his identity and his fame, is "an augur and program for life," [9] a sign of what his future conduct will be. (Perhaps that is why Bercilak so carefully conceals his name until the initial bargain is fulfilled.) Thus, in *Floriant et Florete*, Floriant's son is baptized "Froart" because so many shields will be "frouez" (broken in pieces) by him when he is grown.[10] Other knights, like the young Perceval, must discover their own names and simultaneously their destinies. Once one has a name, his duty as a knight is to maintain the standard of conduct that it implies. When the author of *Aiol* wants to summarize an honorable life, he writes:

> Del fort roi Mibrien vos conterai la vie;
> Il se fist baptisier el non sainte Marie,
> Son non li gardent bien, et nel remuerent mie.
>
> (vv. 10964–66)

[I shall tell you the life of stout King Mibrien. He had himself baptized in the name of Saint Mary; he guarded his name well and never changed again.]

Gawain was especially proud of his name. He never concealed it,[11] and in *Le Chevalier à l'épée*, in which he is tested by a hunter-host, he announces proudly:

"Sire," fet il, "j'e non Gauvain.
Et sui nies au bon roi Artur.
De ce soiez tot aseür,
Que onques mon non ne chanjai."

(vv. 742–45)

["Sir," he said, "I am named Gawain, and I am nephew to the good King Arthur. Of this be entirely sure, that I never change my name."]

When Bercilak's lady doubts Gawain's identity, she thus invokes a powerful concept, and Gawain, intent on guarding his name well, has little choice but to grant her the kisses. Furthermore, her use of the concept of identity and the link she establishes between it, Gawain's fame, and his actions are more than clever devices for winning the kisses. Her arguments deepen the theme of renown and connect it to the change that Gawain's character undergoes in the course of the action. Like the "fol chevalier" of *Perceval* and its descendants, Gawain finds himself in an adventure that involves his very identity. In *Perceval*, as we have seen, the hero discovers his identity and gains renown as a last step in his education as a knight; in *Sir Gawain* the hero loses his identity. He begins secure in his good name, and when the lady first greets him, she acknowledges that she knows "wel, iwysse, Sir Wowen ʒe are" (v. 1226). During his stay at Bercilak's castle, as living up to his reputation becomes more difficult, his identity becomes less secure, and the lady begins to doubt that he is the famous Gawain: "ʒif ʒe be Wawen, wonder me þynnkeȝ." Finally, at the Green Chapel, the challenger has no doubts. He tells the hero, "Þou art not Gawayn . . . þat is so goud halden" (v. 2270). The Green Knight is stating a fact; the man who betrays his host and conceals the lace beneath his armor is no longer the perfect Gawain who "watȝ for gode knawen" (v. 633) at the adventure's beginning.

Gawain accepts the lace, just as Arthur fails in the opening scene, because he does not really understand the nature of the test. Arthur had not recognized that courtesy as well as bravery is involved in the test. Gawain does not understand that anything but courtesy, and continence, of course, is involved. More gentlemanly than warlike, he forgets that bravery too is expected of the knight and, when he thinks he has successfully defended both his courtesy and his continence, he accepts the lace and thereby becomes guilty of cowardice.

By accepting the lace he also accepts the lady's (and, though he does not know it, her husband's) deceitful mode of conduct. Throughout these scenes, as in the scene at Camelot, the knight and his antagonist confront one another, each demanding that the other adopt an opposing mode of conduct. The lady urges that Gawain accept the intimate, and in this context churlish, relationship that she offers, while he strives manfully to keep the conversation at a safely courteous and formal level. This struggle, like that of Arthur and the Green Knight, is reflected in the manners of the participants, although in this scene the manners are contrasted in a far more subtle way than at Camelot. This is that delicate but important point of courtesy, the use of the second personal pronoun. The lady repeatedly shifts from "ȝe" to "þou." By her example she invites Gawain to do the same and to allow their relationship to take on the intimacy that the singular pronoun implies in the sophisticated literature of this period (espe-

cially the alliterative romances).[12] Gawain invariably uses
"ʒe" and thus attempts to keep the lady at a respectable
and courteous distance. The measure of his success is apparent in the pronouns that she uses. When she is winning
and the relationship is becoming dangerously intimate, she
uses "þou." Her "ʒe" is an indication that Gawain has man-
aged to force the conversation back to a more formal level.
Gawain, unlike Arthur in the opening scene, stoutly refuses to adopt his opponent's manners, and when finally he
seizes the opportunity to tell her courteously that he has
no mistress, "Ne non wil welde þe quile" (v. 1791), she
sees that she has failed; she sighs, kisses him, and rises to
leave.

But then, just as she did when she rose to leave halfway
through the first day's meeting, she turns back and resumes the temptation on a new plane. Gawain, like the
fox, is caught off his guard. Thinking his courtesy is safe,
he even uses a singular pronoun (v. 1802), but the lady is
not now concerned with his manners. She offers him the
lace simply as a means of self-preservation, and she does
not refer to his fame or his knighthood when she makes the
offer. It is thus easy for Gawain to accept the lace as if it
had nothing to do with his renowned knighthood, as if he
has not deserted his "nurture" and become what he most
feared, a "traytor to þat tolke þat þat telde aʒte." He ra-
tionalizes his betrayal as a noble "sleʒt," and he even goes
to confession with an apparently clear conscience, though
he obviously intends to make no restitution to his host.[13]
Yet his mind is a bit troubled by this betrayal, for when
he pays the host the three kisses he is careful to recall, for
his own comfort rather than his host's information, the
conditions under which the bargain was made—"þer
spared watʒ no drynk" (v. 1935).

He cannot know that he is echoing the narrator's original condemnation of the court—"Men ben mery in mynde

quen þay han mayn drynk" (v. 497). Nor does he know that
the host and his challenger are the same, that in betraying
one he is betraying the other and that in failing either he
is failing to live up to his famous courtly perfection. Most
important, he is ignorant of the churlish fault within him
that is symbolized by the concealed lace. His knightly
nature, so he thinks, is still intact.

The guide's temptation of Gawain

If *Sir Gawain and the Green Knight* were really to be as
tragic as Gawain thinks it is at the end of the adventure,
the hero would go immediately from his betrayal of the
host to the scene in which the return-blow is delivered.
From his own point of view, he has fallen into the worst
of chivalric sins, disloyalty and cowardice. However, *Sir
Gawain* is essentially a comic poem, and the poet has no
intention of allowing the audience to judge the hero as
harshly as Gawain insists upon judging himself. He is
therefore subjected to one final temptation, the guide's attempt to dissuade him from keeping his appointment with
the Green Knight. Gawain stoutly resists it. Whatever the
danger, he will keep to his agreement and trusting only to
God—and perhaps to the untested lace—he will submit to
the return-blow. His action assures us that his one failing
is indeed slight, and our last impression of Gawain before
he arrives at the Green Chapel is thus not of a traitor but
of a brave and loyal knight—not perfect, for he has the
lace, but as nearly perfect as a knight in this world can be.

This episode deserves more attention than critics have
given to it, for it is one of the poet's most significant additions to the challenge tale (Kay's remarks on the impossi-
bility of the adventure in *Caradoc* provide only the faint-
est suggestion for it),[14] and it is pivotal to the entire ac-

tion. It draws together a number of previously separate minor themes, and it firmly links them with the major theme of renown and with the series of bargains that Gawain has made. Perhaps its most important function is the emphatic reassertion of the major theme. Renown is of great implicit importance in the lady's last temptation of Gawain, but explicitly it has little connection with the lace, for the lady changed the basis of her argument and appealed not to Gawain's knightly concern for his fame but to his human desire for self-preservation. In the guide's temptation these two concerns are united, since he offers a way for Gawain to preserve both his life and his fame. Furthermore, the subsidiary themes of appearance and reality and of disguise are here interwoven with the theme of renown. Gawain himself is now disguised; he has left Bercilak's castle with the appearance of knighthood concealing the reality of the lace. The guide now offers him a means of extending that disguise to cover an even more shameful action. In this manner, renown, the abstract quality to which Gawain must be true, is linked to the network of bargains, the specific agreements that he must fulfill. Thus, the bargains, the unifying actions of the plot, are joined with renown, the unifying theme of the poem.

To understand fully the function of the guide's offer to conceal Gawain's flight, one must be aware that loyalty, Gawain's greatest virtue, is "trawþe" rather than the abstract quality that we designate by "loyalty" today. "Trawþe" is more a matter of *lex* than of *fides*, for the loyal knight is one who is not only faithful to an ideal but who faithfully keeps his plighted word, the contracts he has made, whether with a host or his liege lord. It is to a series of such definite contractual obligations that Gawain must be faithful if he is to remain the "tulk of tale most trwe." At the beginning of the adventure he swears to appear for the return-blow. There is nothing in that agreement that obliges him to abjure any sort of charms that might be helpful. His Pentangle and brown diamonds are such charms, and the green lace is another. Accepting that lace from the lady does not break his initial agreement with the challenger. Gawain's second bargain is with the host; three times over the two agree that they will exchange their "winnings" at the end of each day. The lady offers Gawain yet another bargain, though it is less formally expressed; she will give him the green lace if he agrees to conceal it from her husband. He does so, and he is thus guilty of betraying his host. Compared to the initial bargain with the challenger, the agreement with the host, so Gawain thinks, is a mere trifle. Breaking it will indeed be "noble," for the girdle is only a "little thing" that may help him in the coming encounter, and obviously it pleases the lady to give it to him. He believes that he has kept two of the three bargains he has made and that his contract with the Green Knight is still unbroken.

In order that Gawain shall be tested completely, the plot requires an episode that will have the same relation to the initial bargain as the lady's temptation has to his agreement with the host. The scene between Gawain and the guide is such an episode. As the lady did, the guide offers him a chance to break one agreement by entering into another. Like both the lady and the Green Knight, the guide begins the test on a purely physical plane. He vividly describes the hopelessness of Gawain's position, and he characterizes the challenger as the embodiment of merciless terror. In his description the Green Knight is a completely fearful giant—"More is he þen any mon vpon myddelerde" (v. 2100), and he has none of the merry and attractive qualities that modified his grotesqueness at Camelot. The guide tells Gawain flatly that if he goes to the Green Chapel he will be killed. When Gawain is apparently unmoved by this threat, the temptation shifts to a more subtle plane and the theme of fame is invoked. Now, however, Gawain has accepted the lace, and the guide does not argue that the hero should live up to his fame. Instead, he offers him a chance to move more deeply into error. Flee, the guide advises,

> "And I schal hyȝ me hom aȝayn, and hete yow fyrre
> Þat I schal swere bi God and alle his gode halȝeȝ.
> As help me God and þe halydam, and oþeȝ innoghe.
> Þat I schal lelly yow layne, and lance neuer tale
> Þat euer ȝe fondet to fle for freke þat I wyst."
>
> (vv. 2121–25)

In effect, Gawain is offered a chance to realize in action what is already implied by his possession of the lace, to retain the appearance of knighthood without its reality. He rises to the occasion:

> "Grant merci," quoþ Gawayn, and gruchyng he sayde:
> "Wel worth þe, wyȝe, þat woldeȝ my gode,
> And þat lelly me layne, I leue wel þou woldeȝ.
> Bot helde þou hit neuer so holde, and I here passed,
> Founded for ferde for to fle, in fourme þat þou telleȝ,
> I were a knyȝt kowarde, I myȝt not be excused."
>
> (vv. 2126–31)

Gawain may be tempted by the guide's offer, for he answers "gruchyng," but he will have no part of it. He is again the knight that he was when he left Camelot, and his last words to the guide have the same tone of chivalric forbearance that he displayed when he left Camelot:

> "Ful wel con dryȝtyn schape
> His seruaunteȝ for to saue."
>
> (vv. 2138–39)

The guide, recognizing that his temptation has failed, displays a churlish anger:

"Mary!" quoþ þat oþer mon, "now þou so much spelleʒ,
Þat þou wilt þyn awen nye nyme to þyseluen,
And þe lyst lese þy lyf, þe lette I ne kepe.
Haf her þi helme on þy hede, þi spere in þi honde."

(vv. 2140–43)

The shift from "ʒe," which he had used almost exclusively until now, to "þou," the anger, and the poet's later designation of the guide as "þe wyʒe in þe wod" (v. 2152), which suggests a wild man, may show that Gawain's tempter is, as some critics believe, Bercilak in another shape.[15] Whoever he is, whether Bercilak or one of his men, he has offered the hero a villainous means of preserving his fame and yet escaping its obligations. Gawain remains true to his knighthood and refuses to adopt this mode of conduct. The guide himself pays tribute to Gawain's virtue, for when he hands him the helm and spear, he addresses Gawain in the elaborate fashion suitable to the knight who now carries them—"Now fareʒ wel, on Godeʒ half, Gawayn þe noble!" (v. 2149). He is again Gawain the noble, however ironically the guide may have intended that epithet, and from this point forward the poet returns to the small, chivalric vocabulary for designating Gawain that he had used in the opening scene. The hero is "Gawain," "knyʒt" or "prynce" from the moment he rejects the guide's temptation to the moment the return-blow is delivered.

The rehabilitation of Gawain accomplished in this scene is the end of a process that began before his departure from Bercilak's castle. Just as he did when he left Camelot, he ceremoniously dons his armor, though he does not forget to put on the green lace first. The poet intends this to remind us of Gawain's original departure from Camelot, for he is careful to tell us that "Al watʒ fresch as vpon fyrst" (v. 2019). As Gawain's knighthood is reestablished, so is the Green Knight's churlishness brought again to the foreground. This begins with the guide's characterization of the terrible opponent that Gawain must face. Then comes the Green Chapel, the last variation upon Camelot and the opposite of that seat of "kydde cortaysye." At last, the Green Knight himself appears on the scene. First there is a great noise, the rushing and ringing as he sharpens his axe. Then there is a shout from above Gawain's head, more whetting of the blade, and finally, with characteristic vigor and haste, the challenger comes "Whyrlande out of a wro wyth a felle weppen" (v. 2222):

> And þe gome in þe grene gered as fyrst
> Boþ þe lyre and þe leggez, lokkez and berde.
>
> (vv. 2227–28)

Like Gawain, he is "gered as fyrst," though there is little suggestion here of the merriment that tempered his churlishness at Camelot. Both Gawain and the Green Knight are as they were at "fyrst," and the poet emphasizes the essential qualities of each as he prepares for their final encounter.

The new test at the Green Chapel

At the Green Chapel Gawain fulfills the initial bargain and submits to the return-blow, but a great deal has happened since the agreement was made at Camelot and more than his submission to the blow is now involved. Even as he fulfills the requirements of the first test he is tested further, and here Gawain, like Arthur at Camelot, becomes for the moment a churl. He temporarily loses both his famous courtesy and his knightly identity. It is this new testing rather than the return-blow itself that shapes the action in the last encounter of the challenger and the hero. The two interruptions of the return-blow and its final delivery are, of course, linked to the temptations, but the poet utilizes that parallel in action to develop the theme of his romance even further.

When Gawain appears at the Green Chapel, he calls out for the challenger to show himself, and he announces his coming by "Now is gode Gawayn goande ryȝt here" (v. 2214). He may feel that he has a right to this flattering epithet, for he has kept the initial agreement, something that only "gode Gawayn" would do. The Green Knight seems to agree, since he congratulates him for appearing "as truee mon schulde" (v. 2241). The challenger warns him to "Busk no more debate þen I þe bede þenne" (v. 2248), and Gawain complies, briefly announcing that he will stand still and receive the blow. The Green Knight heaves the great axe aloft and brings it downward. But then the blow is interrupted; Gawain "schranke a lytel with þe schulderes for þe scharp yrne" (v. 2267). The situation is the same as that in *Caradoc,* except that the change in location requires a different reason for the interruption of the blow, but Gawain's shrinking leads to a new development altogether. The poet invents a long speech for the Green Knight to replace Éliavres' words to the king, and in it, as in most of the Gawain-poet's additions to *Caradoc,* the new theme of *Sir Gawain* accounts for the most important features:

> "Þou art not Gawayn," quoþ þe gome, "þat is so goud halden,
> Þat neuer arȝed for no here by hylle no be vale,
> And nou þou fles for ferde er þou fele harmeȝ!
> Such cowardise of þat knyȝt cowþe I neuer here."
>
> "My hede flaȝ to my fote, and ȝet flaȝ I neuer;
> And þou, er any harme hent, arȝeȝ in hert;
> Wherfore þe better burne me burde be called
> þerfore."
>
> (vv. 2270–73, 2276–79)

Here the theme of renown is emphatically introduced. The accusation of cowardice is the same as that with which the challenger had taunted the court—"What, is þis Arþureȝ hous? . . . Al dares for drede withoute dynt schewed!" (vv. 309, 315)—and the statement that this is not the Gawain "þat is so goud halden" (v. 2270) echoes the lady's doubts that one "So god as Gawayn gaynly is halden" (v. 1297) could resist a lady. As Bercilak and the audience know, Gawain is no longer the knight who was "Voyded of vche vylany" (v. 634). That was the knight who left Camelot; the man Bercilak now addresses is one who has acquired a touch of villainy and wears the green lace.

In the last line of this speech the Green Knight emphasizes yet another aspect of the challenge. It now becomes clear that the manner in which Gawain receives the blow is as important as the blow itself. Indeed, the Green Knight seems to think it is more important, for when Gawain shunts and "arȝeȝ in hert" the challenger concludes "Wherfore þe better burne me burde be called/ þerfore." It is as if the test were concluded. Gawain seems to think it is, for he quickly offers a new bargain, one that binds him not only to receive the blow but to bear it as bravely as the challenger did at Camelot. This had not been an express part of the original agreement, and at the beginning of the scene Gawain had merely said that he would stand still. Now he formally pledges himself:

> "For I schal stonde þe a strok, and start no more
> Til þyn ax haue me hitte: haf here my trawþe."
> (vv. 2286–87)

With this assurance the Green Knight is ready to continue the test. Like the previous tests, it continues with a shift from a purely physical to a more abstract plane, and, as usual, the courtier does not realize the changed conditions. Gawain, like Arthur in the opening scene, thinks that now only bravery is involved, for bravery was all that the Green Knight emphasized when he interrupted the first swing of the axe. Now the challenger raises his weapon again and "wayteʒ as wroþely as he wode were" (v. 2289). Gawain bravely keeps his word to stand still:

> Gawayn grayþely hit bydeʒ, and glent with no membre,
> Bot stode stylle as þe ston, oþer a stubbe auþer
> þat raþeled is in roché grounde with roteʒ a hundreth.
>
> (vv. 2292–94)

But again the blow is withheld. Why does the Green Knight delay this time? The reason is apparent in the manner in which Gawain has kept his word. This time he shows that he can pass the test of bravery, but in doing so he has acquired some of the qualities of the Green Knight and his wild chapel. Formerly it was Bercilak who was associated with wild natural imagery, the grass and the bush. Now it is Gawain, just as Arthur was ("as wroþ as wynde") when he was about to give way to churlishness at Camelot. The Green Knight's purpose in withholding the axe a second time is to goad Gawain into the mode of conduct this natural imagery implies.

Merriment had reduced Arthur to uncourtly anger in Camelot, and the Green Knight adopts the same strategy here when he announces his satisfaction with the hero's new mode of action:

> þen muryly efte con he mele, þe mon in þe grene:
> "So, now þou hatʒ þi hert holle, hitte me bihous.
> Halde þe now þe hyʒe hode þat Arþur þe raʒt."
>
> (vv. 2295–97)

Knighthood is too serious a matter to bear calmly amusement at its own expense, and the challenger's merry words bring Gawain to the same churlish anger that Arthur displayed, even though the speech contains a reminder of Gawain's "hyȝe hode," his essential courtesy. Gawain becomes enraged, and his speech becomes as uncourtly as the challenger's:

> "Wy! þresch on, þou þro mon, þou þreteȝ to longe;
> I hope þat þi hert arȝe wyth þyn awen seluen."
>
> (vv. 2300–01)

The former master of "talkyng noble" has adopted the tone of the churl, with its interjections, epithets, insults, and ungentlemanly anger. Only when he has been brought to this state, to the churlish level to which Arthur descended, to the point at which his concealed villainy has become public, is the Green Knight ready to strike:

> "For soþe," quoþ þat oþer freke, "so felly þou spekeȝ,
> I wyl no lenger on lyte lette þyn ernde."
>
> (vv. 2302–03)

When the blow falls, Gawain's new personality becomes even more obvious. When Gawain sees his blood on the snow, the poet changes the manner of designating the hero that he has used since the guide's temptation, and he now begins to apply the same vocabulary to Gawain as he uses for the Green Knight. As many critics have pointed out, Gawain feels as if he has undergone a kind of rebirth, a new initiation into life. In a sense he has, for the poet retains elements of the initiation into knighthood involved in the beheading episode of *Caradoc*, but here again the sense of the initiation is reversed and Gawain, the perfect courtier, begins to act in a manner altogether new to him. He snatches up his helm, just as the Green Knight snatched up his head at Camelot, he leaps forward "more than a spear's length," exactly as far as Éliavres had to move to get his head ("plus loing qu'unge lance n'est longue"), and

Schot with his schulderez his fayre schelde vnder,
Braydez out a bryzt sworde, and bremely he spekez—
Neuer syn þat he watz burne borne of his moder
Watz he neuer in þis worlde wyze half so blyþe—
"Blynne, burne, of þy bur, bede me no mo!
I haf a stroke in þis sted withoute stryf hent,
And if þou rechez me any mo, I redyly schal quyte,
And zelde zederly azayn—and þerto ze tryst—
    and foo.
  Bot on stroke here me fallez—
  Þe couenaunt schop ryzt so,
  Fermed in Arþurez hallez—
  And þerfore, hende, now hoo!"

           (vv. 2318–30)

Gawain is so delighted that he has survived and so
pleased that he has kept the initial agreement that his manner becomes the antithesis of the ceremonial, elaborately
courteous fashion in which he first took up the adventure.
He is no longer the perfect, almost wooden courtier of that
first scene. He is an excited and relieved young man, ready
now to fight if he must.

We admire him for this, but the contrast between this
violent activity and the ceremonial restraint he displayed
when the bargain was made in "Arþurez hallez" reminds
us that by the abstemious standards of perfect courtesy
Gawain's relief and exuberance are excessive. He leaps
about like the Green Knight and he adopts that character's manner of speech, with its boasts ("I redyly schal
quyte"), its shouts ("now hoo"), its ironic epithets
("hende"), and its "breme" manner. Gawain has become
churlish, a point that the Green Knight makes clear in his
use of "vnmanerly" in his very next speech. He can now
use that word without irony, because at the same time Gawain becomes churlish in his manner the Green Knight
becomes almost a gentleman. Significantly, even in that
speech quoted above Gawain begins addressing the Green

Knight as "ȝe," and he continues to use that form throughout the rest of this scene. When Gawain leaps wildly
about, the Green Knight becomes uncharacteristically motionless, just as he was when Arthur whirled the axe about
at Camelot. He leans on his axe, pleased with the sight of
Gawain, now a doughty warrior, "Armed, ful aȝleȝ," and he
gently reminds the hero of the uncourtly anger he is now
displaying:

> "Bolde burne, on þis bent be not so gryndel.
> No mon here vnmanerly þe mysboden habbeȝ."
>
> (vv. 2338–39)

Laughing, the Green Knight explains the adventure to
Gawain, praising him for what he has accomplished and
excusing him for his one slight fault. Yet Gawain feels only
shame for what he has done:

> Alle þe blode of his brest blende in his face,
> Þat al he schrank for schome þat þe schalk talked.
>
> (vv. 2371–72)

The shamed blush—another parallel between his action
and Arthur's (cf. v. 317)—leads Gawain to a violent denunciation of himself:

> "Corsed worth cowarddyse and couetyse boþe!
> In yow is vylany and vyse þat vertue disstryeȝ."

> "For care of þy knokke cowardyse me taȝt
> To acorde me with couetyse, my kynde to forsake,
> Þat is larges and lewté þat longeȝ to knyȝteȝ."
>
> (vv. 2374–75, 2379–81)

At this point Gawain finally realizes the truth of the Green
Knight's statement "þou are not Gawayn," and he acknowledges that he has forsaken his "kynde."

Yet neither knighthood nor churlishness is to be completely defeated in this poem. As the hero and challenger have exchanged physical positions for the return-blow, so have they momentarily exchanged characters; Gawain has become a churl, and the Green Knight, who refused to adopt Arthur's courtly manner in the first scene, is now almost a gentleman. The exchange does not last long. Each retains his integrity, and at the end of the episode the Green Knight is still a churl and Gawain is once again a chevalier. The hero must therefore be restored to his knightly station, and the Green Knight, who reduced him first to churlishness and then to contrition, now becomes the agent of his restoration. He returns to Gawain both the green lace, the symbol of his touch of villainy, and his knighthood, symbolized by the formal mode of address that the Green Knight here uses for the first time in the poem. The change is marked by an explicit image of rebirth, and the lace and Gawain's knightly station are restored at precisely the same moment:

> "I halde þe polysed of þat plyȝt, and pured as clene
> As þou hadeȝ neuer forfeted syþen þou watȝ fryst borne;
> And I gif þe, sir, þe gurdel þat is golde-hemmed,
> For hit is grene as my goune. Sir Gawayn, ȝe maye
> Þenk vpon þis ilke þrepe, þer þou forth þryngeȝ
> Among prynces of prys."
>
> (vv. 2393–98)

At exactly the point Gawain receives the lace, the Green Knight changes his manner of addressing him, and the poet calls our attention to this important change by placing it in a most unusual metrical structure. When the girdle is mentioned, the respectful "sir" is set off from the rest of the half-line by an uncommon internal pause, and it is suspended between the pronoun "þe" on one side and the "gurdel" on the other—"I gif þe, *sir*, þe gurdel." At the end of the sentence, when the Green Knight presumably hands the lace to Gawain, the shift to formal address is complete—"*Sir* Gawayn, ʒe maye." A full stop at the end of the first half-line and a run-on in the second half-line is relatively uncommon in Middle English alliterative verse. Its presence here and the consequent sudden shift in rhythm insures that the audience will not miss noticing the restoration of Gawain's knightly identity, now modified by the green girdle, that allows him once again to ride forth among "prynces of prys."

Gawain is reconciled. He can now excuse his fault, something that he could not do in his previous speech and that he thought impossible when he spoke to the guide. He had told the guide that if he proved disloyal and cowardly, "I myʒt not be excused" (v. 2131). Now he recognizes that "Me burde be excused" (v. 2428). The greatest men have fallen, and even the heroes of biblical antiquity have committed the same blunder. Adam, Solomon, Samson, and David were all similarly "biwyled" by women.[16] Therefore, Gawain will return to the world of renown, but this time renown will not lead him into pride, for the lace, he says, will,

> "When I ride in renoun, remorde to myseluen
> Þe faut and þe fayntyse of þe flesche crabbed,
> How tender hit is to entyse teches of fylþe."
>
> (vv. 2434–36)

The resolution is admirable, and the tone is heavily theological. Gawain will no longer be guilty of pride, of the overweening "surquidré" that is the special danger of the aristocrat famed "for prowes of armes," because he has learned something about knighthood and himself. The "fol chevalier" has become wiser through an initiation into a broader life than knighthood comprehends.

Yet Gawain remains an idealist, and, like all idealists, he takes things too seriously. The extravagance of his humil-

ity in this scene is matched only by the equally extravagant humility of his opening speech, and we are treated to
the diverting spectacle of one of the most famous lovers in
medieval literature breaking into monkish anti-feminism
Pride, "surquidré," is an important part of this adventure,
but it is not as important as Gawain believes, and the poet
does not allow this analysis of the action to stand alone.
First Bercilak explains Morgan's motives, thus reasserting
the importance of renown, and he again praises Gawain
for his "grete trawþe." Then Gawain returns to Camelot,
where the whole adventure is placed in a comic, gently
satiric perspective.

The return to Camelot

The most trying of all Gawain's humiliations at the Green
Chapel is the fact that the Green Knight refuses to take
him seriously. When Gawain, finally brought to true repentance, offers reparation, "Thenn loʒe þat oþer leude"
(v. 2389). It is not the harsh laughter of the moralist but
the tolerant laughter of one who recognizes the comedy
of the situation. Gawain must be his own moralist, solemnly invoking the fall of Adam and Samson without
realizing the absurdity of scaling his bedroom adventure
against their cosmic tragedies. Worse yet, from Gawain's
point of view, is the reaction of his fellow knights. When
he returns to tell his sad tale in Camelot, he groans for
grief and blushes for shame. But Arthur's courtiers only
"Laʒen loude þerat" (v. 2514).

Gawain does not join in the laughter. He remains, in
aspiration at least, the chevalier, and he judges his actions
from the standpoint of that demanding ideal. Much as he
has learned, his character has not been greatly altered. It
is not possible for the poet to allow so drastic a change as

Gawain would have to undergo to accomplish this. As the laughter of the Green Knight and the court shows, what Gawain really learns from his adventure is that chivalry takes itself a bit too seriously, that men become ridiculous and foolish when they attempt to live up to so superhuman an ideal. Yet it would be a failure of tact for Gawain to make light of his own actions, and it would be almost impossible for him to do this without rejecting chivalry itself, and that is not the poet's purpose. Therefore, Gawain remains a knight, unable to judge himself with the uncourtly tolerance of Bercilak.

The court to which he returns can and does change, and it is amused rather than discomfited by the adventure.[17] Gawain was its representative in the adventure, and now it becomes his surrogate in the last stanzas of the poem. It can make light of Gawain's actions without rejecting chivalry, for it is possible for the court to laugh at him and yet receive him back into its membership. The laughter is good-humored, for in laughing at Gawain, their representative, they are laughing at themselves. They accept him with both his one fault and his knighthood into the court, and they decide that in the future he will not be alone in wearing his badge of "blame." They agree that,

> Vche burne of þe broþerhede, a bauderyk schulde haue,
> A bende abelef hym aboute of a bryȝt grene,
> And þat, for sake of þat segge, in swete to were.
> For þat watȝ acorded þe renoun of þe Rounde Table,
> And he honoured þat hit hade euermore after.
>
> (vv. 2516–20)

The renown survives. The touch of villainy did not, as Gawain feared, destroy the virtues "þat longeȝ to knyȝteȝ" (v. 2381), but, as the laughter shows, the fame of the Round Table and the ideal it represents is now modified by the bend of bright green and the tolerant acknowledgment of human limitations that it implies.

This is not the way a romance is supposed to end; the glorious affirmation of the hero's virtues and of the ideal he represents is conspicuously absent. Yet *Sir Gawain* could hardly end in any other way, for this final scene is only an extension of the recurrent alternation of romance and unromantic elements that repeatedly undercuts the high seriousness of the narrative. The poet never allows us to view Gawain's actions in the simple light of romance, and Gawain's heroic deeds and attitudes are constantly juxtaposed with the comic or humiliating. With a grand disregard of consequences and a high romantic sense of duty he rises to accept the challenge; but then, instead of applauding him as a romance narrator should, the poet intrudes with the common-sense, unidealized observation that "Men ben mery in mynde quen þay han mayn drynk." With heroic resolve Gawain departs from the weeping court only to discover that his shining armor is no protection against the wind and the rain and then to be plunged into the comic frustrations he meets at Bercilak's castle. When he does fulfill the bargain and leaps back to give battle to his antagonist, the Green Knight merely laughs and reveals his knowledge of Gawain's encounter with the lady. Gawain, in a reversal of the pattern of romances like *Caradoc* and *Perceval*, starts as a perfect knight and moves downward, ending where the heroes of those romances began, as an imperfect "fol chevalier" who is the object of laughter rather than admiration. From the standpoint of romance, the poem has been a tragedy, and Gawain bitterly laments his fall from his initial perfection into wretchedness. From Bercilak's unromantic viewpoint Gawain has moved upward and the poem has a comic conclusion; the hero began, or so he told the challenger, as the least of knights, and he ends, or so Bercilak tells him, as the best of all.

The Green Knight's judgment on the action must be taken as seriously as Gawain's, for the poet's successful characterization raises him above the status of a merely negative, anti-romantic character. He has an attitude of his own, unromantic rather than anti-romantic in its refusal to take romance seriously. That this attitude is valid and respectable is shown by the narrator's echo of the Green Knight's words after the first beheading and the court's echo of his laughter after the second. The tension between romantic and unromantic elements thus extends even to the possible judgments that the reader can make on the action. He cannot reject Gawain and what he stands for, for the romance ideal is noble, reinforced with the powers of religion and tradition; yet he cannot completely accept it either, for that ideal is slightly absurd, a bit too narrow, and clearly too demanding for a man in this world. The poem is thus both a tragic romance with the sad moral that perfection is beyond our grasp and an unromantic comedy with the happy point that if a man aims high enough he can come as near perfection as this world allows.

Such an ambivalent attitude toward the romance ideal reflects both the underlying seriousness of the Gawain-poet's purposes and his relation to his own time, for the limitations of the ideal were a peculiarly fourteenth-century concern. The genre of romance was still widespread at this time, as it was to remain for another century. Moreover, in theory at least, the romance ideal still offered a code for the conduct of life, and as yet no Castiglione had provided a secular alternative to it. In Edward the Black Prince the previous generation seemed to have had a living embodiment of that code, one whose example, according to the Chandos Herald, could teach all "to take the remembrance of good into their hearts and to achieve honor" ("Pour prendre en lour coers remembrance/ De bien et honour recevoir," vv. 6–7). Yet by the last quarter of the century biographies like the Chandos Herald's *Life of the Black Prince*, romances like *Sir Degrevant*, and even Gawain's ideals seem already "consciously old-fashioned." [18] This is because, as J. D. Bruce wrote, the ideals of romance were no longer in accord with "the spirit of contemporary society":

> Perhaps this may account in part, at least, for the fact that the Middle English romances, on the whole, are inferior to German productions in the same *genre;* for the latter, it will be recalled, fell at the end of the twelfth century and beginning of the thirteenth—that is to say, it was coincident with all but the first period of production in France itself, and so was a vivid representation of actual contemporary ideals. [19]

Most Middle English romances are indeed inferior for this reason, but the best of them, most notably *Sir Gawain*, are also vivid representations of contemporary attitudes, for they show the scrutiny that older values were undergoing as the Middle Ages came to an end.

The sophisticated man of the fourteenth century had only to look about him to see that the romance ideal no longer fit the life he knew. The "crusades" of this century have nothing but the name in common with the great enterprises of the High Middle Ages, and the few examples of chivalric conduct that Froissart admiringly cites are glaring exceptions in his chronicles of a cruel and greedy era. In England, France, and the Low Countries the peasants were asserting themselves in a way that showed clearly that the old feudal order was dying, while the Great Schism and the rise of heresy showed that even the church was not as secure as it once seemed, and plague and famine threatened the existence of society itself, while those who wished to revive the good old days busied themselves with founding ceremonial orders of knighthood that only preserved in an overelaborate fashion the forms of a previous, mainly fictional age. Perhaps such efforts only intensified the disillusionment, especially in England, where Edward III had so closely identified himself with the Arthurian ideal and where, at the end of the fourteenth century, so many of Edward's projects, most obviously the war with France, were yielding such poor results. The old knightly code retained its glamour, and it still seemed admirable that Edward had solemnly proclaimed the restoration of the Round Table and even that, as *Les Voeux de héron* has it, he began the Hundred Years' War to fulfill a chivalric vow made on the carcass of a heron at a great feast, but the results to which such a devotion to chivalry could lead were there for all to see, and none but the most conservative could ignore the disparity between aspiration and fulfillment or overlook the faults of the ideal itself.

This new, more critical attitude toward romantic chivalry is not restricted to England; it is apparent throughout the art and literature of the later medieval period. In the plastic arts it is reflected not only in the general growth of "bourgeois realism" but also in the handling of specific themes; Bernheimer found that in the combat between the wild man and the knight that so frequently appears in medieval art,

> As long as the knightly ideal remained untarnished, the victory in this battle was invariaby accorded the knight. It marks a major turning point in the history of European civilization that . . . the wild man is sometimes allowed to win in works of art describing the combat after the middle of the fourteenth century.[20]

In romance the new attitude is evident in the greater emphasis on religious virtues at the expense of chivalry, beginning with the Benedictine and Cistercian prose romancers of the thirteenth century, and in the new interest in the fall of the Round Table and the death of Arthur, which become popular subjects in fourteenth-century romance, in which Arthur himself is used as a tragic *exemplum* of the workings of fortune.[21] In the major Northern English romances of the later fourteenth and fifteenth centuries the Arthurian court and its code are invariably subjected to moral criticism: the stanzaic *Le Morte Arthur* is a tragedy caused by courtly love and broken allegiance; the alliterative *Morte Arthure* is a tragedy of Arthur's ambition, his "surquidré"; the *Awntyrs of Arthur* contains a long attack on the luxury and vainglory of the Round Table; *Golagros and Gawain* presents a completely debased characterization of Arthur; and *Lancelot of the Laik* seems to have been written mainly for the sake of Amyntas' condemnation of the king for pursuing pleasure rather than the good of his people. Though the existence of these works shows how attractive the romance ideal remained, their unanimous criticism shows that its day of dominance had passed. Significantly, Chaucer's model knight is a man well along toward middle age, old enough to have a twenty-year-old son who shows little promise of becoming the Christian knight his father is. Tournaments and courtly love come off rather badly in *Troilus* and *The Knight's Tale*, and Chaucer's only two "English romances" are *The Wife of Bath's Tale*, in which Arthur's knights are mainly noted for rape, and *Sir Thopas*.

The beauty of *Sir Gawain* is that it takes the old ideals neither too lightly nor too seriously. It has comedy, but none of the burlesque of *Sir Thopas*; it condemns knighthood, but lightly and without the heavy-handed morality that impairs the effect of most of the romances listed above. Their authors also admired the knightly ideal despite their recognition of its faults, and their works are also characterized by the tension between condemnation and admiration that we find in *Sir Gawain*. But the Gawain-poet was able to state with delicacy what most of them could say but crudely. His representative of unromantic vitality can finally praise knighthood for what it is because he has no romantic notions of what it should be, and he therefore does not denounce what he finds and call for a return to an unattainable older order, as do Langland and Gower. Gawain, the representative of knighthood, must denounce himself, and in doing so he shows us its most attractive quality, its nobility of aspiration. The noble desire for perfection remains, and Gawain returns to the court and a life of adventure rather than to the hermitage where Arthur's knights end their days in *Le Morte Arthur*. For Gawain to condemn himself and the Green Knight to praise him is a final reversal of expectation; it is the unromantic figure who is supposed to denounce the knight for his pride—the Brahmin in *Alexander and Dindimus*, the "philosophers" in the alliterative *Morte Arthure*, the ghost in the *Awntyrs of Arthur*. This final reversal of roles, part of the exchange we see in the return-blow, is one of the last and most significant variations in the poem, and it is in the variation, in both contrasting speeches, that the meaning lies, for the attitudes they express, indulgent forgiveness and uncompromising aspiration, are both finally maintained by the poem.

In these parallel but contrasting attitudes toward what has happened we can finally see the meaning that was expressed throughout the poem in the most important variation of all, the carefully drawn parallel contrast between the Green Knight and Gawain. When they momentarily exchange roles, the Green Knight becoming temporarily a gentleman and Gawain an unromantic churl, filled with energy, angry speech, and anti-romantic ideas about women, and when they finally part, Gawain to the court and the undefeated Green Knight whithersoever he would, we recognize that the main characters are themselves variations, two parts of the unstated whole that is life itself. Neither can triumph in their conflict because Gawain's ceremonial idealism and the Green Knight's laughing realism are both essential to the better life that the court with its bend of green—ceremonialized and used in a courtly, heraldic fashion—and its good-natured laughter represents at the end of the poem.

The laughter with which the action concludes is exactly the right note, for whatever deeper concerns it has touched and however serious it almost becomes, *Sir Gawain* is predominantly a festive poem. In that spirit it weighs and gently criticizes the ideal of literature and life that was romance, and it suggests that this noble ideal can survive only if it takes account of the rest of life and of the human limitations of even its best representatives. That the poem still has meaning for the reader today is because, though the vocabulary has changed, the conflict between ideal codes and human limitations still persists. That it evidently appeals even more to readers of the twentieth century than to those of the nineteenth may be because our age, in which absolute ideals derived from theory or literature have again become important forces in life, can more easily recognize the value of a poem in which the juxtaposition of churlishness and knighthood, of humility and laughter, of terror and comedy, yields a finely tolerant, vigorously good-natured, and characteristically Gothic acceptance of life both as it is and as it should be. English literature may offer a few, very few better narratives than *Sir Gawain and the Green Knight,* but none more delightful and humane.

Appendix: *The prose redaction of the* Caradoc *beheading tale*

The following passage is the complete *Caradoc* beheading tale as it appears on folios 78 to 80 of the prose redaction of the First Continuation of *Perceval* in *Le Tresplaisante et Recreative Hystoire du trespreulx et vaillant chevallier Perceval le galloys,* printed at Paris in 1530 for Jehan Longis, Jehan de Sainct Denis, and Galliot du Pré. The many surviving rimes (cf. *feste/appreste* in the first sentence of the passage below) confirm the statement of the "privilege" that Jehan Longis and Jehan de Sainct Denis were publishing an "ancien livre . . . faict en ryme et langaige non usite, lezquelz ilz avoient faict traduyre de ryme en prose et langaige moderne pour imprimer." Their "ancien livre" has since been lost, and their edition itself has now become very rare. Only three copies survive, those at Berlin, at the British Museum, and at the Library of Congress, which also has a rotograph of the British Museum's copy.[1] The passage below is transcribed from the copy at the Library of Congress, its readings confirmed by a comparison with the rotograph of the British Museum's copy. Since it will be of interest mainly to students of English literature, I have silently expanded its many abbreviations, modernized the punctuation and capitalization, changed the usage of "u" and "v" and "i" and "j" to conform to modern practice, and corrected two obvious printer's errors.

Au moys de May fust faicte ceste feste que Dieu eust le jour appreste si beau qu'on ne le scavroit dire; auquel alla le roy la messe ouir. Et entre les seigneurs de sa barroniey fust Carados regarde de moult grande beaulte et de perfaicte maintien, lequel estoit avecques cinquantes jeusnes escuyers qui le roy feist en l'honneur de luy tous chevalliers ce jour—filz de barons, de contes, et aultres grans seigneurs—tous cortois et bien ensiegnez, lesquel on fist laver et bagnier comme allors estoit la costume. Genievre la notable royne se monstra ce jour liberalle; laquelle envoya a Carados et a ses compaignons fines chemisez et richement ouvrees, et leur envoya de telles robes que les puissanz roy en eussent este bien revestus, et pareillement leur envoia des manteaulx fort beaulx et riches, tous fourrez de martres subellines brodes d'estoilles d'or par dessus. L'hystoire nous recite que quant Carados fust de ses riches vestemens aorne et pare que si plaisant apparessoit que bien estoit a chascun advis que nature n'avoit en luy rien oublie ne obmis, car chose n'estoit en son corps qu'il deust ennuyer ou desplaire. Et quant se vint a les faire chevalliers, Gauvain chaussa a Carados l'esperon dextre et messire Yvain le senestre, et le roy lui saignit l'espee et puis luy donna la collee en luy disant que Dieu le face preudhomme et chevallereux. Et puis ce faict. Cent des plus prisez chevalliers de la court ont aux aultres cinquantes escuiers chausse les esperons, sainctes leurs espees, et puis leur donnerent les collees. Ainsy furent faie chevalliers, lesquelz s'en allerent ensemble a l'esglise pour

ouir le divin service que celebra l'archevesque de Can-
torbie et feist l'office de la messe du Sainct Esprit. Et ne
fault doubter que l'offerte fust grande et riche ou y offrit
mainte personne. Ce jour porta le roy couronne que bal-
loit ung moult grant tresor. Quant le divin service fut
acheve et dist, le roy de sa noblesse accompagnie s'en
retirent en la salle en grand joye et grande liesse, ou les
sergens et escuiers appareillerent toutes les tables et les
napes sur lesquelles mirent sel et pain, ou y fust le buffet
si riche qu'ugne chose est inestimable. Et tandis que les
tables on dressoit se pourmenoit le roy avecques sa
baronnie et les nouveaulx chevalliers avant la salle. Et
allors yssit hors d'unge chambre Keux le Seneschal, lequel
tout nud teste au roy s'en vient, tenant le bacin tout
appareille en sa main, luy demander si son bon plaisir
estoit de laver. "Keux," faict le roy, "ne vous hastez, car
vous scavez long temps y a que quant court planiere ay
tenue que jamais ne voullus menger ains que nouvelles
ou merveilles ne fussent devers moy venues, et encores ne
veuil coustume laisser ne abollir." Ainsy qu'ensemble y
parlerent fust advise ung chevallier venir parmi la porte
qui chevaulchoit a moult grand haste. Et s'en venoit
chantant une chançon bien doulcement; et avoit dessus
le bonnet ung cercle ou pendoit ung chapeau de fleurs; et
estoit vestu de satin verd fourre de erminnes; et avoit une
espee saincte dont puis eust la teste couppee, et en estoient
les renges ou saincture de fine soie batue en or et force
perles semees par dessus. Lequel s'en vint devant le roy
que tres humblement sallua en ceste maniere. "Sire," dist
il, "je vous sallue comme le meilleur et le plus hault roy
qui pour ce jour sur terre regne, et sachez que vous viens
ung don requirir, lequel s'il vous plaist me octroayrez."
"Amy," faict le roy, "je le vous accorde mais que le don
vous m'aiez dist moiennant qu'il soit raisonnable." "Roy,"
faict il, "je ne quiers personne decepvior et le don que je

vous demande est seullement collee pour colle, ou aultre-
ment pour une collee recepvoir pour une aultre collee
rendre." "Comment entendez vous cella?" faict le roy. "Je
le veulx scavoir." "Sire, je vous apprendray," dist le chevallier. "Cest espee devant vostre royalle majeste et devant
toute la compagniee a ung chevallier bailleray s'il m'en
peult a ung coup la teste trencher; et que ce de coup je
garisse la collee luy rendray." "A mon dieu," se luy a dist
Keux. "Ceste chose ne ferois je pas pour tout l'avoir qu'il
soit au monde, et pour fol le chevallier tendroie qui ceste
chose entreprendroit." Et allors le chevallier dist: "Sire,"
faict il, "d'ung don vous ay requis; et si m'en aviez es-
conduit il seroit dist par tout le monde que je avroie failly
a voustre grande feste a ung don de vous impetrer duquel
je vous en fis la requeste, et pource vous prie ne me le
refuser quant n'en povez acquerir blasme." Lors l'espee a
du fourreau traicte en la presentant ça et la, de quoy le
roy fort se dehaite, et si en sont tant les grands que les
petis esbahis en pensant en leur cueur quel honneur on
peult avoir de ferir et luy couper la teste. Adonc ne si
peult contenir Carados le nouveau chevallier qu'il ne se
vint presenter pour satisfaire a la requeste du chevallier,
et si tost qu'il eust aproche, mist le manteau jus, et prent
l'espee qu'il tenoit. Et le chevallier luy demanda: "Estes
vous," dist il, "pour ung des meilleurs esleu?" "Non," faict
Carados, "mais pour ung des plus folz." Allors le chevallier
le col estend lequel la chouche sur ung bloc, de quoy le
roy fust fort dollent et tous les barons de sa court, et a
petit de chose tint que Yvain ne luy court l'espee hors
des mains oster. Adonc Carados, en son entreprise per-
sistant, haulsa l'espee qu'il tenoit de laquelle en donna au
chevallier telle collee qu'elle coulla jusques au doigtz, et
s'en est la teste vollee plus loing qu'unge lance n'est
longue, et le corps comme s'il fust vif de si pres la teste
suivat que nul ne se donna de garde que la teste ne fust

reunye bien joincte * et bien aderee. Et adonc saillist le chevallier en place que dist au roy. "Sire," faict il, "maintenant me debvez mon droict rendre, et pource que collee ay receve en vostre court tant estimee raison est qu'elle soit rendue, et de ce vous en fais le juge; mais je veuil bien le terme attrendre du jourdhuy jusques a ung an court planiere † vous tiendrez." Et allors, sans faire long sejour, le roy tous ses barons invita de retourner au bout de l'an au jour assigne par le chevallier que la collee il debvra rendre. Et ainsy que le chevalleur fust remonte dist a Carados. "Carados," fist il, "vous m'avez devant le roy grant collee donnee, mais je vous semons que d'huy en ung an vous avrez la mienne." Et a tant se part et s'en va. Et le roy en si grant yre demeura que nul ne le vous scavroit dire, pensant comment Carados pourroit eviter sans mort de cest affaire, et en print ung deuil si tres grand que nul ne l'en scavroit retraire. Et vous prometz qu'il n'y eust chevalliers ne dames qui tout ne fondant en larmes du regret et de la craincte qu'il ont de Carados. Certainnement tost furent les ris et les jeus en pleurs et en cris convertis. O que malheureux est, qui par sa couppe ou par une folle plaisance mect tant de monde en dolleur et en peine, et en le fin le plaisir seul est en cent tourmens converti! O effimine et plus que enraige enchanteur, comment as tu ose entreprendre ung si criminel delict par lequel tant se en ensuivra de perte dommaige a ton propre sang et a celle que tant tu as aimee? Quant le chevallier enchanteur que nul ne congnoissoit s'en fust retourne, se mist le roy et les barons a table ou ne fust propos tenu qui de ceste matiere en gectant souvent grand souspirs. Mais Carados n'en prent soussy, disant qu'il en actendra la fortune.

Pour Carados furent maintes larmes gectees a Cardeuil,

* *bien joincte*]—bien io ioincte
† *planiere*]—plauiere

ou les barons se doibvent trouver a l'autre an le jour de la Penthecouste. Et fust ceste nouvelle ouye par Carados roy de Vaigne et par sa femme la belle Ysenne, qui de l'ennuy de leur enfant en eurent au cueur grand tristesse laquelle ne dellaisserent tout le long de l'annee. Et le jeusne Carados, actendant que cest an fust revollu et accomply, ne voullut en la court du roy son oncle sejourner, mais nous dict le compte qu'il faist de tant chevalleureux faictz que chevallier vivant en terre n'en a tant faict en peu d'espace, si que par tout en fust si grande la renommee que chascun reputoit ses euvres estre plustost faictes divinement que corporellement. Et quant veit que le terme approchoit que la court se debvoit rassembler, se retira droit a Cardeuil, ou se trouverent tous ceulx et celles qui pour y venir furent invitez pour l'aventure regarder. Mais n'y comparurent a ceste fois le roy Carados ne sa femme, parce qu'il n'y osent venir pour la craincte et la doulleur qu'il ont de leur enfant; lesquelz gueres n'eurent de joye pendant que la court si tenoit et ne se scevent a aultre sainct vouer fors que a Dieu pour lequel prier firent de belles et grandes aulmosnes affin de leur enfant preserver et garder de la mort.

Comment le chevallier enchanteur qui pere estoit de Carados vint au bout de l'an faignant vaulloir coupper le chef du dict Carados son filz.

Quant a Cardeuil fust la court ung jour de la Penthecouste assemblee, les processions faictes, et les messes aux esglises chantees, et aussy que l'on voulloit donner leave au roy pour aller menger, arriva le chevallier en la salle comme auparavant, avoit faict son espee saincte, que bien sembloit estre delibere et prest de faire son exploict; lequel dist au roy de plain sault tost apres qu'il eust sallue. "Sire," faict il, "si vous plaist, vous ferez icy Carados comparoir ainsy comme il a este dict il y a maintenant ung an." Et en ce disant, advisa Carados auquel a dist: "Carados," faict il, "Metz icy la teste, car tu scez qu'y mis la mienne; parquoy y dois la tienne mettre, et par ainsy tu congnoistras comme je scay d'espee ferir en te rendant une collee." Alors Carados plus n'atent si s'en vient et sault en avant, puis mest sa teste sur le bloc et dist au chevallier: "Tenez," faist il, "Vous me voiez. Faictes du pis que vous pourrez." Adonc se escria le roy au chevallier en disant. "Chevallier," faict il, "je vous prie que vous montriez estre courtois; mettez Carados a rançon." "Et a quoy?" dist le chevallier. "Je vous doneray," faict le roy, "voulluntiers toute la vaisselle que vous trouverez en ma court que conques l'y ait apportee tant soit a moy come a aultruy avecques tout la harnois de Carados, qui est mon nepveu legitime." Et il dist que point ne la prendra mais que luy ostera la teste. Encores luy dist le roy, "Je vous doneray tous les tresors tant en pierrerie qu'en aultre chose qui present sont en ceste terre, en Engleterre, et en Bretaigne, et par toutes mes seigneuries." "Certes," dist le chevallier, "point je n'en veuil, mais je luy osteray le chief." Et alors haulce son espee pour le ferir, de quoy le roy en eust grand deuil. Et Carados luy dist par yre, "Pourquoy ne frapez vous, beau sire? De deux mors me faictes mourir. Que tant vous metez a frapper il semble que couart soiez!" Adonc est la royne hors de sa chambre yssue avec les dames et les pucelles pour luy prier de pitie en avoir. Puys luy dist: "Je vous requiers, franc chevallier," faict elle, "qu'a Carados vous ne touchez. Car ung trop grand peche seroit et doumaige s'il estoit en ce point occis. Pour Dieu aiez de luy merci et je vous prometz que quant sa mort luy aurez pardonnee que bon guerdon recepverez. Croiez conseil, je vous en prie, et se jamais voullez quelque bien pour Dieu me faire, je vous requiers de faire cestuy pour moy et clamez quite mon nepveu de la collee que pretendes luy rendre. Vous voyez tant de damoiselles et de si honnestes pucelles qui de ce faire vous requierent." "Dame," respond le chevallier, "pour toutes les femmes de ce monde je ne luy vouldrois pardonner, pource veuil qu'il y perde la vie. Se vous ne l'osez regarder, cachez vous dedens vostre chambre." Adonc se retira la royne, la teste baissee, et les dames en sa chambre, ou grand deuil et plaincte menerent pour Carados qu'il n'ont sceu delivrer.

Comment le roy Arthus avec ses chevalliers, dames, et damoiselles furent an grande tristesse pour la craincte de la mort du jeune Carados, et comment le chevallier enchanteur declara au dict Carados qu'il estoit son filz.

Le roy et tous les chevalliers enprindrent si tres grand courroux qu'il ne scevrent que devinir et ne croyent pas que homme charnel ne veit jamais tel deuil mener. Lors s'est remis Carados voulluntairement sur le bloc, son col estendu au plaisir du chevallier. Et cil a l'espee haulcee qui du plat fiert tant seullement, et puis a dist: "Carados," dist il, "or te lieve, car se seroit grand oultraige se t'avoie occis et domiage; mais apart veuil parler a toy." Et quant ilz furent arriere mis, luy a dict en ceste maniere: "Scez tu," faict il, "pourquoy je ne t'ay occis? C'est pourtant que je suis ton pere et tu es mon filz naturel." "Certes," dist Carados, "j'en deffenderay ma mere en soubtenant que jamais ne fust vostre amye et que jamais avec elle ne geustes, par quoy vous prie de vous taire." Et alors le chevallier a relate a Carados de point en point come la chose estoit allee, comment avecques sa mere geust par trois nuictz. Mais Carados, qui ce ne creust, voullut au chevallier tencer quant si estrange chose et si nouvelle luy comptoit, de quoy tant triste et tant dollent estoit que plusieurs fois le dementit et dist qu'il en feroit desdire. Mais de chose qu'il sache dire de rien n'en chault au chevallier, qui sans aultre propos tenir remonta dessus son cheval, puis print conge, et s'en retourne, que delaissa la court en joye voiant Carados delivre. Alors fist Keux les grailles ou l'assiete soner pour le roy et les barons laver et eux mectre a table, ou y convierent les dames, damoiselles, et les pucelles fort rejouis de l'adventure de Carados. Et quant a table furent tous assis, servis furent de metz precieux et delectables, lesquelz je ne vous specifie a cause de bresvete et craincte de allonger mon compte. Quant les barons furent levez apres la joyeuse repeu, s'en allerent tous pour ceste nuict reposer et l'endemain apres la messe chascun vint au roy demander son conge; mais avant leur departement le roy les remunera en beaulx dons comme chevaulx, bagues, joyaulx or et argent, et bons oyseulx. Lors ne vint nul si povrre en court que riche il ne s'en retournast. Chascun a sa contree s'en retourna joyeusement, et le roy a son prive demeure avecques la chevallerie se deduisant joyeusement. Et Carados s'en va en Bretaigne ou pieça n'y avoit este et tant diligenta qu'il arriva a Nantes ou il trouva le roy son pere a sejour avec la belle Ysenne sa mere.

Abbreviations

Alex A	Alexander A
CE	College English
CFMA	Classiques français du moyen âge
Cheu	Cheualere Assigne
Clean	Cleanness (Purity)
ClkT	Clerk's Tale
DT	Destruction of Troy (Geste Hystoriale of the Destruction of Troy)
EETS	Early English Text Society
ELH	Journal of English Literary History
Erk	St. Erkenwald
ES	English Studies
GenPro	General Prologue to The Canterbury Tales
JEGP	Journal of English and Germanic Philology
KT	Knight's Tale
MA	Morte Arthure
MÆ	Medium Ævum
MED	Middle English Dictionary
MLN	Modern Language Notes
MP	Modern Philology
MLQ	Modern Language Quarterly
MLR	Modern Language Review
MS	Medieval Studies
Mum and Soth	Mum and the Sothsegger

NPT	*Nun's Priest's Tale*
N&Q	*Notes and Queries*
OED	*Oxford English Dictionary*
PAPS	*Proceedings of the American Philosophical Society*
Parl	*Parlement of the Thre Ages*
ParsT	*Parson's Tale*
Pat	*Patience*
Perc	*Sir Perceval of Gales*
Pistill	*The Pistill of Susan*
PMLA	*PMLA: Publications of the Modern Language Association*
PP	*Piers Plowman*
PPCr	*Pierce the Ploughmans Crede*
PQ	*Philological Quarterly*
RES	*Review of English Studies*
RP	*Romance Philology*
SATF	Societé des anciens textes français
SG	*Sir Gawain and the Green Knight*
SHF	Societé de l'histoire de France
SirThop	*Sir Thopas*
SJ	*The Siege of Jerusalem*
SN	*Studia Neophilologica*
SP	*Studies in Philology*
SqT	*Squire's Tale*
STS	Scottish Texts Society
Quatrefoil	*The Quatrefoil of Love*
Traitié	*Traitié pour essampler les amantz marietz*
WA	*The Wars of Alexander*
ZFSL	*Zeitschrift für französische Sprache und Literatur*

Notes

Preface

(Since there is a bibliography of all primary texts cited, I use only titles when citing the editions of medieval works in the notes. Tolkien and Gordon's edition is used for all quotations from *Sir Gawain*.)

1. Émile Pons (ed.), *Sire Gauvain et le chevalier vert*, p. 15.
2. The poem must have existed in more than one manuscript, since our copy is not the author's own and since the influence of our poem is apparent in *The Grene Knight* (a fifteenth-century redaction of *Sir Gawain*) and in a work by Humphrey Newton; see R. H. Robbins, "A Gawain Epigone," *MLN*, LVIII (1943), 361–66. For the editions of *Sir Gawain* see the bibliography. For a list of translations, see the bibliography in Gollancz' edition, p. lxvii, to which should be added the translations of Ormerod Greenwood (London, 1946), M. R. Ridley (London, 1944), J. L. Rosenberg (New York, 1959), Brian Stone (London, 1960), and B. J. Whiting in *College Survey of English Literature*, ed. B. J. Whiting *et al.* (New York, 1948), I, 114–38. The French translation is in Pons' edition; the Breton is *Gaovan Hag an den Gwer*, tr. Roparz Hemon, Brezhoneg Eeun, Niv. 2 [La Baule, 19–?].
3. Eduard Stucken, *Gawân, ein Mysterium* (Berlin, 1902); James Yeames, *Sir Gawain and the Green Knight, a Play* (Detroit,

1911); C. M. Lewis, *Gawain and the Green Knight, a Fairy Tale* (Boston, 1903). For an example of *Sir Gawain* in the work of a modern poet (and an interesting gloss on the poem itself) see Yvor Winters, "Sir Gawain and the Green Knight," in *Collected Poems* (Denver, 1952), p. 113.

4. See George Kane, *Middle English Literature* (London, 1951), pp. 73–74; J. R. Kreuzer, Introduction to Rosenberg's translation, pp. xiii–xiv. Obviously such apologies are necessary, and their presence is no reflection on these two very good essays.

5. More precise localizations are based on internal, geographical evidence from the poem or on assumptions about authorship rather than on linguistic criteria; Morton W. Bloomfield, "*Sir Gawain and the Green Knight*," *PMLA*, LXXVI (1961), 10, raises telling objections to this procedure.

6. R. M. Wilson, *The Lost Literature of Medieval England* (London, 1952). Wilson cautiously restricts himself to works for which there is some evidence that they once existed. Many other manuscripts must have disappeared without leaving a trace, and orally composed alliterative verse, which probably still existed in the early fourteenth century, was never recorded at all.

7. Aside from Huchown and Strode, whom older scholars identified with the Gawain-poet, the candidates are John Donne and John Pratt, both suggested by O. Cargill and M. Schlauch, "*The Pearl* and Its Jeweler," *PMLA*, XLIII (1928), 105–23; John Erghome, suggested by C. O. Chapman, "The Authorship of *The Pearl*," *PMLA*, XLVII (1932), 346–53; and Hugh Mascy, nominated by Ormerod Greenwood in the Introduction to his translation of *Sir Gawain*. The argument for multiple authorship has been put most forcibly by J. W. Clark in his series of articles, "Observations on Certain Differences in Vocabulary Between *Cleanness* and *Sir Gawain and the Green Knight*," *PQ*, XXVIII (1949), 261–73; "The Gawain-poet and the Substantival Adjective," *JEGP*, XLIX (1950), 60–66; "Paraphrases for 'God' in the Poems Attributed to the Gawain-poet," *MLN*, LXV (1950), 232–36; "On Certain 'Alliterative' and Poetic Words in the Poems Attributed to the Gawain-poet," *MLQ*, XII (1951), 387–98. The first three articles are of little value, since the arguments are based not on the poems themselves but on their editors' glossaries or upon the examples gathered by Oakden, who did not claim that his lists were complete. Thus Clark was led to believe that there are no periphrases for "God" in *Pearl* and that there are only three substantival adjectives in *Patience* and *Cleanness* together. There are periphrases for "God" in *Pearl*—cf. vv. 705, 799, 811–12, among others. A hasty count

shows at least four substantival adjectives in *Patience* (vv. 163, 169, 175, 502), and eight in the first four hundred lines of *Cleanness* (vv. 114, 116, 126, 127, 130, 163, 276, 362, 387). Clark's last article is more convincing, since it is based on a full study of *Cleanness*, though not of any of the other poems, and it raises some important questions. However, the assumption of his study is that a person's verbal habits never change and that minor differences in usage between *Sir Gawain* and *Cleanness* are significant. Yet Chaucer is very fond of the construction "Whan that" in *The General Prologue*, where he uses it seven times in the first nine hundred lines (vv. 1, 266, 697, 711, 760, 800, 822). In *The Book of the Duchess* this construction appears only once (v. 697). In *The Book of the Duchess* Chaucer frequently uses "therewith"—vv. 275, 385, 888, 1015, 1059, 1064, 1324—but that word appears only once in *The General Prologue*—v. 678. Clark's argument is therefore suggestive, but it must remain unproven until we have a full concordance of the Cotton Nero poems and a bit more knowledge about the significance of vocabulary in tests of authorship.

8. It is often assumed that the Gawain-poet also wrote *St. Erkenwald*, but this is very unlikely. I discuss this matter in detail in "The Authorship of *St. Erkenwald*," *JEGP*, LXIV (1965), 393 ff.

The Sources

1. Jean Bodel, *Chanson des Saisnes*, v. 6; quoted by A. C. Baugh in his discussion of English romance in *A Literary History of England*, ed. A. C. Baugh *et al.* (New York, 1948), pp. 173–99, which the reader should consult for a good discussion of the subject.

2. For a general discussion of this distinction see Ian Watt, *The Rise of the Novel* (Berkeley and Los Angeles, 1957), Ch. I (mainly philosophic in its emphasis), and Harry Levin, *The Gates of Horn* (Oxford, 1963), Ch. II (mainly literary).

3. Cf. Alain Renoir, "Thebes, Troy, Criseyde, and Pandarus: An Instance of Chaucerian Irony," *SN*, XXXII (1960), 14–17.

4. For the function of "authentication" in narrative see Morton W. Bloomfield, "Authenticating Realism and the Realism of Chaucer," *Thought*, XXXIX (1964), 335–58.

5. Cf. Geoffrey of Monmouth, *Historia Regum Britanniae*, XII, 20: "Librum istum Britannici sermonis, quem Gvalterus Oxenefordensis archdiaconus ex Britannia aduexit" ("The book in British speech which Archdeacon Walter of Oxford brought from Britain" [i.e., Wales]); Chrétien de Troyes, *Perceval*, vv. 66–67:

"Ce est li contes del graal./ Don li cuens li baille le liure" ("This is the story of the grail, for which the count furnishes him the book"); Wolfram von Eschenbach, *Parzifal,* 419, 25–27; "Kîôt ist ein Provenzâl/ der dise âventiur von Parzifâl/ heidensch geschriben sach" (Kîôt is a Provençal who saw this story of Parzifal written in the heathen language). In the Merlin romances the production of the authenticating book is built into the plot; Merlin periodically returns to his old master Blaise, who records faithfully the events that Merlin relates to him.

6. *Lancelot,* vv. 1–33; *NPT,* 3443; cf. D. W. Robertson, "Some Medieval Literary Terminology, with Special Reference to Chrétien de Troyes," *SP,* XLVIII (1951), 669–92.

7. *ClkT,* vv. 27, 54. In v. 54 Chaucer refers only to the "prohemye," but, as J. B. Severs points out, "Chaucer made significant changes in characterization, in narrative technique, and in the whole tone and spirit which informs the tale" (*Sources and Analogues of Chaucer's Canterbury Tales,* ed. W. F. Bryan and Germaine Dempster [New York, 1941], p. 290).

8. For an illuminating discussion see A. C. Baugh, "Improvisation in the Middle English Romance," *PAPS,* CIII (1959), 418–54.

9. E. Vinaver (ed.), *The Works of Sir Thomas Malory,* I, lxvi. The bit of green lace, which the author of *Caradoc* added to the challenger's weapon, illustrates this principle. In *Sir Gawain* the lace, extended now to the temptation episode, becomes an emblem of the whole action; in the fifteenth-century *Grene Knight* the cloth, now changed to white and no longer connected with the weapon, becomes the emblem of the order of chivalry which that poem was written to glorify.

10. G. L. Kittredge, *A Study of Gawain and the Green Knight* (Cambridge, Mass., 1916), contains useful summaries of all the versions. For speculations about the lost versions see, in addition to Kittredge, L. L. Ball, *The Relation of Diu Crône of Heinrich von dem Türlîn to Paiens' La Mule sanz frain* (Washington, 1935), although both scholars base their assumptions of other versions on the theory that *Sir Gawain* has only an indirect relation to *Caradoc.*

11. For the best treatment of *Sir Gawain* as a seasonal myth see R. S. Loomis, *Wales and the Arthurian Legend* (Cardiff, 1955), pp. 77–90. In all treatments of the mythic aspects of *Sir Gawain* there is a confusion of origins with the final product in *Sir Gawain.* As my discussion shows, whatever the ultimate origin of a romance plot, its original nature is changed in the literary tradition. For examples of the "exchange of blows" see Kittredge, *A Study of Gawain* . . . , pp. 21–23, 218–223.

12. See Kittredge, *A Study of Gawain* . . . , pp. 22, 221–22. In *Wallace* see Bk. II, 27–45, where the "carl" offers Wallace a chance to strike him for a small payment.

13. "Other books say that they made that bargain with him—namely Loigaire to cut off his head the first day—and that he [Loigaire] avoided him [did not appear to receive Uath's blow in return], and that Conall avoided him in the same way." The translation and glosses are by Kittredge, *A Study of Gawain* . . . , p. 18.

14. This and the following summaries of the Irish beheading episodes are drawn from the translation in Henderson's edition of the *Fled Bricrend*, pp. 96–101 for the "Terror" version, pp. 116–29 for "The Champions' Bargain."

15. For a convenient discussion of the problem see R. S. Loomis, "The Oral Diffusion of the Arthurian Legend," in *Arthurian Literature in the Middle Ages*, ed. R. S. Loomis (Oxford, 1961), pp. 52–63.

16. "Caradoc, ou es tu?" "Je suis toz prez" (vv. 2382–83); Curoi asks "Where is Cuchulainn?" "Here am I," Cuchulainn answers. Later redactors omitted this passage, which occurs only in the "short" metrical version, the earliest redaction; see note 20 below.

17. Potvin's text appears in Vol. III, pp. 117–221, of his *Perceval le Gallois* (Mons, 1866); Potvin based this edition on the Mons Ms., designated Ms. P in Roach's edition.

18. For a more detailed discussion see my "The Source of the Beheading Episode in *Sir Gawain and the Green Knight*," MP, LIX (1961), 1–12.

19. Paul J. Ketrick, *The Relation of Golagros and Gawane to the Old French Perceval* (Washington, D.C., 1931), pp. 67–85.

20. This summary is based on the prose redaction (see Appendix). The "long" is in Roach's edition, II, vv. 7037–7425; the "short" redaction is in Vol. I, vv. 3300–3583; the "mixed" in III, vv. 2208–2491 (in Ms. L), vv. 2214–2497 (in Mss. A, S, P).

21. *La Mule*, vv. 496–1035; *Hunbaut*, vv. 1462–1539; *Perlesvaus*, pp. 136–38, 283–86.

22. See Arthur Dickson, *Valentine and Orson* (New York, 1929), pp. 128 ff., for a full discussion of the tradition.

23. See Henderson's note in his edition of the *Fled Bricrend*, p. 211. (However, I quote here from Kittredge's translation of the line.) Of course, many other commentators have remarked upon this. When Éliavres visits Ysanne, there is also a great deal of supernatural light, but this detail could have come to the French poet from the Alexander romances as well as from the Irish. There are elements in *Caradoc* that originated in folklore, but the poet seems more concerned with the literary aspects of

his work than folklorists have recognized, and he draws more from the traditions of *Perceval* and the Alexander romances than from folklore.

24. See W. A. Nitze, "Is the Green Knight Story a Vegetation Myth?" *MP*, XXXIII (1936), 351–66.

25. Roach edition, Vol. II, vv. 10487–88: " 'Certes,' fait il, 'je suis li pire/ Hom qui onques alast par terre.' " This scene is central to the meaning of *Le Livre de Caradoc,* which has more formal unity, once one recognizes its penitential theme, than critics have generally believed.

26. Child edition, 29; cf. Hales and Furnivall (eds.), *Bishop Percy's Folio Manuscript,* II, 304.

27. E.g., Jesse Weston, *The Legend of Sir Perceval* (London, 1906), I, 309–18.

28. See the examples cited by J. Campion and F. Holthausen (eds.), *Sir Perceval of Gales,* v. 485 n., p. 93. The *Morte Arthure* evidently contains a similar shift in date. Lucius' ambassadors arrive at Pentecost in Geoffrey of Monmouth, Laȝamon, and Wace, but they appear at the court on New Year's Day in the *Morte Arthure.*

29. In *Hunbaut* Gawain grasps the *vilain* by the clothes and thus prevents him from reaching the head; in *Caradoc* the poet tells us that the challenger is so quick that no one can prevent him from reaching it; in *Sir Gawain* "Fele hit foyned wyth her fete, þere hit forth roled" (v. 428). See the discussion on p. 6 of the article cited in note 18 above.

30. The prose version is slightly different: "Je vous accorde mais que le don vous m'aiez dist moiennant qu'il soit raissonable." Likewise, the prose differs slightly from verses quoted at the end of this paragraph; the prose has "si vint" rather than "si vet corant." These differences may be due to the prose redactor, or it may be that his manuscript differed in small details from that used by the Gawain-poet. However, the differences are minor.

31. For the latest discussion of the problems see Mother Angela Carson, O.S.U., "Morgain la Feé as the Principle of Unity in *Gawain and the Green Knight,*" *MLQ,* XXIII (1962), 3–16; Albert B. Friedman, "Morgan le Fay in *Sir Gawain and the Green Knight,*" *Speculum,* XXXV (1960), 260–74.

32. Bredbeddle's wife loves Gawain, though she has never seen him. Aggteb, her mother and a witch, sends Bredbeddle to Camelot. Bredbeddle knows of his wife's love for Gawain, but he goes to Camelot for adventure, not knowing that he is being sent to fetch Gawain for his wife's sake. This turns the tale into something very close to a "fairy mistress" story. J. R. Hulbert believed that *The Grene Knight* is earlier than *Sir Gawain,* and

he used this work as evidence for his "fairy mistress" theory of our poem; "*Gawain and the Green Knight*," MP, XIII (1915), 433–62, 689–730. Kittredge demonstrated the dependence of *The Grene Knight* on *Sir Gawain* in his *A Study of Gawain* . . . , pp. 282–89, and the fact that the Gawain-poet was the original combiner of the beheading and temptation lends further, though unneeded, support to Kittredge's position.

33. Kittredge, *A Study of Gawain* . . . , p. 118.

34. R. S. Loomis, *Wales and the Arthurian Legend*, pp. 79–90; Hulbert (see note 32 above); M. C. Thomas, *Gawayne and the Green Knight: A Comparison with the French Perceval* (Zurich, 1883); Mabel Day, Introduction to Gollancz' edition of *Sir Gawain*; L. H. Loomis, "Sir Gawain and the Green Knight," in *Arthurian Literature in the Middle Ages*, ed. R. S. Loomis (Oxford, 1961), pp. 528–40.

35. Summarized from *Yder*, vv. 185–508; see Kittredge, *A Study of Gawain* . . . , pp. 83–85, for a fuller summary. We should note that although *Yder* survives in but one manuscript, that manuscript is Anglo-Norman. See H. Gelzer's edition for a discussion of its provenance. It may be that the Gawain-poet knew the Yder story in some version which combined that tale with elements drawn from other romances, such as *Le Chevalier à l'épée*, in which the passages recounting Gawain's sight of the castle, his reception, his disarming, and his meeting with his host are very similar to *Sir Gawain*. However, the Gawain-poet himself is most likely the combiner.

36. Day, Introduction to Gollancz' edition of *Sir Gawain*, p. xxxiv.

37. R. S. Loomis, *Wales and the Arthurian Legend*, pp. 79–90.

38. For examples in romance see M. A. Gist, *Love and War in the Middle English Romances* (Philadelphia, 1947), pp. 101–02; for a more general treatment, see F. E. Faverty, "The Story of Joseph and Potiphar's Wife in Medieval Literature," *Harvard Studies and Notes in Philology*, XIII (1931), 81–127. The relation of this traditional tale to *Sir Gawain* is noted very briefly by Gist, p. 101, and by Morton W. Bloomfield, "*Sir Gawain and the Green Knight*," PMLA, LXXVI (1961), 15, n. 35.

39. See the notes in the editions of Gollancz (vv. 1323–64) and of Tolkien and Gordon (vv. 1139 ff.).

40. See Alain Renoir, "A Minor Analogue of *Sir Gawain and the Green Knight*," *Neophilologus*, XLIV (1960), 37–38; Hulbert, MP, XIII, 699.

41. R. S. Loomis, *Wales and the Arthurian Legend*, pp. 79–90, cites some examples of continence before battle. English preachers stressed the idea as a refutation of the opposite belief that there was a connection between sexual prowess and success in battle;

see Morton W. Bloomfield's discussion of the *Sermo epicinus* ascribed to Thomas Bradwardine, *PMLA*, LXXVI (1961), 14. Note that in Malory, Lancelot states the same belief: "As for to sey to take my pleasance with peramours, that woll I refuse: in prencipall for drede of God, for knyghtes that bene adventures sholde nat be advoutrers nothir lecherous, for than they be nat happy nother fortunate unto the werrys . . . they shall be overcom with a sympler knyght than they be hemself" (VI, x).

42. P. 35 in Gragg's translation; since the entire Latin ms. remains unpublished, this translation is the only available edition of this passage.

43. Vv. 1876–84. The confession is bad, of course, because Gawain is evidently not contrite about concealing the lace from the host, and he does not intend to make restitution to him. See John Burrow, "The Two Confession Scenes in *Sir Gawain and the Green Knight*," *MP*, LVII (1959–60), 73–79; Robert Ackerman, "Gawain's Shield; Penitential Doctrine in *Gawain and the Green Knight*," *Anglia*, LXXVI (1958), 254–65. R. H. Greene, "Gawain's Shield and the Quest for Perfection," *ELH*, XXIX (1962), p. 138, denies that the confession is bad; he argues that Gawain cannot acknowledge his sin even to himself, for "There are moral issues the rational mind will not face."

44. Kittredge, *A Study of Gawain* . . . , pp. 101–04; Henry James, *The Europeans* (London, 1952), Ch. XII, p. 163.

45. Gist, *Love and War in the Middle English Romances*, p. 101; as Gist notes, this is the answer of the Gawain in *The Grene Knight*, vv. 388–93. He is, writes Gist, "too shocked to be tactful."

46. Gollancz prints line 1284 as "þaʒ [ho] were burde bryʒtest, þe bur[n]e in mynde hade." Émile Pons, Francis Berry, and R. T. Jones accept the emendation; it has passed into standard anthologies such as that of Fernand Mossé, *A Handbook of Middle English*, tr. J. A. Walker (Baltimore, 1952); it also appears in the most recent popular translations of the poem, those of J. L. Rosenberg (New York, 1961), and Brian Stone (Baltimore, 1959). Its currency is unfortunate, for it changes the whole meaning of a very important part of the poem.

47. *Joseph Andrews*, Bk. I, Ch. vii, in Henry Fielding, *Works*, ed. George Saintsbury (London [1926]), VII, 42–45.

48. See J. F. Kitely, "The *De honeste amandi* of Andreas Capellanus and the Concept of Courtesy in *Sir Gawain and the Green Knight*," *Anglia*, LXXIX (1961), 7–16, for a discussion of the lady's knowledge of courtly love. Kitely notes that her blunt offer of her body is not in keeping with the rules.

49. See Hulbert, *MP*, XIII, 433–62, 689–730.

50. They love Lancelot because, as a damsel explains to him, "For the renowne and bounté that they here of you they woll have your love" (VI, iv).
51. I quote from the long redaction, though the redactions differ only in minute details. The prose version is slightly more condensed (and therefore makes the lady's proposal seem slightly more abrupt), but otherwise it differs little from the others.

Literary Convention and Characterization in *Sir Gawain*

1. W. P. Ker, *Epic and Romance* (New York, 1957), p. 342.
2. See W. C. Curry, *The Middle English Ideal of Personal Beauty* (Baltimore, 1916), p. 3; D. S. Brewer, "Medieval Conceptions of Beauty," *MLR*, L (1955), 257–69. On the knowledge and use of this convention by the Gawain-poet and his fellow alliterative romancers see D. L. Pearsall, "Rhetorical 'Descriptio' in *Sir Gawain and the Green Knight*," *MLR*, L (1955), 129–34.
3. J. F. Eagen, "The Import of Color Symbolism in *Sir Gawain and the Green Knight*," *St. Louis University Studies*, Series A, I (1949), 27. Despite this error, this is a valuable work.
4. John Speirs, "*Sir Gawain and the Green Knight*" in *Medieval English Poetry: The Non-Chaucerian Tradition* (London, 1957), p. 234; G. L. Kittredge, *A Study of Gawain and the Green Knight* (Cambridge, Mass., 1916), p. 199; both Alice Buchanan, "The Irish Framework of *Gawain and the Green Knight*," *PMLA*, XLVII (1932), 234, and R. S. Loomis, *Arthurian Tradition and Chrétien de Troyes* (New York, 1961), p. 288, take the red eyes as a Celtic "solar" feature.
5. Alan Markman, "The Meaning of *Gawain and the Green Knight*," *PMLA*, LXXII (1957), 574–86; H. L. Savage, *The Gawain-Poet* (Chapel Hill, 1956); Speirs, *Medieval English Poetry*, p. 225.
6. Marie Borroff, *Sir Gawain and the Green Knight: A Stylistic and Metrical Study* (New Haven, 1962), pp. 107, 114, notes that the use of "myriest" is unusual here but that there is no doubt the poet intends this aspect of the Green Knight to be attractive. W. C. Curry, *Middle English Ideal of Personal Beauty*, shows how often the Green Knight's features appear in other handsome knights (e.g., p. 114). Hans Schnyder, *Sir Gawain and the Green Knight*, The Cooper Monographs, 6 (Bern, 1961), p. 41, is so taken by the challenger's handsome side that he denies that the character has any grotesqueness at all and argues that the Green Knight is "described as a superior, even

majestic being who inspires respectful awe, and certainly not as a wild man of the woods whose savagery provokes terror."

7. The resemblances between Youth and the Green Knight are noted by M. Y. Offord (ed.), *The Parlement of the Thre Ages,* v. 109 note.

8. For examples see G. L. Marsh, *Sources and Analogues of The Flower and the Leaf* (Chicago, 1906), pp. 23–37.

9. E. K. Chambers, *The English Folk Play* (Oxford, 1933), discusses this history from the point of view of folklore.

10. Chambers, p. 197, suggests a relation between this play and *Sir Gawain,* for which he had long before suggested a ritual origin; see his *The Medieval Stage* (Oxford, 1903), I, 185–86.

11. See Sir James Frazer, *The Golden Bough,* Abridged Edition (New York, 1942), Ch. XXVIII, "The Killing of the Tree Spirit"; Wilhelm Mannhardt, *Wald- und Feldkulte* (Berlin, 1875), I, esp. pp. 322 ff.

12. London, 1941, Pl. 69. See also the eighteenth-century Jack o' the Green, Pl. 52.

13. Speirs, *Medieval English Poetry,* p. 225.

14. *Ibid.,* pp. 219–20.

15. C. J. P. Cave, *Roof Bosses in Medieval Churches* (Cambridge, 1948), p. 67; Lady Raglan, "The Green Man in Church Architecture," *Folk Lore,* L (1938), 45. Lady Raglan noted how realistic these grotesques seem and she concluded that they must therefore be portraits.

16. *The Canterbury Psalter,* intro. M. R. James (London, 1935), esp. Pl. 11; for Farnese's Book of Hours see *Exhibition of Illuminated Manuscripts,* Pierpont Morgan Library (New York, 1934), Ms. 69. In the plates to Richard Bernheimer's *Wild Men in the Middle Ages* (Cambridge, Mass., 1952) there are several such green men, and the margins of almost any illuminated manuscript of the fourteenth century (especially a manuscript of the celebrated East Anglian school) will contain further examples. Some of the best are found in a fourteenth-century French work, in which English influence is apparent, *Les Heures dites de Jean Pucelle,* ed. L. Deslisle (Paris, 1910), Pl. 47. Modern descendants of these figures are still to be found in the colophons of printed books.

17. A monochrome reproduction of this page of the Windmill Psalter is printed in the Morgan *Exhibition* (see note 16 above), Ms. 102. Since the shrubbery in this painting is blue, brown, and orange rather than green, none of these men is green. However, the green-skinned grotesque is very common in medieval art.

18. See the discussion in G. G. Coulton, *Art and the Reformation*

(Oxford, 1928), pp. 371–87. Like almost all reformers, the Lollards and the author of *Pierce the Ploughmans Crede* shared this attitude, but most English preachers approved of art and even of grotesques. See G. R. Owst, *Literature and Pulpit in Medieval England,* Second Revised Edition (Oxford, 1961), pp. 136–48.

19. A. E. Schönbach, "Zu Ulrich von Lichtenstein," *Zeitschrift für deutsches Alterthum, Neue Folge,* XXVI (1882), 314, n. 1. The occurrence of "green as the grass" in both *Sir Gawain* and Ulrich's poem is, of course, without significance, for the phrase is a common formula in German as well as English; see Adèle Stoecklin, *Die Schilderung der Natur im deutschen Minnesang und im älteren deutschen Volkslied* (Strassburg, 1913), p. 33.

20. Ethel Seaton, "*Le Songe vert:* Its Occasion of Writing and Its Author," *MÆ,* XX (1950), 1–16; the attribution to Gower is not convincing. The poem has received little attention; P. Meyer, who discovered it, wrote, "Je ne me suis pas cru obligé de le lire, car il appartient à un genre peu récréatif, le genre allégorique" (*Romania,* V [1876], 63), and C. Langlois in the *Histoire littéraire de la France,* XXXVI (Paris, 1927), characterizes the poem as "Verbose et médiocre, mais non pas sans agrément ça et là." For the possible influence of the poem see W. O. Sypherd, "*Le Songe vert* and Chaucer's Dream Poems," *MLN,* XXIV (1909), 46–47, and Miss Seaton's article, in which the relation of *Le Songe* to *The Black Knight* is discussed.

21. See A. S. Cook, "The European Sky God," *Folk Lore,* XVII (1906), 340–41; G. L. Henderson, "Arthurian Motifs in Gadhelic Literature," *Miscellany Presented to Kuno Meyer* (Halle, 1912), p. 26.

22. For a general discussion of the wild man see Richard Bernheimer's valuable work, *Wild Men in the Middle Ages;* for the wild man in romance see Arthur Dickson, *Valentine and Orson* (New York, 1929), pp. 97–156; a useful study of the wild man in English art is G. C. Druce, "Some Abnormal and Composite Forms in English Church Architecture," *Archeological Journal,* LXXII (1915), esp. pp. 150–70; for the wild man in pageantry see R. S. Loomis, "The Allegorical Siege in the Art of the Middle Ages," *American Journal of Archeology,* Second Series, XXIII (1919), 255–69. In the discussion that follows I draw most heavily on the works of Dickson and Bernheimer.

23. Gollancz glosses "staue" as "axe," apparently considering it a synecdoche like "schaft," but Tolkien and Gordon take it as "club," remarking in their note on the appropriateness of a club to a mound-dweller like the Green Knight. Cf. *OED,* s.v. "staff," *sb.*¹, 2: "A stick, pole, or club used as a weapon."

24. See the discussions by Frazer and Mannhardt cited in note 11 above, and cf. *OED*, s.v. "wodewose" and "ivyman," where it appears the two words are used interchangeably.
25. See Bernheimer, *Wild Men in the Middle Ages*, p. 47.
26. R. S. Loomis, *Arthurian Tradition and Chrétien de Troyes*, pp. 285–89. However, Celtic influence played only a part, though perhaps an important one, in shaping this tradition. See W. Mulertt, "Der wilde Mann im Frankreich," *ZFSL*, LVI (1932), 69–88, for the French tradition of the wild man before Chrétien. Bernheimer, *Wild Men in the Middle Ages*, p. 194, n. 12, notes the contribution of the classical tradition.
27. On *bachlach* see R. S. Loomis, *Celtic Myth and Arthurian Literature* (New York, 1927), pp. 59–60, and *PMLA*, XLVIII (1933), 1024. Loomis even derives the name "Bercilak" from *bachlach*. The derivation is based on the assumption that *Sir Gawain* has a lost source more Celtic than *Caradoc*. For other objections to this derivation see R. M. Smith, "Guinganbresil and the Green Knight," *JEGP*, XLV (1946), 1–25; Smith believes the Green Knight's name is derived from "breslach" and related to Guinganbresil. J. R. Hulbert, "The Name of the Green Knight: Bercilak or Bertilak," *The Manly Anniversary Studies in Language and Literature* (Chicago, 1933), pp. 12–19, offers the more probable explanation. He derives the name from Bertolais, one of Arthur's enemies in the Vulgate *Merlin*. The name appears as "Bertelak" in the English prose *Merlin*. Gollancz therefore prints the name as "Bertilak." Usage among scholars is divided; I use the form "Bercilak" in order to conform to the usage of Tolkien and Gordon, whose edition I use for quotations.
28. On the relation of the wild man in *Le Livre d'Artus* to *Yvain* see L. A. Paton, "The Story of Grisandole: A Study in the Legend of Merlin," *PMLA*, XXII (1907), esp. pp. 268–69. In Spenser see *Fairy Queen*, IV, vii, 5. The editors of the Variorum Spenser search a great variety of sources in an attempt to account for this "carl's" strange features, but they overlook the medieval romance tradition.
29. To the brief account of the wild man in the Latin source, quoted by Skeat in his note to line 4171, the English poet adds enough details to expand the description from two lines in Latin to ten in English.
30. The description of Paradise in *Pearl* (vv. 73–84), in which the trees are blue and silver, is influenced, I believe, by medieval painting, since such nonrepresentational coloring is rare in the literary *plaisance* but relatively common in illuminated books, such as the Windmill Psalter, cited in note 17 above.

31. *English Illuminated Manuscripts of the XIVth and XVth Centuries,* ed. E. G. Millar (Paris, 1928), Pl. 82.
32. *Les Heures dites de Jean Pucelle,* Pl. 61.
33. I. P. McKeehan, "St. Edmund of East Anglia: The Development of a Romantic Legend," *University of Colorado Studies,* XV (1925), 13–74, believed that the beheaded St. Edmund was reflected in *Sir Gawain,* but C. G. Loomis, *White Magic* (Cambridge, Mass., 1948), p. 93, shows that this was a widespread theme.
34. *"Sir Gawain and the Green Knight," JEGP,* XXXIV (1935), 158.
35. See the account in Froissart, *Chroniques,* XV, 84–92.
36. The Wardrobe Accounts list payment for "vizards"—twelve woodwose heads. See Sir N. H. Nicholas, "Observations on the Institution of the Most Noble Order of the Garter," *Archeologica,* XXI (1846), 43, 122.
37. "Attempt nothyng surmountyng your myght/ Ne that to finish passeth your power," v. 29. The sentiment, of course, is a commonplace of fourteenth-century moralizing.
38. V. 992: "þe kyng comaundet lyȝt." The line does not require the alliteration "lord" supplies; none of the rimes in this wheel alliterates.
39. See the discussion in Bernheimer, pp. 106–20. The idea of a wild man as a philosopher may perhaps be involved in the scene in *Mum and the Sothsegger* in which Witt enters the great hall. He is dressed in a simple, old-fashioned, "wholesome guise" in contrast to the elaborately dressed courtiers. Furthermore, the courtiers are all "beardless burnes" (III, 235), whereas he is "With grette browis y-bente and a berde eke" (III, 214). Perhaps the beard should be related to his generally old-fashioned dress, for beards were going out of style in this period, but the combination of the great brows with the beard is reminiscent of the wild man. In romance the most famous of the wise wild men is, of course, Merlin.
40. The illustrations in the Taymouth Hours provide the evidence for its existence. See R. S. Loomis, "A Phantom Tale of Feminine Ingratitude," *MP,* XIV (1917), 751–55.
41. Bernheimer, *Wild Men in the Middle Ages,* p. 123.
42. The lines quoted are from the earlier Porkington Ms., which is dated 1453–1500 (though the romance itself is probably older). In the Percy Ms. (around 1650) the beard is not so prominent: "His mouth was wyde & his beard was gray,/ his lockes on his shoulders lay" (vv. 177–78). This carl also has "2 great eyen brening as ffyer" (v. 181).
43. For a full discussion of the sources of *The Carl of Carlisle* see Auvo Kurvinen's introduction to her edition, pp. 80–111.

44. Kittredge, *A Study of Gawain* . . . , pp. 257–73; R. S. Loomis, *Wales and the Arthurian Legend* (Cardiff, 1955), pp. 77–90.

45. P. 61: "Puis a pris unce hache grant & pesant. . . . Et il estoit li hons el monde qui plus amoit hache en grant mellee." P. 38: "Vns riches roi poissans qui a non claudas de la terre deserte." ("Then he took a great and heavy axe. . . . And he was the man in the world who most loved an axe in battle." "A rich, powerful king called Claudas de la Terre Deserte".) In *Lestoire de Merlin* Claudas is one of Arthur's and Gawain's greatest enemies; he hunts boar (p. 18); when Arthur is young, he visits his court in disguise (pp. 28–29); and he also fights with a club or stick—".j. baston en sa main" (p. 95). R. S. Loomis, *Arthurian Tradition and Chrétien de Troyes*, pp. 282 ff., notes some of the resemblances between Claudas and Bercilak.

46. In French romance, Gollancz notes in his edition (p. 104), the name is "le sauage," and Doddinaual is a mighty hunter.

47. Cf. *Yvain*, vv. 31–32: "Qu'ancor viaut miaux, c'est m'avis,/ Uns cortois morz qu'un vilain vis" ("In my view, a dead courteous man is better than a live churl"). The figure of the *vilain* seems to have been necessary to romance. In the *chansons de geste* he seldom appears, but in romance one needed a figure of the "other fellow" not only as an enemy for the knight but also as a means of defining what knighthood is. See Per Nykrog, *Les Fabliaux* (Copenhagen, 1957), pp. 176–96, 227–41.

48. *Le Roman* is the only secular work the Gawain-poet mentions by name (*Clean*, 1057); see R. J. Menner (ed.), *Purity*, pp. xli–xlii.

49. E.g., *Fairy Queen*, I, iv, 33; VI, vii, 41. Langlois, in his note to v. 2920 of his edition of *Le Roman*, gives many examples of this and Dangier's other features in previous romance.

50. *Sir Perceval*, v. 596. The German version also makes Perceval explicitly wild. See E. Brugger, "Bliocadran," in *Medieval Studies in Memory of G. S. Loomis* (New York, 1957), p. 167–68, where Brugger also cites Weston's emendation, which would make the French Perceval explicitly wild.

51. Else van der ven-ten Bensel, *The Character of Arthur in English Literature* (Amsterdam, 1925), p. 137; Hans Schnyder, "Aspects of Kingship in *Sir Gawain and the Green Knight*," *ES*, XL (1959), 289.

52. There are some green-skinned characters in folklore; see Lewis Spence, *The Fairy Tradition in Britain* (London, 1948), p. 136, and Kittredge, *A Study of Gawain* . . . , pp. 195–99.

53. Cf. J. R. Hulbert, "*Gawain and the Green Knight*," *MP*, XVII (1915), 715. In this period "fayrye" may mean "fantasy" rather than the modern word "fairy." Spence, *The Fairy Tradition*,

pp. 116–17, points this out and cites *Piers Plowman:* "Me befel a ferly of faerie," "a sleight of fantasy," as Spence translates it. Spence also derives the word "fairy" from Latin "fadus," as used by Gervase of Tillbury, *Otia Imperialis,* Diss. III, c. 94, and it has been suggested that "fadus" is a likely explanation for the puzzling word "fade" in the description of the Green Knight. See I. Jackson, *N&Q,* CXCV (1950), 24, and G. V. Smithers, *N&Q,* CXCV (1950), 134–36.

54. For an interpretation of the Green Knight as Death see A. H. Krappe, "Who Was the Green Knight?" *Speculum,* XIII (1938), 206–15; Heinrich Zimmer, *The King and the Corpse,* ed. Joseph Campbell (New York, 1948), pp. 76–77. In a note Campbell adds, " 'Life' and 'Death' are equally *nomina dei.* Green stands for either or both." Yet Zimmer takes it to stand for death, even though this forces him to take the revelation of Bercilak's name as "still another joke of disguise, played this time not on the hero alone but on the readers and the poet too," p. 80. The lyric quoted is "A Light Is Come to the World," No. 24, v. 44, *English Lyrics of the Thirteenth Century,* ed. Carlton Brown (Oxford, 1932). The ambiguous word "fade," taken by some to mean "enchanted" (see note 53 above), by most to mean "hostile," is sometimes used to mean "faded" with the sense of "dead." See *OED,* s.v. "fade," and cf. *Pearl,* v. 29: "Flor and fryte may not be fede."

55. See Dale B. J. Randall, "Is the Green Knight a Fiend?" *SP,* LVII (1960), 479–91. To the objection that Bercilak has some attractive features Randall answers, "We should remember that it is an easy trick for Satan and his cohorts to masquerade as angels of light" (p. 485). D. W. Robertson, in "Why the Devil Wears Green," *MLN,* LXIX (1959), 472, n. 6. remarks that the green devil is not quite comparable to the Green Knight. Hans Schnyder takes the Green Knight as "the Word of God and—on a different allegorical level—anagogically as Christ" (*Sir Gawain,* p. 41).

56. Editors commonly translate "broun" in "Diamaunteȝ a deuys/ þat boþe were bryȝt and broun" (vv. 617–18) as "shining." That is a possible translation, but brown diamonds and their special virtues were evidently well known in this period. Mandeville in his *Travels,* p. 107, tells of brown diamonds that protect one from evil spirits and turn away witchcraft so long as their wearer avoids incontinence. The Gawain-poet probably knew this passage in Mandeville, since he uses the *Travels* as a source for part of *Cleanness;* see Carleton F. Brown, "Note on the Dependence of *Cleanness* on the *Book of Mandeville,*" *PMLA,* XIX (1904), 149–53, and Menner's *Purity,* pp. xli–xliii. Fur-

thermore, brown diamonds (which do exist) were discussed in almost all the medieval lapidaries, where they are credited with the same power Mandeville ascribes to them. See *English Medieval Lapidaries,* ed. J. Evans and M. S. Serjeantson, EETS, CXC (1933).

57. For a brief explanation of this principle see Robertson's article, cited in note 55; for the various symbolic meanings of green see Joseph Eagen, cited in note 3 above.

58. *Eger and Grime,* vv. 69, 291–94. The green elixir is life-giving, but the green complexion may indicate merely that Eger is pale and sickly, still weakened from his wound.

59. "More than one critic has remarked that Gawain is probably more fully represented in English literature before Malory than Arthur himself," R. W. Ackerman, "English Rimed and Prose Romances," *Arthurian Literature in the Middle Ages,* ed. R. S. Loomis (Oxford, 1961), p. 493. Ackerman surveys the extant Gawain-romances, pp. 493–505.

60. For a full discussion see B. J. Whiting, "Gawain: His Reputation, His Courtesy, and His Appearance in Chaucer's *Squire's Tale,*" *MS,* IX (1947), 189–234.

61. This point is touched upon by Hans Schnyder, *ES,* XL (1959), 289.

62. D. E. Baughan, "The Role of Morgan la Fay in *Sir Gawain and the Green Knight,*" *ELH,* XVII (1950), 241–51, comments from a much different point of view on the contrast between the court in *Sir Gawain* and the Arthurian court of tradition.

63. Sister Imogene Baker, *The King's Household in the Arthurian Court from Geoffrey of Monmouth to Malory* (Washington, D.C., 1937), p. 79, notes that next to Arthur and Gawain, Kay is the most common character in Arthurian romance.

64. Kay leaps up and shouts "I shall strike his neck in tooe." The court in *The Grene Knight* is much more traditional than that in *Sir Gawain.* The king is not disturbed by the challenge, and all the knights there are willing to accept the adventure. Such changes show the force of the conventions that the Gawain-poet is breaking. They make the challenge in *The Grene Knight* closer to that in the early redactions of *Caradoc* than to that in *Sir Gawain.* This is not because the author of *The Grene Knight* knew those versions; it is only because he, like the authors of those redactions, is using the material to write a more conventional romance than *Sir Gawain.*

65. "Ce *premerain vers,* joyeux, ensoleillé, printanier est suivi des peines et douleurs, de tout ce qu'il y a de sérieux dans l'amour du troubadour comme dans l'aventure du roman." Reto R.

Bezzola, *Le Sens de l'aventure et de l'amour* (Paris, 1947), p. 88. I have slightly changed Bezzola's meaning by translating "comme" as "or," since in his argument he is moving from the lyric to the romance.

66. See Albert B. Friedman, "Morgan le Fay in *Sir Gawain and the Green Knight*," *Speculum*, XXXV (1960), 260–74.

67. See, for example, the arming of Gawain in *Le Chevalier à l'épée*, vv. 36–46.

68. This is shown not only by the attention to heraldry in the later romances but in the use of purely decorative heraldic devices in the illuminated books of the fourteenth century.

69. The relation of Gawain's shield to the action is discussed by G. J. Englehardt, "The Predicament of Gawain," *MLQ*, XVI (1955), 218–25; R. W. Ackerman, "Gawain's Shield; Penitential Doctrine in *Gawain and the Green Knight*," *Anglia*, LXXVI (1958), 254–65; R. H. Greene, "Gawain's Shield and the Quest for Perfection," *ELH*, XXIX (1962), 121–39.

70. See F. Bogdanow, "The Character of Gawain in the Thirteenth-Century Prose Romances," *MÆ*, XXVII (1958), 154–61.

71. Jean Frappier, "Le Personnage de Gauvain dans la Première Continuation de *Perceval (Conte du Graal)*," *RP*, XI (1958), 331–44.

72. The adventure is told in Malory, IV, xxii.

73. *Le Chevalier à l'épée*, vv. 624–31; *Hunbaut*, vv. 490–850; *Carl of Carlisle*, vv. 335–46.

74. *Perlesvaus*, p. 95. The passage is discussed in more detail in my last chapter.

75. J. F. Kitely, "The Knight Who Cared for His Life," *Anglia*, LXXIX (1962), 131–37, shows that Gawain was traditionally characterized as "willing to accept a draw," especially in the English romances.

76. "Fayled neuer þe freke in his fyue fengereȝ" may refer not to Gawain's strength but to his virtue; see Ackerman, *Anglia*, LXXVI, 263, and Greene, *ELH*, XXIX, 134. Gawain's prowess is implied by "forsnes" in v. 646, but even there the sense is ambiguous. Tolkien and Gordon emend to "fersnes" and translate "pride, high courage." Gollancz allows the word to stand and glosses "forsnes" as "strength." "Forsnes," which appears nowhere else in Middle English, is probably closer to "fortitude" than to "strength" or even "courage." See *MED*, s.v. "fors," and note that when Mary does come to Gawain's aid (v. 1769), fortitude, in its older sense of the power to resist sin, is the aid she gives. G. R. Owst, *Literature and Pulpit in Medieval England*, pp. 331–38, discusses fourteenth-century

knighthood from the preachers' point of view and notes (p. 336) that participation in tournaments, such as those at Camelot, was no guarantee of military prowess.
77. *Pars T,* l. 952.
78. Cf. *Erec and Enide,* vv. 2536 ff.

The Style

1. A beginning in this direction has been made by Marie Borroff, *Sir Gawain and the Green Knight: A Stylistic and Metrical Study* (New Haven, 1962), esp. Ch. IV, although Miss Borroff's main emphasis is on diction.
2. E.g., Richard Garnett and Edmund Gosse, *English Literature, an Illustrated Record* (London, 1903), I, 111.
3. *Parson's Prologue,* vv. 42–43.
4. For a discussion of "traits" and "tendencies" in style see Meyer Shapiro, "Style," in *Anthropology Today,* ed. A. L. Kroeber (Chicago, 1953), pp. 287–312. Shapiro is not primarily concerned with literary style, but his essay and rich bibliography are very useful to the literary student.
5. Ben Jonson, *Timber,* in *Works,* ed. Simpson and Herford (Oxford, 1924), VIII, 625: "Language most shewes a man; speak that I may see thee." For the medieval theory see R. H. Robbins, *Ancient and Medieval Grammatical Theory* (London, 1951), esp. the discussion of the "Modistae," pp. 77–90. Medieval literary critics, however, did not share the assumption of the grammarians that the form of language was important. Geoffrey of Vinsauf quotes the opening lines of the *Aeneid* and then comments, "Quod nihil aliud est quam 'Describo Aeneam.'" *Documentum de arte versificandi,* II, 2, 11, p. 273 in Faral.
6. Marie Borroff, *Sir Gawain,* pp. 133–210, has the most recent discussion of the Middle English alliterative line. Her theory is that there are two lifts in every half-line, without exception, but it is clear from her discussion of "The Extended Form," pp. 190–210, that extensions (by means of secondary stresses) usually occur in the first half-line.
7. See the discussions by Dorothy Everett, *Essays on Middle English Literature* (Oxford, 1955), pp. 23 ff.; R. M. Wilson, *Early Middle English Literature,* Second Edition (London, 1951), pp. 207–09; and, most important, J. P. Oakden, *Alliterative Poetry in Middle English: The Dialectal and Metrical Survey,* Publications of the University of Manchester, CCV, English Series, XIII (1930), and *Alliterative Poetry in Middle English:*

A Survey of the Traditions, Publications of the University of Manchester, CCXXXVI, English Series, XXII (1935).

8. See Kemp Malone, *A Literary History of England,* ed. A. C. Baugh *et al.* (New York, 1948), pp. 26–28, for a perceptive and useful discussion of Old English "run-on" and "end-stopped" styles. In Middle English, of course, the lines are not uniformly end-stopped. Here, as elsewhere in this chapter, I speak of the dominant tendencies of the style. Morton W. Bloomfield's remark on Langland's alliterative line (in *Piers Plowman as a Fourteenth-Century Apocalypse* [New Brunswick, N.J., 1962], p. 39) could apply to most alliterative verse in this period: "It would be too much to say his lines are end-stopped, for he writes in rather long sentences . . . with parallel and parenthetical clauses; but the end of a line tends to be the end of a clause or at least a thought unit. When Langland does use . . . a violent enjambement dividing a syntactic unit in two, we are brought up short." For want of a better term I have retained "end-stopped" to describe this style. That the Middle English writers did consider the full line rather than the half-line as the significant unit is shown by the manner in which they added rime to the alliterative line. In the older tradition when a writer such as Cynewulf or, much later, Laȝamon, added end-rime, he added it to the ends of the half-lines, riming within the line. In the Middle English tradition rime was usually added at the end of the full line. Likewise, the Old English formula is usually a half-line unit; in Middle English, though the half-line unit still predominates, formulas that extend beyond the caesura are not uncommon. See note 19 below.

9. W. P. Lehmann, *The Origin of Germanic Verse Form* (Austin, Texas, 1956), shows how profoundly linguistic change affected the alliterative style of all the Germanic languages.

10. "Alwaldende kyng," however, did remain as a fixed epithet.

11. See E. S. Olszewska, "Norse Alliterative Tradition in Middle English, I," *Leeds Studies in English and Kindred Languages,* VI (1937), 50–66.

12. The date of *Somer Soneday* is still disputed, but no one has yet offered a convincing alternative to Brown's argument (in the introduction to his edition) for an early fourteenth-century date. In *Ane Schort Treatise* King James VI calls the line "tumbling verse," and the example he uses to illustrate it shows that it was associated with "flytings." The late flytings of Dunbar and Kennedy, and even one of those by Skelton (the first of the poems "Against Garnesche"), contain enough touches of alliteration and archaic diction to justify James' association of the

line with this genre; perhaps such traces originally lent the flytings a touch of mock-heroic humor.

13. See Gustav Plessow, *Gotische Tektonik im Wortkunstwerk: Kunsterliches im Bau der mittelenglischen Romanze von Gawain und dem grünen Ritter* (Munich, 1931).

14. Oakden, *A Survey of the Traditions*, Appendix I; see also August Brink, *Stab und Wort im Gawain* (Halle, 1920); Max Kullnick, *Studien über den Wortschatz in Sir Gawayne and the grene Knyzt* (Berlin, 1902).

15. F. P. Magoun, Jr., "Oral-Formulaic Character of Anglo-Saxon Narrative Poetry," *Speculum*, XXVIII (1953), 446–67. See also Albert Lord, *The Singer of Tales* (Cambridge, Mass., 1960).

16. R. A. Waldron, "Oral Formulaic Technique and Middle English Alliterative Poetry," *Speculum*, XXXII (1957), 792–804. This is a most important article upon which, as my discussion shows, I depend heavily. J. P. Oakden, in *A Survey of the Traditions*, assembled lists of "alliterative formulas" that showed how heavily these poets depended on past tradition, but Oakden listed alliterating words without reference to the structure in which they appear, a procedure to which Waldron rightly objects.

17. I quote here from the manuscript (British Museum Add. Mss. 31042), adding punctuation and silently expanding abbreviations. Gollancz moves line 22 to an earlier passage and prints this one as:

> Whylome were lordes in londe þat loued in thaire hertis
> To here makers of myrthes, þat matirs couthe fynde,
> Wyse wordes with-inn, þat wr[iten] were neuer,
> Ne redde in no romance þat euer renke herde.
>
> (vv. 20–23)

This makes the allusion more clear, but the passage makes sense even with the parenthetical line 22, and a recognition of the oral tradition allows us to retain the original "wroghte," referring not to the writing of the poem but to its composition.

18. A. C. Baugh, "Improvisation in the Middle English Romances," *PAPS*, CIII (1959), 418–54.

19. In the following citations I quote first the similar phrases to be found elsewhere in *Sir Gawain* and the other Cotton Nero poems and then examples gathered from other alliterative works. They are only examples, for I have not made an exhaustive search. Doubtless a full study of the formulas in Middle English poetry should be undertaken.

1. *SG*, 2525, After þe segge and þe asaute watȝ sesed at Troye.
   WA, 1452, And he settes on a sawte and seses it beliue.
   WA, 2380, Has he noȝt cites butt saute sesyd out of nounbre? (Cf. *WA*, 1431, 1766; *SJ*, 833.)

1a. *Parl*, 303, þat þaire cite assegede and saylid it full ȝerne.
    DT, 3532, Sone after þis saute, sothely to telle.
    (Cf. *Wynnere*, 1, Sithen that Bretayne was biggede, and Bruyttus it aughte.)

1b. *WA*, 3020, Was neuer sene, I suppose, sen þe sege of troye.

2. *Clean*, 1292, And syþen bet doun þe burȝ and brend hit in askeȝ.
   SJ, 1288, Bot doun betyn & brent into blake erþe.
   DT, 5007, Betyn and brent doun vnto bare askeȝ.

2a. *Pistill*, 147, I be bretenet and brent in baret to byde.
    MA, 3520, Are they brettenede, or brynte, or broughte owte of lyue?

2b. *SJ*, 716, & brenten euereche bon into þe browne askeȝ.
    Cheu, 344, And brente here in þe balowe fyer alle to browne askes.

3. *SG*, 22b, tene þat wroȝten; 1775, And be traytor to þat tolke þat þat telde aȝt. (See the next section in the text for a discussion of the pattern in 3b.)
   SJ, 723, In tokne of tresoun & trey þat he wroȝt.
   MA, 3901, Trynnys in with a trayne treson to wirke.
   WA, 5028, Qua suld þat trecherous trayne of treson him wirke.

4. *SG*, 2098b, "þe worst vpon erthe." (Cf. also the frequent use of "upon earth" as the final foot of the line in both *Sir Gawain* and *Cleanness*.)

4a. *WA*, 3439, Quen tried was a trechory þe tolkis to be hedid.
    WA, 3192, þire traitours on þis trechoure trowthis has strakid.

4b. See below in the text for a discussion of this common formulaic pattern, and cf. *Parl*, 298b, "witest on erthe," *MA*, 4344b, "praysed in erthe," etc.

5. *SG*, 1110, Gawayne þe gode; *Pat* 245a, Jonas þe Jwe; *SG*, 844b, and of hyghe eldee.

5a. *WA*, 620a, Alexander þe athill.
    Alex A, 79a, Phillip þe fre. (The pattern is very common.)

5b. *WA*, 3316a, It commes wel of hyghe kyn.

6. *WA*, 1941, Deperset all our prouince & purely distroyde.

7. *SG*, 50a, With alle þe wele of þe worlde.
   WA, 20, And all rialme & þe riches in-to þe rede est.

7a. *Erk*, 119a, þat welneghe al þe nyȝt.
    Quatrefoil, 19, Alle þe wele of þis worlde.

8. *Pat*, 90a, Jonas toward port Japhe; *Clean*, 1361, Balþasar
   þurȝ Babiloyn. (See also lines 11 and 12 ff.) *SG*, 2259b,
   grayþed hym swyþe.
8a. *SJ*, 49, Nathan toward Nero nome on his way.
   Parl, 547a, And that Emperour at Egremorte. (The construction is very common.)
8b. *Parl*, 369b, & bashed hem swithe.
   Mum and Soth, III, 60, dineth hem swyþe. (The construction is very common.)
9. *SG*, 528b, þat ros vpon fyrst.
   WA, 5415, þou has a blisful burȝe bigged to þi name.
   Erk, 207, After þat Brutus þis burghe had buggid on first.
   DT, 5216, That biggid þe burgh bigly hym-seluyn/
   And callid it Messan be mowthe, in mynd of his nome.
9a. *WA*, 4431, In bigging of burgis & bilding of toures (cf.
   WA, 2256).
9b. *WA*, 1366b, bigget was frist.
10. *Clean*, 410, Noe þat ofte nevened þe nome of our Lorde.
   WA, 1119, And neuenes hit his awen name þat neuer
   syn chaungid.
   Parl, 108, And to ȝowe neuen thaire nomes naytly
   there-aftir.
   (Cf. *Parl*, 297, 580; *WA*, 293, 619, 1456, 2187, 5655.)
11. See verse 8 above; for 11b cf. *Clean*, 280b, ful wroþly
   bygynneȝ, and 359b, 1401b; *SG*, 1606b, lufly bigynneȝ.
11a. *MA*, 3586, And tendirly to Tuskayne take tente alls I
   byde (cf. *MA*, 431).
12. See vv. 8 and 11 above. For 12b cf. *Clean*, 717, to lyfte
   such domez.
12b. *SJ*, 997b, he lifte vp þe eyen.
13. *Pat*, 126, For he watȝ fer in þe flod foundade to Tarce.
13a. *DT*, 5800a, þat fer from þe flod.
14. *SG*, 195a, þer mony belleȝ ful bryȝt; *Pat*, 254a, Bi mony
   rokkes ful roȝe; *Clean*, 43a, With mony blame ful bigge;
   Pat, 117a, ȝise, he blusched ful brode; *Clean*, 636b, and
   by þe bred settez.
   Erk, 32, By alle Bretaynes bonkes were bot othire twayne.
14a. *Parl*, 125a, With many dyamandes full dere.
   Death and Life, 25, Broad on þeir bankes. (The construction is common.)
14b. *WA*, 1143b, & þare hys tentis settis (cf. *WA*, 397b,
   1850b, 2142b). Cf. *MA*, 4346a, Into Bretayne the brode.

20. J. R. Hulbert, "A Hypothesis Concerning the Alliterative Revival," *MP*, XXVIII (1931), 405–22. Some of the satiric alliterative poems do take a "baronial" point of view; *Richard the
Redeles* is the most obvious example, but, like the other satires,
it was composed well after the Revival had begun. Likewise,

some barons did support alliterative verse, but the only one we can identify is Humphrey of Bohun, a member of the "royal party" in politics.

21. The abandonment of Anglo-Norman as a literary language in the fourteenth century certainly helped create the conditions in which the Revival took place. See Fitzroy Pyle, "The Place of Anglo-Norman in the History of English Versification," *Hermathena*, XLIX (1935), 22–42.

22. Cf. Oakden, *A Survey of the Traditions*, and Baugh (note 18 above).

23. *KT*, v. 2605. Cited by Dorothy Everett, who discusses Chaucer's knowledge of alliterative verse in "Chaucer's 'Good Ear,'" in *Essays on Middle English Literature*, pp. 139–48.

24. J. D. Bruce, *The Evolution of Arthurian Romance* (Baltimore, 1923), I, 125; John Speirs, "*Sir Gawain and the Green Knight*," *Medieval English Poetry: The Non-Chaucerian Tradition* (London, 1957), esp. pp. 267–71; Waldron, *Speculum*, XXXIII, 800. Waldron cautiously limits his speculation to *Morte Arthure*.

25. J. A. Burrow, "The Audience of *Piers Plowman*," *Anglia*, LXXV (1957), 373–84; Morton W. Bloomfield, *Piers Plowman*, pp. 42–43.

26. In the introduction to his edition Skeat notes that the poem is faultless in the use of the second personal pronoun (pp. xli–xliii). Considering the early date of this poem, this usage is evidence of a remarkable degree of sophistication.

27. Vv. 75–82: "I mad noght for no disours/ Ne for no seggers no harpours,/ Bot for þe luf of symple men/ þat strange Inglis can not ken./ for many it ere þat strange Inglis/ In ryme wat neuer what it is." Robert lived in the Northeast Midlands, and the poems of which he speaks are not necessarily alliterative. However, the alliterative tradition was probably strong in this part of England in Robert's time and earlier, for the later tail-rime romances from this area are characterized by many features of the alliterative tradition. See A. M. Trounce, "The English Tail-Rhyme Romances," *MÆ*, I (1932), 87–108, 168–82; II (1933), 34–57, 189–98; III (1934), 30–50.

28. *NPT*, v. 3347. For discussions of medieval rhetorical theory see C. S. Baldwin, *Medieval Rhetoric and Poetic* (New York, 1928); J. W. H. Atkins, *English Literary Criticism: The Medieval Phase* (New York, 1943); Edmond Faral, *Les Arts poétiques du XIIᵉ et du XIIIᵉ siècle* (Paris, 1923; repr. 1958), pp. 54–103; Richard McKeon, "Rhetoric in the Middle Ages," "Poetry and Philosophy in the Twelfth Century: The Renaissance of Rhetoric," *Critics and Criticism*, ed. R. S. Crane (Chicago, 1952), pp. 260–96, 297–318.

29. Quoted by Charles Muscatine, *Chaucer and the French Tradition* (Berkeley, 1957), p. 244.

30. A. G. Brodeur, *The Art of Beowulf* (Berkeley, 1959), p. 40.

31. Alan M. F. Gunn, *The Mirror of Love* (Lubbock, Texas, 1953), p. 89, finds *expolitio* "easily the most important" means of amplification, so important that he takes *expolitio* and *amplificatio* as synonyms. Cf. Faral, *Les Arts poétiques*, p. 61: *expolitio* is "la grande chose."

32. See John Finlayson, "Rhetorical 'Descriptio' of Place in the Alliterative *Morte Arthure*," *MP*, LXI (1963), 1–11.

33. C. O. Chapman, "Virgil and the Gawain-poet," *PMLA*, LX (1945), 16–23, bases almost the whole of his argument on the many smaller details of style (e.g., asyndeton) that appear in both Virgil and *Sir Gawain*. Tom Burns Haber, *A Comparative Study of Beowulf and the Aeneid* (Princeton, 1931), makes a good case for the influence of Virgil on *Beowulf*, but part of his argument is based on the many parallels in phraseology that are traditional rather than "borrowed."

34. See Klaeber's Introduction, *Beowulf*, p. xxxii; see also Malone, *Literary History of England*, pp. 28–29. J. S. P. Tatlock, in "Laʒamon's Poetic Style and Its Literary Relations," *Manly Anniversary Studies in Language and Literature*, p. 8, discusses variation in the *Brut*, noting how the poet likes to pause to examine an object or action from all angles. (One need not halt the narrative to do this; see W. K. Wimsatt's analysis of variation in a passage from *Beowulf* in *The Verbal Icon* [Louisville, 1954], p. 193.) Dorothy Everett, *Essays on Middle English Literature*, p. 23, touches on descriptions in Middle English alliterative verse from this point of view.

35. In the short poem *Patience* Jonah is designated by a dozen different words—*Jonas, prophete, Jue, renk, wyʒe, gome, sege, burne, lede, haþel, freke,* and *schalk*. In *Cleanness* the poet uses eight different synonyms for Abraham in the less than ninety lines that narrate the angels' visit (vv. 601–88).

36. Tolkien and Gordon, *Sir Gawain*, p. vi.

37. *A Survey of the Traditions*, pp. 394–99; see also K. R. Schmittbetz, *Das Adjectiv im Vers von Syr Gawayne and the grene Knyʒt* (Berlin, 1908), and *Anglia*, XXXII (1909), 1–59, 163–89, 359–93.

38. The adjectives are (with the verse number of their first appearance): þat hende, 946; þe ʒonge, 951; þat on, 952; þat gay, 970; þe loueloker, 973, þat swete, 1222, þe menskful, 1268; worþy, 1276; þe clere, 1489; dere, 1492; fre, 1545, þat cortays, 2411; þat lufsum, 1814; þat comly, 1755. The nouns are lady, 941;

burde, 1010; Madame, 1263; dame, 1316; prynces, 1770; þat lif, 1780; þat wyght, 1792; wyf, 2369; fere, 2411.

39. In the first 251 lines of Chaucer's *Parliament of Fowls* there are thirty-four constructions consisting of a noun plus a prepositional phrase. They have no special structure, for they range from three to seven syllables in length and they occur in any position in the line. In the first 251 long lines of *Sir Gawain* (that is, not counting the bobs and wheels) there are fifty-seven such constructions (I do not count the prepositional phrases that occur in series—there are five of them); forty-seven of these occur in exactly the same metrical position—at the end of the first half-line—and the great majority have the same metrical structure—"cóurce in þe cóurt," "móst vpon mólde." Nine of the other ten occur in the second half-line and they fall into another formulaic pattern—noun plus preposition plus modifier plus object, with the noun and the modifier alliterating. The only prepositional phrase in these lines that does not fall into either of these two patterns is the anomalous v. 3: "þe tulk þat þe trammes of tresoun þer wroȝt." The syntactic structure and meter of the phrase is quite ordinary, but the caesura falls in the middle of the construction. It is worth noting that the line is also anomalous in its handling of the relative clause (see note 40).

40. In the first 251 lines of *The Parliament of the Fowls* there are twenty-three constructions consisting of a noun plus a relative clause introduced by *that*. Again these constructions have no special syntactic or metrical characteristics. They can occur anywhere in the line, and it is not unusual for the *that* clause to be separated by one or more words from the noun on which it depends. There are six examples of this in the twenty-three constructions. In the first 251 long lines of *Sir Gawain* there are thirty-one examples of this construction. All but one—line 3—are contained within the half-line, occurring either as the two alliterating syllables nearest the caesura ("þe fyrst word þat he warp") or as a construction consisting of a noun at the end of the preceding half-line followed by the *þat*-clause which completely fills the next half-line. In only three of the thirty-one examples is the noun separated from the relative clause.

41. Although the characteristic had been noted by earlier scholars, Menner was the first to discuss it fully in his Introduction to *Purity* (*Cleanness*), pp. xvi–xix. For a recent restatement see J. D. Ebbs, "Stylistic Mannerisms of the Gawain-poet," *JEGP*, LVII (1958), 522–25. For a discussion of its use throughout the tradition see my article, "The Authorship of *St. Erkenwald*," *JEGP*, LXIV (1965), 393 ff.

42. "Haþel" is an exception only in those poems in which initial "h" is not pronounced.

43. George Kane, *Piers Plowman: The A Version,* emends III, 95: "Vnwittily,[wy], wroȝt hast þou ofte." This is a kind of variation Langland carefully avoids. J. A. Burrow notes that when a traditional word, "burde" (III, 14), is used of Mede, its rarity gives it a special, here ironic, effect that Langland fully exploits (*Anglia,* LXXV, 381). On Langland's "middle" style as opposed to the "aristocratic" (and more traditional) style of *Sir Gawain,* see Morton W. Bloomfield, *Piers Plowman,* pp. 34–41.

44. In the first thousand lines Arthur is once "þe gome" (v. 85), once "þe bolde" (v. 79), once "þat worthiliche wy" (v. 695), once "þat nobel of names" (v. 524), once "roy reall" (v. 411). He is three times "souverayn," ten times "Arthur," fourteen times "conquerour," and twenty-five times "kyng." The old lady who is the giant's captive on St. Michael's mount does not recognize Arthur and addresses him as "careman" (v. 957) and "berne" (v. 962).

45. He is "knyȝt" at vv. 366, 381, 482; "Gawain" at vv. 110, 339, 343, 365, 375, 377, 381, 387, 390, 398, 405, 416, 421, 448, 463, 476, 487; Arthur once warmly addresses him as "cosyn," and the churlish Green Knight addresses him once each as "haþel," "lude," and "segge."

46. "Leude" refers to Gawain in vv. 2333 and 2505, and to the Green Knight in vv. 2389 and 2499; "haþel" is used for the Green Knight in v. 2331 and for Gawain in v. 2467.

47. The phrase is Milton's description of his own verse, applied to alliterative poetry by W. P. Ker, *English Literature: Medieval,* Home University Library (London, n.d.), p. 41. It is interesting but not entirely surprising that Milton's verse, itself distantly related to an oral heroic tradition, should share some stylistic similarities with alliterative verse.

48. "Mit Unterbrechung des syntaktischen Zusammenhang," Walter Paetzel, *Die Variationen in der altgermanische Alliterationspoesie,* Palaestra, XLVIII (Berlin, 1913), p. 3.

49. The Latin (quoted in Magoun's note) reads: "Deinde amoto exercitu venit ad[r]Osidraces. Oxidraces enim non sunt superbi homines neque pugnant cum aliqua gente. Nudi ambulant et habitant in tiguriis et in spelluncis, non habentes ciuitatem neque habitationem et uocantur Gi[m]nosophyste."
The English translator writes:

> When þis weith at his wil weduring hadde,
> Ful raþe rommede he rydinge þedirre.
> To Oxidrace with his ost Alixandre wendus,

þere wilde contré was wist and wonderful peple,
þat weren proved ful proude and prys of hem helde.
Of bodi went þai bar wiþ-oute any wede,
And hadde grave on þe ground many grete cavys,
þere here wonnynge was wyntyrus and somerus.

(vv. 1–8)

Only in v. 7 does the second half-line carry the translation.

50. See vv. 43 ff. in *The Squire of Low Degree*; see *The Parliament of Fowls*, vv. 337–64, for a more successful use of this common device. See R. A. Waldron, *Speculum*, XXXII, pp. 800–01, for a discussion of the sentence in the *Morte Arthure*, which begins at v. 26 and ends at v. 59, though a good many complete clauses are contained in those lines.

51. A. Bonjour, "Werre and wrake and wonder (*Sir Gawain*, l. 16)," *ES*, XXXII (1951), 70–72.

52. See Ernst Curtius, *European Literature and the Latin Middle Ages*, tr. W. R. Trask (New York, 1953), pp. 70–72.

53. Malone, *Literary History of England*, p. 20, remarks that all variation involves ellipsis, even appositive constructions.

54. See Cornelius Novelle, "The Demonstrative Adjective *This:* Chaucer's Use of a Colloquial Narrative Device," *MS*, XIX (1957), 246–49.

55. Ruth Crosby, "Chaucer and the Custom of Oral Delivery," *Speculum*, XIII (1938), 413–22.

56. "The Significance of the Hunting Scenes in *Sir Gawain and the Green Knight*," *JEGP*, XXVII (1928), 1–15. Now reprinted as Chapter II in Savage's *The Gawain-Poet*.

57. Else von Schaubert, "Der englische Ursprung von *Syr Gawayn and the Grene Knyȝt*," *Englische Studien*, LVII (1923), 330–46.

58. See Sylvan Barnett, "A Note on the Structure of *Sir Gawain and the Green Knight*," *MLN*, LXXI (1956), 319.

59. For a full discussion see Brodeur, *Art of Beowulf*; A. C. Bartlett, *The Larger Rhetorical Patterns in Anglo-Saxon Poetry* (New York, 1935); Jean Bloomfield, "The Style and Structure of *Beowulf*," *RES*, XIV (1938), 396–403.

60. See William Matthews, *The Tragedy of Arthur* (Berkeley, 1960), which includes a discussion of the structure of *Morte Arthure* and, on pp. 157–77, of the structures of *Awntyrs of Arthur* and *Golagros and Gawane*. E. von Schaubert (note 57 above) discusses the general resemblance of the structure of *Sir Gawain* to the structure of these works.

61. Arnold Hauser, *The Social History of Art*, tr. Stanley Goodman in collaboration with the author (New York, 1957), I, 240. See

Charles Muscatine, *Chaucer and the French Tradition,* pp. 167–73, for a discussion of Gothic form in Chaucer.

62. The Gawain-poet was apparently familiar with these works, for he not only drew on the conventions of painting for his description of Paradise in *Pearl* (see note 30, p. 272), he shares with the East Anglian school an interest in heraldry, wild men, and hunting, and his technique of visual description (see Ch. IV) seems to have some affinities with Gothic painting. See Erec G. Millar, Introduction, *English Illuminated Manuscripts of the XIVth and XVth Centuries* (Paris, 1928); Margaret Rickert, *Painting in Britain: The Middle Ages* (Baltimore, 1954), Ch. VI; Joan Evans, *English Art, 1307–1461* (London, 1955), Ch. III; for examples see also the British Museum's *Schools of Illumination, Part III; English, A.D. 1300 to 1350* (London, 1921).

63. Émile Pons (ed.), *Sire Gauvain et le chevalier vert,* p. 37; Erich Auerbach, *Mimesis,* tr. W. R. Trask (New York, 1957), p. 216.

The Narrative and Descriptive Techniques

1. George Kane, *Middle English Literature* (London, 1951), p. 76; see also G. L. Kittredge, *A Study of Gawain and the Green Knight* (Cambridge, Mass., 1916), p. 3; J. E. Wells, *A Manual of the Writings in Middle English* (New Haven, 1916), p. 47; John Speirs, "Sir Gawain and the Green Knight," in *Medieval English Poetry: The Non-Chaucerian Tradition* (London, 1957), p. 231; John Berry, "Sir Gawain and the Green Knight," in *The Age of Chaucer,* ed. Boris Ford, Pelican Guide to English Literature, I (London, 1954), p. 149.

2. Wells, *Manual,* p. 47; the quoted phrase is from Dorothy Everett, *Essays on Middle English Literature* (Oxford, 1955), p. 79.

3. Everett, p. 81; Werner Habicht, *Die Gebärde in englischen Dichtungen des Mittelalters* (Munich, 1959), pp. 148–56; Alain Renoir, "Descriptive Technique in *Sir Gawain and the Green Knight," Orbis Litterarum,* XIII (1958), 126–32. My discussion depends heavily on Renoir's study. See also Marie Borroff, *Sir Gawain and the Green Knight: A Stylistic and Metrical Study* (New Haven, 1962), esp. pp. 126–28.

4. Hugo Sanctis Victoriensis, *Didascalicon,* p. 59; "Ordo . . . attenditur . . . in narratione secundum dispositionem, quae duplex est; naturalis scilicet quando res eo refertur ordine quo gestu est; artificialis, scilicet quando in quod postea gestum est prius narratur, et quod prius postmodum dicitur." Edmond

Faral, who cites this passage, discusses theories of narrative in *Les Arts poétiques du XIIe et du XIIIe siècle* (Paris, 1923; repr. 1958), pp. 55–59; see also J. W. H. Atkins, *English Literary Criticism: The Medieval Phase* (New York, 1943), pp. 100–01.

5. "Amet artificialem ordinem et spernat naturalem." So a medieval commentator glosses Horace, *Ars poetica*, vv. 42–45; quoted by Faral, *Les Arts poétiques*, p. 56.

6. The rhetoricians also recognized this possibility. Faral (*Les Arts poétiques*, p. 57) quotes Bernard of Utrecht, who holds that the orders of narrative may be "artificialis vel naturalis vel commixtus." However, the major medieval critics gave little attention to the "mixed" order.

7. This is most apparent in the "disenchantment scenes" in romances like *William of Palerne* and *The Carl of Carlisle*. See Sarah F. Barrow, *The Medieval Society Romances* (New York, 1924), pp. 77–78.

8. See Manfred Gsteiger, *Die Landschaftbilderungen in den Romanen Chrestiens de Troyes* (Bern, 1958), for a full discussion of Chrétien's usual descriptive techniques.

9. J. Huizinga, *The Waning of the Middle Ages* (London, 1924), Ch. XII.

10. Dorothy Everett, *Essays on Middle English Literature*, p. 81.

11. Frederick W. Moorman, *The Interpretation of Nature in English Poetry* (Strassburg, 1905), provides what is still the best survey of the subject, though he did not recognize the existence of a tradition and considered the alliterative descriptions purely representational. Ernst Curtius, *European Literature and the Latin Middle Ages*, tr. W. R. Trask (New York, 1953), Ch. X, discusses the *locus amoenus* and *gaste forest*. However, it should be noted that the passage quoted in this paragraph is based on an unusually long description of a storm in the poet's source, Guido delle Colonne, *Historia destructionis Troiae*, p. 243.

12. See, for example, *The Siege of Jerusalem*, vv. 53–60; *Cleanness*, vv. 947–60; *The Wars of Alexander*, vv. 550–68.

13. *Biblia Vulgata*, Jonah, i, 4.

14. SG, 1998–2005. The description of the passing of the seasons, though necessarily somewhat more general, is organized on the same principle; SG, 500–31.

15. SG, 2160–84. Other examples are discussed in the text below.

16. John Speirs, *Medieval English Poetry*, p. 231.

17. This passage is discussed briefly by Dorothy Everett, *Essays on Middle English Literature*, p. 81.

18. See Helmut Hatzfeld, "A Note on de Joinville's Prose Style" in *Medieval Studies in Honor of J. M. Ford* (Cambridge, Mass.,

1948), pp. 67–80. On the "eyewitness" technique in Froissart see my "The Use of a Physical Viewpoint in Berners' Froissart," *MLQ*, XX (1959), 333–38.

19. See Alain Renoir, "The Progressive Magnification: An Instance of Psychological Description in *Sir Gawain and the Green Knight*," *Moderna Språk*, LIV (1960), 245–53; D. L. Pearsall, "Rhetorical 'Descriptio' in *Sir Gawain and the Green Knight*," *MLR*, L (1955), 129–34.

20. Habicht, *Die Gebärde*, p. 149.

21. Huizinga, *Waning of the Middle Ages*, pp. 245–46, quotes the familiar words of Thomas Aquinas: "Three things . . . are required for beauty: first, integrity or perfection . . . next, true proportion or consonance; lastly, brightness, because we call beautiful whatever has a brilliant color." Edgar de Bruyne, *L'Esthétique du moyen âge* (Louvain, 1947), provides a good brief discussion of the whole problem.

22. See, for example, the feasting scene in Queen Mary's Psalter, reproduced in *English Illuminated Manuscripts of the XIVth and XVth Centuries*, ed. Eric G. Millar (Paris, 1928).

23. Edgar de Bruyne, *Études d'esthétique médiévale* (Bruges, 1940), II, 224, quotes Hugo of St. Victor: "In his quattor . . . situs, motus, species, qualitas . . . motum excellentiorem locum habere dubium non est, quia viciniora vitae sunt mobilia quam ea quae moveri non possunt."

The Meaning

1. As a sample of the variety of answers offered, see Charles Moorman, "Myth and Medieval Literature: *Sir Gawain and the Green Knight*," *MS*, XVI (1956), 158–72, in which the poem is regarded as a kind of *rite du passage* and the conflict as an initiation ritual; William Goldhurst, "The Green and the Gold: The Major Theme of *Gawain and the Green Knight*," *CE*, XX (1958), 61–65, regards the conflict as one between courtly civilization and nature; Joseph Eagen, "The Import of Color Symbolism in *Sir Gawain and the Green Knight*," *St. Louis University Studies*, Series A, Humanities I, 2 (1949), 11–86, regards the conflict as essentially satiric, an attack on romance ideals; and George J. Englehardt, "The Predicament of Gawain," *MLQ*, XVI (1955), 218–25, sees the conflict as mainly religious. I mention these works because, as my discussion will show, I have found them very useful. For a full summary of criticism of the poem see Morton W. Bloomfield's excellent "*Sir Gawain and the Green Knight*," *PMLA*, LXXVI (1961), 7–19.

2. For a discussion of the romance ideal see M. A. Gist, *Love and War in the Middle English Romances* (Philadelphia, 1947); as Miss Gist remarks, p. 141, "The primary interest of every knight was his reputation."

3. Quoted by Gist, p. 142.

4. The entire passage, vv. 140–68, is an interesting statement of the importance of renown to knighthood.

5. Quoted by Gist, p. 179, from *Charles the Great*, p. 174.

6. The incident is discussed and Arthur's failure is defined in varying ways by D. E. Baughan, "The Role of Morgan la Fay in *Sir Gawain and the Green Knight*," *ELH*, XVII (1950), 241–51 (however, his interpretation is based on a misreading of v. 331; Englehardt discusses this error in the article cited in note 1 above); Else van der ven-ten Bensel, *The Character of Arthur in English Literature* (Amsterdam, 1925) (she notes that this is a failure in courtesy, p. 138); Hans Schnyder, "Aspects of Kingship in *Sir Gawain and the Green Knight*," *ES*, XL (1959), 289–94; Albert B. Friedman, "Morgan le Fay in *Sir Gawain and the Green Knight*," *Speculum*, XXXV (1960), 260–74.

7. Editors gloss it as "fearful," deriving it from O.N. *hræddr*, but elsewhere in the poem the word means "swiftly"—v. 862. Cf. *OED*, s.v. "rad."

8. This analogue was first noted by M. C. Thomas, *Gawayne and the Green Knight: A Comparison with the French Perceval* (Zurich, 1883), p. 60.

9. Reto R. Bezzola, *Le Sens de l'aventure et de l'amour* (Paris, 1947), p. 58.

10. Cited by J. D. Bruce, *The Evolution of Arthurian Romance* (Baltimore, 1923), II, 257, n. 14.

11. As B. J. Whiting shows in "Gawain: His Reputation, His Courtesy, and His Appearance in Chaucer's *Squire's Tale*," *MS*, IX (1947), 189–234, it was Gawain's traditional boast that he never once concealed or changed his name.

12. On this point see Herbert Koziol, *Grundzüge der Syntax der mittelenglischen Stabreimdichtungen*, Wiener Beiträge zur englischen Philologie, LVIII (Vienna, 1932), pp. 64–65.

13. This point has been discussed by a number of critics; see above, Ch. I, note 43.

14. Mabel Day, Introduction to Gollancz' edition of *Sir Gawain*, pp. xxxvi–xxxvii, cites an analogue for this episode in the Vulgate *Lancelot* (Sommer, IV, 108–09, 116), in which a vavasour's squire is assigned to lead Galeshin, Duke of Clarence, to the Dolorous Tower, where Gawain is imprisoned. The squire, like the guide in *Sir Gawain*, attempts to persuade the hero to turn

back, and he warns Galeshin that he will be killed if he persists in the undertaking.

15. Day, Introduction, p. xxxvi. Miss Day argues that it would "be unchivalrous to let a servant into the plot." This is true, but Bercilak is not especially chivalrous.

16. The biblical names that Gawain cites show that the poet is using here the "*Minnesklaven* Topos," which is widespread in the literature of the period. See the discussion and further references cited by Morton W. Bloomfield in his discussion of this topos in *Piers Plowman*, "*Piers Plowman* and the Three Grades of Chastity," *Anglia*, LXXVI (1958), esp. pp. 231–45.

17. The courtiers' laughter has been interpreted in widely differing ways. Charles Moorman, *MS*, XVI, 170, believes that the laughter indicates that Arthur's courtiers have misunderstood Gawain, indeed cannot understand him, for he is now an initiate and they are not. R. H. Greene, "Gawain's Shield and the Quest for Perfection," *ELH*, XXIX (1962), 139, believes that Arthur's court has probably not learned anything from the adventure but that "some of the laughter is directed at themselves."

18. Gervase Mathew, "Ideals of Knighthood in Late Fourteenth-Century England," *Studies in Medieval History Presented to F. M. Powicke* (Oxford, 1948), p. 362. Mathew includes *Sir Gawain* among the "old-fashioned works." This is true of what Gawain represents, but not of the whole poem.

19. J. D. Bruce, *Arthurian Romance*, I, 125.

20. Richard Bernheimer, *Wild Men in the Middle Ages* (Cambridge, Mass., 1952), p. 122 (Bernheimer is discussing a battle for possession of a woman).

21. See Karl J. Höltgen, "König Arthur und Fortuna," *Anglia*, LXXV (1957), 35–54.

Appendix: The Prose Redaction of the *Caradoc Beheading Tale*

1. A. W. Thompson, *The Elucidation* (New York, 1931), pp. 9–13, and Alfons Hilka, *Percevalroman* (Halle, 1935), pp. vii–viii, give full bibliographic details. As an appendix to his *Percevalroman*, Hilka prints the sections concerning Perceval in the 1530 edition. Those sections also appear in a modernized French version, *Le Tresplaisante et Recreative Histoire*, ed. G. Apollinaire (Paris, 1918). However, the sections concerning Gawain still remain unpublished.

Bibliography

EDITIONS OF THE GAWAIN-POET'S WORKS

Sir Gawain and the Green Knight, ed. J. R. R. Tolkien and E. V. Gordon. Corrected Edition. Oxford, 1930.

Syr Gawayne, ed. Sir Frederick Madden. Bannatyne Club Publications, 61. London, 1839.

Sir Gawayne and the Grene Knight, ed. Sir Israel Gollancz. EETS, 210. London, 1940.

Sire Gauvain et le chevalier vert, ed. Émile Pons. Bibliothèque de Philologie Germanique, IX. Paris, 1946.

Sir Gawayne and the Grene Knight, ed. Francis Berry in *The Age of Chaucer,* ed. Boris Ford. Pelican Guide to English Literature, I. London, 1954. Pp. 351–430.

Sir Gawain and the Grene Gome, ed. R. T. Jones. Natal University Press, 1960.

Sir Gawain and the Green Knight in *Pearl and Sir Gawain and the Green Knight,* ed. A. C. Cawley. Everyman's Library, 346. London, 1962, Pp. 51–146.

Cleanness. See *Purity.*

Patience, ed. Hartley Bateson. Second Edition. Publications of the University of Manchester, English Series, 3. Manchester, 1918.

Pearl, ed. E. V. Gordon. Oxford, 1953.

Purity, ed. R. J. Menner. Yale Studies in English, 61. New Haven, 1920.

EDITIONS OF MEDIEVAL TEXTS CITED

Adenès li Rois. *Cléomadès,* ed. André von Hasselt. Académie Royale de Belgique. Brussels, 1865.

Aiol, ed. Jacques Normand and Gaston Raynaud. SATF. Paris, 1877.

Aeneas Sylvius (Pius II). *Memoirs of a Renaissance Pope: The Commentaries of Pius II,* tr. Florence A. Gragg, ed. Leona C. Gabel. New York, 1959.

Alexander A in *The Gests of King Alexander of Macedon,* ed. F. P. Magoun, Jr. Cambridge, Mass., 1929. Pp. 121–70.

Alexander and Dindimus (Alexander B) in *The Gests of King Alexander of Macedon,* ed. F. P. Magoun, Jr. Cambridge, Mass., 1929. Pp. 171–216.

Andreas Capellanus. *De amore,* ed. E. Trojel. Hanover, 1892.

Aucassin et Nicolette, ed. Mario Roques. Second Edition. CFMA, 41. Paris, 1936.

Awntyrs of Arthur in *Scottish Alliterative Poems,* ed. F. J. Amours,. STS. Edinburgh, 1892–1897. I, 115–71.

Barbour, John. *Bruce,* ed. W. W. Skeat. EETS, Extra Series, 11, 21, 29, 55. London, 1870–1879.

Beowulf and the Fight at Finnsburg, ed. Fr. Klaeber. Third Edition with Supplements. Boston, 1936.

The Romance of Sir Beues of Hamptoun, ed. Eugen Kölbing. EETS, Extra Series, 46, 48, 65. London, 1885–1894.

Biblia Sacra, ed. Alberto Colunga and Laurentio Turrado. Third Edition. Biblioteca de Autores Cristianos. Madrid, 1959.

The Black Knight. See *The Complaint of the Black Knight.*

Boccaccio, Giovanni. *Il Decameron,* ed. Pietro Fanfani. Florence, 1897.

Bodel, Jean. *Chanson des saisnes. Jean Bodels Saxenlied,* ed. F. Menzel and E. Strengel. Ausgaben und Abhundlungen, 99–100. Marburg, 1909.

The Boy and the Mantle in *The English and Scottish Popular Ballads,* ed. F. J. Child. Boston, 1885–1886. No. 29, II, 257–74.

Brun de Branlant in *Continuations of the Old French Perceval: The First Continuation,* ed. W. R. Roach. Philadelphia, 1949–1955. I, 56–84; II, 161–95; III, 74–131.

The Carl of Carlisle. See *Sir Gawain and the Carl of Carlisle.*

Le Chanson de Roland, ed. F. Whitehead. Blackwell's French Texts. Oxford, 1947.

Chapman, George. *The Tragedy of Alphonsus, Emperor of Germany* in *The Plays and Poems of George Chapman: The Tragedies,* ed. Thomas M. Parrott. London, 1910. Pp. 403–71.

The Lyfe of the Noble and Crysten Prynce Charles the Grete, tr. William Caxton, ed. S. J. Herrtage. EETS, Extra Series, 36–37. London, 1881.

La Chastelaine de Vergi, ed. Gaston Raynaud. Third Edition, rev. by Lucien Foulet. CFMA, 1. Paris, 1921.

Chaucer, Geoffrey. *The Works of Geoffrey Chaucer,* ed. F. N. Robinson. Second Edition. Cambridge, Mass., 1957.

Cheualere Assigne, ed. H. H. Gibbs. EETS, Extra Series, 4. London, 1868.

Le Chevalier à l'épée, ed. Edward C. Armstrong. Baltimore, 1897.

"Chevy Chase" in *Bishop Percey's Folio Manuscript,* ed. J. W. Hales and F. J. Furnivall. London, 1868. II, 1–16.

Chrétien de Troyes. *Cligés,* ed. Alexandre Micha. CFMA. Paris, 1957.

———. *Eric et Enide,* ed. Alexandre Micha. CFMA. Paris, 1957.

———. *Lancelot (Le Chevalier de la charette)* in *Christian von Troyes sämtliche Werke,* ed. Wendelin Foerster, Vol. IV. Halle, 1899.

———. *Percevalroman,* ed. Alfons Hilka. *Sämtliche Werke,* ed. Wendelin Foerster, Vol. V. Halle, 1932.

———. *Yvain.* ed. Wendelin Foerster, notes by T. B. W. Reid. Manchester, 1942.

Cléomadès. See Adenès li Rois.

Colin, Philipp, and Claus Wisse. *Parzifal,* ed. Karl Schorbach. Elsässiche Litteraturdenkmäler aus den XIV–XVII Jahrhundert, V. Strassburg, 1888.

The Complaint of the Black Knight in *Chaucerian and Other Pieces,* ed. W. W. Skeat. Oxford, 1897. Pp. 245–65.

Cynewulf. *Elene* in *The Vercelli Book,* ed. George P. Krapp. The Anglo-Saxon Poetic Records, II. New York, 1932.

Dante Alighieri. *La Divina Commedia,* ed. C. H. Grandgent. New York, 1933.

Death and Life, ed. Sir Israel Gollancz. Select Early English Poems, V. London, 1930.

Deguilleville, Guillaume de. *Pilgrimage of the Life of Man,* tr. John Lydgate, ed. F. J. Furnivall. EETS, Extra Series, 77, 88. London, 1898–1901.

The Destruction of Troy. See *The Geste Hystoriale of the Destruction of Troy.*

Diu Crône. See Heinrich von dem Türlîn.

Dunbar, William. *The Poems of William Dunbar,* ed. W. McKay MacKenzie. London, 1932.

Eger and Grime, ed. J. R. Caldwell. Harvard Studies in Comparative Literature, IX. Cambridge, Mass., 1933.

The Elucidation, ed. Albert W. Thompson. New York, 1931.

English Medieval Lapidaries, ed. J. Evans and M. S. Serjeantson. EETS, 190. London, 1933.

Fled Bricrend, ed. and tr. G. Henderson. Irish Texts Society, II. London, 1899.

Floriant et Florete, ed. Harry F. Williams. University of Michigan Publications Language and Literature, 23. Ann Arbor, 1947.

The Flower and the Leaf in *Chaucerian and Other Pieces,* ed. W. W. Skeat. Oxford, 1897. Pp. 361–79.

Froissart, Jean. *Chroniques* in *Œuvres de Froissart,* ed. Baron Kervyn de Lettenhove. Brussels, 1868.

Generydes, ed. W. Aldis Wright. EETS, 55, 70. London, 1873–1878.

Geoffrey of Monmouth. *Historia Regum Britanniae,* ed. Acton Griscom. London, 1929.

Geoffrey of Vinsauf. *Documentum de arte versificandi* in *Les Arts poétiques du XIIe et du XIIIe siècle,* ed. Edmond Faral. Bibliothèque de l'École des Hautes Études, 238. Paris, 1923; repr. 1958. Pp. 263–320.

———. *Poetria Nova* in *Les Arts poétiques,* ed. Faral. Pp. 194–262.

The Geste Hystoriale of the Destruction of Troy, ed. G. A. Panton and D. Donaldson. EETS, 39, 56. London, 1869–1874.

A Geste of Robyn Hode in *The English and Scottish Popular Ballads,* ed. F. J. Child. Boston, 1885–1886. No. 117; V, 39–89.

Golagros and Gawane in *Scottish Alliterative Poems,* ed. F. J. Amours. STS. Edinburgh, 1892–1897. I, 1–46.

Gower, John. *The Complete Works of John Gower,* ed. G. C. Macaulay. Oxford, 1899. 4 vols.

The Grene Knight in *Bishop Percy's Folio Manuscript,* ed. J. W. Hales and F. J. Furnivall. London, 1868. II, 56–57.

Guido delle Colonne. *Historia destructionis Troiae,* ed. N. E. Griffin. Medieval Academy of America Publications, 26. Cambridge, Mass., 1936.

Guillaume de Lorris and Jean de Meun. *Le Roman de la rose,* ed. Ernest Langlois. SATF. Paris, 1914–1924. 5 vols.

Heinrich von dem Türlîn. *Diu Crône,* ed. G. H. F. Scholl, Litterarischer Verein in Stuttgart, 27. Stuttgart, 1852.

Henryson, Robert. *The Poems of Robert Henryson,* ed. G. Gregory Smith. STS, 55, 58, 64. Edinburgh, 1906–1914.

Hugo of St. Victor. *Didascalicon de studio legendi,* ed. Br. Chas. H. Buttimer. Catholic University of America Studies in Medieval and Renaissance Latin, X. Washington, D.C., 1939.

Hunbaut, ed. Jakob Stürzinger. Gesellschaft für romanische Literatur, 35. Dresden, 1914.

Huon de Bordeux, tr. Sir John Bourchier, Lord Berners, ed. S. L. Lee. *English Charlemagne Romances,* VII–VIII. EETS, Extra Series, 40, 41. London, 1882–1883.

The Interlude of Youth in *Dodsley's Old English Plays,* ed. W. Carew Hazlitt. London, 1874. II, 5–40.

James VI of Scotland (I of England). *Ane Schort Treatise* in *The Poems of King James VI of Scotland,* ed. James Craigie. STS, Third Series, 22, 26. Edinburgh, 1948–1952. I, 66–83.

The Jeaste of Syr Gawayne in *Syr Gawayne,* ed. Sir Frederic Madden. Bannatyne Club Publications, 61. London, 1839. Pp. 207–23.

Jehan. *Les Mervelles de Rigomer,* ed. Wendelin Foerster. Gesellschaft für romanische Literatur, 19, 39. Dresden, 1908–1915.

Kyng Alisaunder, ed. G. V. Smithers. EETS, 227, 237. London, 1952–1957.

Laȝamon. *Brut,* ed. Sir Frederic Madden. Society of Antiquaries. London, 1847.

Lancelot in *The Vulgate Version of the Arthurian Romances,* ed. H. O. Sommer. Washington, D.C., 1908–1916. Vols. III, IV, V.

Langland, William. *Piers Plowman: The A Version,* ed. George Kane. Oxford, 1960.

———. *The Vision of William Concerning Piers the Plowman, in Three Parallel Texts,* ed. W. W. Skeat. Oxford, 1866.

Lestoire de Merlin in *The Vulgate Version of the Arthurian Romances,* ed. H. O. Sommer. Washington, D.C., Vol. II.

The Life of the Black Prince by the Herald of Sir John Chandos, ed. M. K. Pope and E. C. Lodge. Oxford, 1910.

"A Light Is Come to the World" in *English Lyrics of the XIII Century,* ed. Carleton F. Brown. Oxford, 1950. No. 24, pp. 34–37.

Le Livre d'Artus in *The Vulgate Version of the Arthurian Romances,* ed. H. O. Sommer. Washington, D.C., 1908–1916. Vol. VI.

Le Livre de Caradoc in *Continuations of the Old French Perceval: The First Continuation,* ed. W. R. Roach. Philadelphia, 1949–1955. I, 84–238 (Mixed Redaction); II, 195–377 (Long Redaction); III, 131–205 (Short Redaction). The prose redaction is in *Tresplaisante et Recreative Hystoire du trespreulx et vaillant chevallier Perceval le galloys.* Avec Privilege . . . Jehan longis et Jehan sainct denis. Paris, 1530 [Library of Congress; *MLA* Rotographs, 8]. Folios, LXXXIX–CI.

Lovelich, Henry. *Merlin,* ed. Ernst A. Kock. EETS, Extra Series, 93, 112. London, 1904–1916.

Lydgate, John, tr. *Pilgrimage of the Life of Man.* See Deguilleville.

Malory, Thomas. *The Works of Sir Thomas Malory,* ed. Eugène Vinaver. Oxford, 1947. 3 vols.

Mandeville, John. *The Travels of Sir John Mandeville,* ed. P. Hamelius. EETS, 153, 154. London, 1919–1923.

Merlin, a Prose Romance, ed. D. W. Nash. EETS, 10, 21, 36. Second Edition, revised. London, 1875–1877.

Miles Gloriosus in *Origines latines du théâtre moderne,* ed. E. du Méril. Paris, 1847.

Le Morte Arthur, ed. J. D. Bruce. EETS, Extra Series, 88. London, 1903.

Morte Arthure, ed. Edmund Brock. EETS, 8. New Edition. London, 1871.

La Mule sanz frain. See Paiens de Maisières.

Mum and the Sothsegger, ed. Mabel Day and Robert Steele. EETS, 199. London, 1936.

A Mumming of the Seven Philosophers in *Secular Lyrics of the XIV and XV Centuries*, ed. R. H. Robbins. Second Edition. London, 1955. No. 120, pp. 110–13.

Newton, Humphrey. "The Poems of Humfrey Newton, Esq., 1466–1536," ed. R. H. Robbins, *PMLA*, LXV (1950), 276–79.

Der Nibelunge Not, ed. E. Sievers. Rept. Leipzig, 1955.

Paiens de Maisières. *La Damoisele à la mule (La Mule sanz frain)*, ed. Boreslas Orlowski. Paris, 1911.

The Parlement of the Thre Ages, ed. M. Y. Offord. EETS, 246. London, 1959.

Perlesvaus, ed. William Nitze and T. A. Jenkins. Chicago, 1937. 2 vols.

The Pilgrimage of the Life of Man. See Deguilleville.

Pierce the Ploughmans Crede, ed. W. W. Skeat. EETS, 30. London, 1867.

The Pistill of Susan in *Scottish Alliterative Poems*, ed. F. J. Amours. STS. Edinburgh, 1896–1897. II, 190–245.

Pwyll Prince of Dyfed in *The Mabinogion*, tr. Gwyn Jones and Thomas Jones. Everyman's Library, 97. London, 1949.

The Quatrefoil of Love, ed. Sir Israel Gollancz and Magdalene M. Weale. EETS, 195. London, 1934.

The Revesby Folk Play in *The English Folk-Play*, ed. E. K. Chambers. Oxford, 1933. Pp. 104–20.

Rhetorica ad Herennium (Ad C. Herennium, de ratione dicendi), ed. Harry Caplan. Loeb Classical Library. Cambridge, Mass., 1954.

Richard Coeur de Lion, Der mittelenglischen Versroman über Richard Lowenherz, ed. Karl Brunner. Wiener Beiträge zur englischen Philologie, 42. Vienna, 1913.

Richard the Redeles. See *Mum and the Sothsegger*.

Rigomer. See Jehan.

St. Erkenwald, ed. H. L. Savage. Yale Studies in English, 72. New Haven, 1926.

St. John the Evangelist (*Of Sayne Iohan the Euaungelist*) in *Religious Pieces*, ed. George C. Perry. EETS, 26. Revised Edition. London, 1889.

Schir William Wallace, ed. James Moir. STS, 6, 7, 17. Edinburgh, 1885–1889.

The Siege of Jerusalem, ed. E. Kölbing and Mabel Day. EETS, 188. London, 1932.

Sir Gawain and the Carl of Carlisle in Two Versions, ed. Auvo Kurvinen. Annales Academiae Scientarum Fennicae, Series B, 71. Helsinki, 1951.

Sir Perceval of Gales, ed. J. Campion and F. Holthausen. Alt- und mittelenglische Texte, 5. Heidelberg, 1913.

Sir Tristrem, ed. George P. McNeill. STS, 8. Edinburgh, 1886.

Skelton, John. *Works*, ed. Alexander Dyce. London, 1843. 2 vols.

Somer Soneday, ed. Carleton Brown in *Studies in English Philology: A Miscellany in Honor of Frederic Klaeber*, ed. Kemp Malone and Martin B. Rudd. Minneapolis, 1929. Pp. 362–74.

Le Songe vert, ed. L. Constans. *Romania*, XXXIII (1904), 490–539.

The Sowdone of Babylone, ed. Emil Hausknecht. EETS, Extra Series, 38. London, 1881.

Speculum Gy de Warewyke, ed. G. L. Morrill. EETS, Extra Series, 75. London, 1898.

Spenser, Edmund. *Works, Variorum Edition*, ed. Edwin Greenlaw, C. G. Osgood, F. M. Padelford, and others. Baltimore, 1932–1949.

The Tournament of Tottenham in *Middle English Metrical Romances*, ed. W. H. French and C. B. Hale. New York, 1930.

The Turk and Gawain in *Bishop Percy's Folio Manuscript*, ed. J. W. Hales and F. J. Furnivall. London, 1868. I, 88–102.

Ulrich von Lichtenstein. *Frauendienst*, ed. Reinhold Bechstein. Deutsche Dichtungen des Mittelalters, 6, 7. Leipzig, 1888.

Ulrich von Tatzikhoven. *Lanzelet*, ed. K. A. Hahn. Frankfurt a. M., 1845.

Valentine and Orson, tr. Henry Watson, ed. Arthur Dickson. EETS, 204. London, 1937.

Voeux du héron, ed. Thomas Wright, in *Political Poems and Songs . . . from the Accession of Edw. III to that of Ric. III*. London, 1859. I, 1–25.

The Wars of Alexander, ed. W. W. Skeat. EETS, Extra Series, 47. London, 1886.

The Weddynge of Syr Gawen and Dame Ragnell in *Syr Gawayne,* ed. Sir Frederic Madden. Bannatyne Club Publications, 61. London, 1839. Pp. 298ª–298ʸ

William of Palerne, ed. W. W. Skeat. EETS, Extra Series, I. London, 1867.

Wynnere and Wastoure in *The Parlement of the Thre Ages,* ed. Sir Israel Gollancz. Roxburghe Club Publications, 132. London, 1897. Appendix I.

Wolfram von Eschenbach. *Parzifal,* ed. Albert Leitzmann. Halle, 1947–1950. 3 vols.

Yder, ed. H. Gelzer. Gesellschaft für romanische Literatur, 31. Dresden, 1914.

Yvain and Gawain, ed. Gustav Schleich. Oppeln, 1887.

Index

About the author

LARRY D. BENSON is on the English faculty at Harvard University, and since 1963 has been Allston Burr Senior Tutor of Quincy House. Mr. Benson holds degrees from the University of California at Berkeley. He is a contributor to *Modern Language Quarterly, Speculum, English Studies,* the *Journal of English and Germanic Philology,* and *Modern Philology.*

The type face used in this book is Linotype Caledonia with Glamour Light display type. The book was printed by letterpress on 50# Warren's No. 66 Antique and bound in Holliston Payco with endpapers of Multicolor Endleaf. It was designed by Adrianne Onderdonk and manufactured by H. Wolff Book Manufacturing Co., Inc., New York.